Lynn,

Many thanks for your help, encouragement and many contributions to this. I look forward to our continued colleagueship.

John

Multivariate Analysis in
The Human Services

INTERNATIONAL SERIES IN SOCIAL WELFARE

Previously Published Books in the Series:

Crane, J.A., *The Evaluation of Social Policies,* 1982.

Multivariate Analysis in the Human Services

John R. Schuerman
University of Chicago

Kluwer-Nijhoff Publishing
Boston   The Hague   Dordrecht   Lancaster

Distributors for North America:
Kluwer Boston, Inc.
190 Old Derby Street
Hingham, MA 02043, U.S.A.

Distributors Outside North America:
Kluwer Academic Publishers Group
Distribution Center
P.O. Box 322
3300AH Dordrecht, The Netherlands

Library of Congress Cataloging in Publication Data

Schuerman, John R.
  Multivariate analysis in the human services.

  Bibliography: p.
  Includes index.
  1. Social service—Research—Statistical methods.
2. Multivariate analysis. I. Title.
HV11.S382   1983   361'.0072   82-20328
ISBN 0-89838-105-3

Printed in the United States of America

Contents

List of Tables and Figures

Tables

Acknowledgments

Several classes at the School of Social Service Administration at the University of Chicago made use of various versions of this book over the past few years. I am grateful for their forbearance and their suggestions. I appreciate helpful advice from a number of colleagues who reviewed parts of this manuscript: Jeanne Marsh, William Reid, John Tropman, Lynn Videka-Sherman, and Lynn Harold Vogel. Gwen Graham meticulously typed early drafts of this material with great care. Deborah Siegel and Lynn Videka-Sherman graciously consented to use data from their dissertations for examples used in the book.

All of the figures in this book except for figure 8-1 were produced with the Tell-A-Graf graphics system, a product of Integrated Software Systems Corporation (ISSCO). Figure 8-1 was drawn using the graphing facilities in the SAS computer system. The examples of computer output (the tables) were produced with the SPSS system.

Finally, I am indebted to my family, Charlotte, Gabrielle, and Matthew for their support and understanding in the course of this project.

Multivariate Analysis in
The Human Services

1 INTRODUCTION

Research and evaluation in the human services usually involves a relatively large number of variables. We are interested in phenomena that have many aspects and many causes. The techniques needed to deal with many variables go beyond those of introductory statistics. Elementary procedures in statistics are limited in usefulness to situations in which we have two or three variables. When we have more than that, application of elementary techniques will often yield misleading results.

Why are elementary techniques inadequate when applied to many variables? Why, for example, should we not simply interpret a series of correlations of independent and dependent variables? The answer lies in the fact that these correlations are not independent pieces of information. The correlations of variables x and z with y are affected by the association of x with z. Hence, talk about the "effect" of x on y will be somewhat ambiguous, since we will be including in that effect some of the effects of z. We would like to be able to sort out these effects. This is the problem of "estimation," that is, estimating the relationships or effects between variables, taking into account their relationships with other variables.

A second problem arises when we construct confidence intervals or test hypotheses about the population from which our sample was drawn. When we test

1

hypotheses about relationships among a large number of variables we increase substantially the risk of Type I error, that is, the error of rejecting a null hypothesis when it is really true. Multivariate analysis is designed to deal with these problems.

This book is intended for research workers and students in the helping professions who wish to deepen their understanding of data analytic techniques beyond that provided in introductory statistics texts. The intent is to provide a beginning, working understanding of certain procedures in multivariate analysis. I emphasize techniques useful for work in evaluation. Many of these techniques are widely used (they are readily available in computer programs) but they are often applied with only a meager understanding of their inner workings. This book attempts to go behind the computer program writeups to explain the ideas that underly the techniques. In addition, I attempt to delineate those situations in which the techniques are appropriate and inappropriate and to explain how to interpret the output of computer programs. Examples from the helping professions are provided.

As developed in this book, multivariate analysis rests on several main ideas. Two ways of thinking about data that are introduced in elementary statistics, regression and the analysis of variance, are important in the foundation of multivariate analysis. Regression and analysis of variance are extended in various ways, in particular, to deal with multiple dependent variables. Elementary regression and analysis of variance are reviewed in chapter 3. To these two conceptual frameworks, multivariate analysis adds a third, the ideas of principal components analysis which is concerned with the *structure* of a set of variables. Although there are hints of ideas from regression, principal components analysis is mostly new. The concepts in it combine with regression and the analysis of variance to form the basis of much of multivariate analysis.

These statistical ideas in turn rest on a number of mathematical concepts, in particular, matrix algebra and a few notions from calculus. Calculus is used primarily to find maxima and minima and maxima and minima subject to constraints. Matrix algebra and calculus come together to give us the concepts of eigenvalues and eigenvectors, which are central notions in multivariate analysis.

After an initial orientation to basic concepts (primarily some matrix algebra) the book considers three categories of techniques. First, multiple regression (which is not considered by purists to be a multivariate technique) is presented in terms of matrix representations. In the process, students may wish to take a diversion into appendix C on the calculus to see how to find regression coefficients. Next, the techniques of principal components analysis and factor analysis are considered, leading up to their use as data simplification and data reduction procedures. Finally, procedures involving multiple dependent variables are presented including simple multiple analysis of variance (multivariate tests of group differences), multivariate multiple regression, discriminate analysis, canonical correlation, multivariate analysis of covariance and repeated measures analysis.

The book is conceptual, intuitive, and geometric in orientation. No formal mathematical proofs are provided, with the exception of a few in the appendices. I attempt to allow readers to "see" things. Nonetheless, it is necessary to employ mathematical terms and to use quite a few symbols, equations, Greek letters, etc. I have tried to keep such symbolism from being an impediment to understanding.

Actual computational techniques are not stressed in this book since the techniques usually require the use of a computer when dealing with real data. In some cases, the computation routines follow directly from the material here. In other cases, there is much more to go through. However, programs are readily available and mastering their details is not necessary for basic understanding.

The approach relies heavily on matrix representations. Some matrix algebra is introduced at the beginning and more is brought in later on. In a few places it is necessary to use some ideas from differential calculus. At those points, the results from the calculus are merely stated. An appendix provides a brief introduction to calculus. At a few other points, results depending on mathematical manipulations are simply quoted and sometimes a more complete discussion is provided in a footnote or appendix.

The book assumes a beginning understanding of statistics such as would be provided in a one- or two-quarter course. I assume familiarity with the ideas of variable, mean, variance, standard deviation, correlation, regression (at a beginning level), probability, sampling distribution (probability distribution), the normal distribution, inference, tests of hypotheses, and confidence intervals; and a beginning understanding of the analysis of variance. Perhaps more importantly, I assume that the reader is comfortable with the representation of ideas in symbols and with the manipulation of symbols, although I try throughout to explain symbolic expressions in words. I also assume comfort with the summation notation (Σ) and with subscripts.

At several points examples of computer analysis are presented. These analyses were all performed using the Statistical Package for the Social Sciences (SPSS), Version 9. Students who want to use SPSS to perform similar analyses will need to consult the relevant SPSS manuals. At this writing those manuals are *SPSS*, second edition and *SPSS Update 7-9*, both published by McGraw-Hill. Most SPSS documentation is well written and thorough, although the write-up in the *Update* on the MANOVA (multiple analysis of variance) program is difficult. SPSS will shortly release Version X which will be compatible with the earlier versions. At the same time new manuals will be published.

It will be helpful for students using this text to perform some of these analyses on real data, using available computer routines. SPSS is the most widely used package of statistical programs for the social sciences. Other programs that are used are the *Statistical Analysis System* (SAS) and *BMDP* (Biomedical Computer Programs, P-series). One of the SAS procedures, PROC MATRIX, is particularly useful for exploring multivariate techniques. An appendix provides a brief introduction to this procedure. Again, SAS manuals should be consulted, although they tend to be difficult to understand.

It is also desirable to work, with paper and pencil, with these ideas, so a number of exercises are included at various points. Further, the reader is asked at times to verify some assertion. I do not mean by this that a general mathematical proof is to be produced, rather the reader should construct a simple example of the assertion and demonstrate the truth of that example.

This book is not exhaustive of the techniques described herein. In addition, there are lots of advanced (and not so advanced) techniques that are not considered at all. The book is suitable for a one-quarter or one-semester course, although some selection of material may be required.

Few readers will be able to approach this material casually. However, those who invest some effort should be rewarded with considerable understanding of these fascinating and useful techniques.

2 MATHEMATICAL PRELIMINARIES

As with all statistical techniques, multivariate analysis is based on certain mathematical ideas. An understanding of at least some basic mathematical concepts is necessary to understand multivariate analysis. The ideas that are most critical have to do with matrices, so most of this chapter is devoted to those. However, before we get to matrices, two other ideas we will need are introduced, functions and probability functions.

Functions of Variables

The concept of functions is a basic idea in mathematics. We will give a formal definition of the idea of a function and then will talk about what it means. We begin with two sets of objects, the set X and the set Y. Members of the set X will be denoted by x and of the set Y by y. In our work the sets will be sets of numbers. By a function we mean a rule that assigns to or associates with each element of one set a single element of the other. Thus we might have a function of the set X that assigns to each x some y. We represent functions of X by symbols like $f(x), g(x), h(x)$. Some examples of functions are:

$$f(x) = x$$

$$f(x) = x^2$$

$$g(x) = 5x^2 + 2x + 3$$

$$h(x) = \sqrt{x}$$

Since x varies, we think of it as a *variable*. The set of values that a function takes can be thought of as another variable, so sometimes we write things like

$$y = f(x) = x^2$$

where y is thought of as another variable that is a function of x.

The rule that constitutes a function can give only one value for each value of x, but it does not have to give a value for every x. For example, the function

$$f(x) = \sqrt{x}$$

is not defined for negative values of x (at least in the real number system, to which we are confining ourselves here). Also, it must be understood that this function means only the positive square root of x, since otherwise the function could take two values for each x (both the positive and negative square roots).

Mathematicians sometimes think of functions in terms of *mappings* or *transformations* of one variable into another.

Probability Functions

A probability function is a function of a particular kind of variable called a *random* variable. It is a function that can only take values greater than or equal to zero and the sum of all the probabilities assigned by the function to the possible values of the random variable must be equal to one. The foregoing is not a rigorous definition of the concept of probability function; but together with the reader's prior understanding of probability, it will suffice for now. We will represent probability functions by the symbol $p(x)$.

The variable x can be either *discrete* or *continuous*. By discrete we mean a variable that can take only certain values, for example, only the integers or only the values one and two. By continuous we mean a variable that can take all possible numeric values within some range. The range could be between plus and minus infinity or some narrower interval. Discrete random variables have probabilities assigned to each of the possible values they can take and these probabilities cannot exceed one for any value.

The idea of the probability of a certain value for a continuous random variable is a bit more problematic. For a continuous variable x, the probability

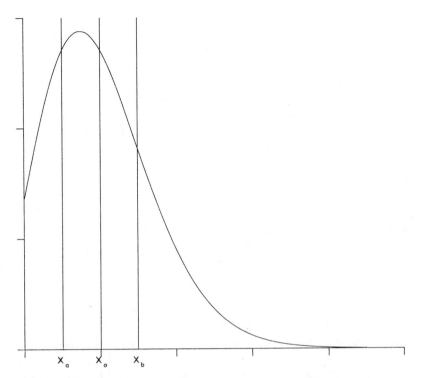

Figure 2-1. Probability Function of a Continuous Variable.

function will be defined (that is, will have a value) for particular values of x; but we will not talk about the probability of a particular value. We encounter here what may appear to be a bit of a paradox. If we had a perfectly accurate measurement procedure, it would be very unlikely that we would get exactly some preselected value for the variable; in fact, the probability will be vanishingly small. On the other hand, if we apply the measurement procedure to a subject, we will get some value for the variable. We get around this problem by refusing to talk about the probability of a particular value (its probability will be undefined, even though the probability function has a value at that point) and instead talk about the probability of getting any value between two specified values of the random variable.

The matter may be somewhat clearer if we remember that for continuous distributions, probabilities can be thought of as areas under probability curves. If we have a probability function $p(x)$ of a random variable x, we can diagram the situation as in figure 2-1.

Consider the point x_o. The probability function has a value at x_o $(p(x_o))$

represented by the height of the curve at that point. However, there is no area under the curve at that point, there is only a straight line and it has no area. We can, however, talk about the area under the curve between x_a and x_b. That area represents the probability of getting a value between x_a and x_b. The total area under a probability function is one.

We will use the term *probability distribution* to mean the same thing as a *probability function*. Another term that is sometimes used is *probability density function*. I assume the reader is familiar with one important probability distribution, the normal distribution.

Functions of More Than One Variable

We will deal frequently with functions that assign values to each possible combination of values of two or more variables. Such functions are represented by expressions like $f(x,y), f(x_1,x_2,x_3), f(x_1, \ldots ,x_n)$.

An example in two variables is

$$f(x,y) = 4x^2 + 5yx + 9y^2$$

We will also deal with probability distributions of more than one variable, by which we mean a function that assigns a probability to each possible combination of values for a set of random variables. An example is the bivariate normal distribution that assigns a probability to each possible combination of two variables and looks something like a fireman's hat (it has to be diagrammed in three dimensions). We will also make use of the idea of a multivariate normal distribution by which we mean a generalization of the idea of a normal distribution to the combination of values of p variables. (It would take $p + 1$ dimensions to diagram such a distribution.)

Linear Combinations

We will often make use of the idea of linear combinations or linear functions of a set of variables. By a linear combination we mean functions that look like this:

$$f(x_1,x_2, \ldots ,x_p) = b_0 + b_1 x_1 + b_2 x_2 + \cdots + b_p x_p$$
$$= b_0 + \sum_i b_i x_i$$

Neither the b's nor the x's are taken to any power or are expressed as other kinds of functions. Therefore, the expression

$$f(x_1,x_2,x_3) = b_0 + b_1 x_1 + b_2 x_2^2 + b_3 x_3^{1/4}$$

is not a linear function. However, this nonlinear function can be written as a linear function of other variables. To do this, define $y_1 = x_1$, $y_2 = x_2^2$, $y_3 = x_3^{1/4}$. We then have

$$f(y_1,y_2,y_3) = b_0 + b_1 y_1 + b_2 y_2 + b_3 y_3$$

which is a linear function "in the y's."

Some nonlinear functions cannot be written as linear functions of other variables. For example: $f(x,y,z) = 5x^2 y^z$.

Polynomials

A polynomial in x is a function like

$$f(x) = a_0 + a_1 x + a_2 x^2 + a_3 x^3 + \ldots +$$

a sum of terms involving various integral powers of x. The *degree* of a polynomial is the highest exponent.

Matrices

Many statistical operations in social science research are readily conceptualized in terms of matrix algebra. It is thus useful to develop some elementary knowledge of matrix theory. First some definitions. A *scalar* is simply an ordinary number, whole, fractional, negative, positive, or irrational (irrational numbers are numbers like π or $\sqrt{2}$). A *matrix* is simply a rectangular array of numbers. For example:

$$\begin{array}{rrr} 5 & 4 & 6 \\ 7 & 9 & 2 \\ 8 & 7 & 4 \\ 82 & 6 & 18 \end{array}$$

The individual numbers in a matrix are called *elements*. Therefore, the numbers 5, 9, 82, and 18 are all elements of the above matrix. We will always limit ourselves to matrices whose elements are numbers, although, of course, we will symbolize those numbers with letters:

$$\begin{matrix} x_{11} & x_{12} & x_{13} \\ x_{21} & x_{22} & x_{23} \\ x_{31} & x_{32} & x_{33} \\ x_{41} & x_{42} & x_{43} \end{matrix}$$

Note that in the subscripts the first number designates the row and the second the column. x_{22}, therefore, refers to the element in the second row and the second column; x_{42} refers to the element in the fourth row and the second column. To designate an array of numbers as a matrix some authors put brackets, parentheses, or double rules around the arrays:

$$\begin{bmatrix} 5 & 3 & 2 \\ 6 & 3 & 7 \end{bmatrix} \quad \begin{pmatrix} 5 & 3 & 2 \\ 6 & 3 & 7 \end{pmatrix} \quad \left\|\begin{matrix} 5 & 3 & 2 \\ 6 & 3 & 7 \end{matrix}\right\|$$

A single rule,

$$\begin{vmatrix} 5 & 3 & 2 \\ 6 & 3 & 7 \\ 8 & 5 & 6 \end{vmatrix}$$

is never used, as this means something else, namely, a determinant. We will discuss determinants later on.

How Matrices Arise

The data collected for a study may often be cast in a matrix that we call the original data matrix. In such a matrix the rows represent cases and the columns variables:

		variables			
		1	2	...	p
	1	x_{11}	x_{12}	...	x_{1p}
	2	x_{21}	x_{22}	...	x_{2p}
cases	3	x_{31}	x_{32}	...	x_{3p}
	...				
	n	x_{n1}	x_{n2}	...	x_{np}

Here x_{22} refers to the value of the second variable for the second case, x_{1p} to the value of pth variable in the first case, and x_{np} to the value of the pth variable in the nth case. Thus, the first index indicates the row (case number) and the second index indicates the column (variable number).

We will only use numbers in matrices. Purely categorical variables (e.g., region, religion) cannot be put directly into matrices unless they have only two categories and can be coded 0, 1. Categorical variables of more than two categories can sometimes be recast into *dummy variables* for the kinds of analyses discussed in this book. In statistical work we start with an original data matrix and then manipulate it in various ways to produce other matrices.

Notation

In what follows, bold-faced letters will represent matrices:

$$\mathbf{X} = \begin{pmatrix} x_{11} & x_{12} & \cdots & x_{1p} \\ \cdots & & & \\ x_{n1} & \cdots & \cdots & x_{np} \end{pmatrix}$$

This means $\mathbf{X}$ is the matrix which has x's as elements and has p columns and n rows.

Order

The order of a matrix is its number of rows and columns, e.g., 4 by 3, 3 by 2, or in general, n by m. This will be written as $n \times m$. Matrices with an equal number of rows and columns are called square matrices of order m. The original data matrix is rarely square but many of the matrices we will derive from it are. If a matrix has only one row or one column, it is called a row or column *vector*. For example, the values on all the cases for a single variable form a vector as do the values for all the variables for a single case. A matrix of only one row and one column is only a single number and is called a *scalar*. In this book a vector will be represented as a bold faced lower-case letter, for example, $\mathbf{x}$ or $\mathbf{a}$. Most vectors start out as column vectors (they are usually vectors having all the values for a single variable), so you can assume that when you see a symbol like $\mathbf{x}$ it means a column vector. A row vector will usually be written $\mathbf{x}'$. Occasionally when we are dealing with lots of vectors, a particular vector will have a subscript like $\mathbf{a}_i$. A scalar will be represented by a lower-case letter which will often have subscripts, for example, x_{ij} or a_i.

In a *square matrix,* the principal diagonal consists of those elements in the diagonal running from the top left to the lower right. They are the elements for which the column index equals the row index (x_{ii}):

$$\begin{matrix} x_{11} & x_{12} & x_{13} \\ x_{21} & x_{22} & x_{23} \\ x_{31} & x_{32} & x_{33} \end{matrix}$$

The sum of the elements in the principal diagonal is called the trace $(\sum_i x_{ij})$.

A square matrix is symmetric if the corresponding elements of rows and columns are equal $(x_{ij} = x_{ji}$ for all i and $j)$. If you turn a symmetric matrix about its principal diagonal it will look the same as before. For example:

$$\begin{matrix} 11 & 4 & 3 \\ 4 & 15 & 10 \\ 3 & 10 & 17 \end{matrix}$$

A *diagonal matrix* is a square matrix with all elements zero except those in the principal diagonal (that is, all $x_{ij} = 0$ except where $i = j$):

$$\begin{matrix} 15 & 0 & 0 \\ 0 & 12 & 0 \\ 0 & 0 & 9 \end{matrix}$$

To save space, a diagonal matrix, is sometimes written diag (x_{11}, x_{22}, x_{33}). The *identity matrix* is a diagonal matrix with ones in the diagonal:

$$\mathbf{I} = \begin{matrix} 1 & 0 & 0 \\ 0 & 1 & 0 \\ 0 & 0 & 1 \end{matrix}$$

It is always square. The letter $\mathbf{I}$ stands for the identity matrix. Sometimes a subscript is used to indicate the order of the particular identity matrix: $\mathbf{I}_4$.

Equality

Two matrices are equal if each element of one is equal to the corresponding element of the other. Equal matrices must be of the same order. For example,

$$\begin{matrix} 1 & 5 & 7 \\ 9 & 8 & 13 \\ 4 & 3 & 12 \end{matrix} = \begin{matrix} 1 & 5 & 7 \\ 9 & 8 & 13 \\ 4 & 3 & 12 \end{matrix}$$

but

$$\begin{matrix} 1 & 5 & 7 \\ 9 & 8 & 13 \\ 4 & 3 & 12 \end{matrix} \neq \begin{matrix} 2 & 8 & 16 \\ 9 & 3 & 1 \\ 4 & 0 & 7 \end{matrix}$$

Transpose

The transpose of a matrix is a second matrix which has as its rows the columns of the first matrix. When the original matrix is designated by $\mathbf{Y}$, the usual symbol for its transposed matrix is $\mathbf{Y}'$ or $\mathbf{Y}^T$. We will use $\mathbf{Y}'$. $\mathbf{y}'$ will mean a row vector which is the transpose of a column vector $\mathbf{y}$. From the definition of a transposed matrix, it is evident that $\mathbf{Y}'$ has the same number of rows as $\mathbf{Y}$ has columns, and $\mathbf{Y}'$ has the same number of columns as $\mathbf{Y}$ has rows. Thus, if the order of $\mathbf{Y}$ is $m \times n$ the order of $\mathbf{Y}'$ is $n \times m$.

$$\mathbf{Y} = \begin{pmatrix} 3 & 2 \\ 2 & 1 \\ 7 & 9 \end{pmatrix} \qquad \mathbf{Y}' = \begin{pmatrix} 3 & 2 & 7 \\ 2 & 1 & 9 \end{pmatrix}$$

Symbolically, $y_{ij} = y'_{ji}$. If we transpose a matrix and then transpose it again we wind up with the original matrix, that is: $(\mathbf{Y}')' = \mathbf{Y}$. It should be obvious that if a matrix is symmetric it is equal to its transpose (i.e., if $\mathbf{S}$ is symmetric then $\mathbf{S}' = \mathbf{S}$).

Matrix Algebra

The algebra of everyday life is called scalar algebra. It deals with single numbers at a time. You are familiar with expressions like

$$x + y = 30$$

$$5a^2 + 6 + c = 0$$

$$a^2 + b^2 = 15$$

and so on. Now we will introduce some matrix algebra. Many computer programs use matrix algebra and thus can manipulate whole data matrices at once (or so it seems).

Addition

Two matrices of the same order may be added by simply adding each element of one to the corresponding element of the other:

$$\begin{pmatrix} 4 & 6 \\ 3 & 7 \\ 2 & 5 \end{pmatrix} + \begin{pmatrix} 3 & 2 \\ 6 & 4 \\ 3 & 6 \end{pmatrix} = \begin{pmatrix} 7 & 8 \\ 9 & 11 \\ 5 & 11 \end{pmatrix}$$

Subtraction works the same way:

$$\begin{pmatrix} 4 & 6 \\ 3 & 7 \\ 2 & 5 \end{pmatrix} - \begin{pmatrix} 3 & 2 \\ 3 & 1 \\ 1 & 2 \end{pmatrix} = \begin{pmatrix} 1 & 4 \\ 0 & 6 \\ 1 & 3 \end{pmatrix}$$

The commutative and associative laws hold for matrix addition. That is, $\mathbf{A} + \mathbf{B} = \mathbf{B} + \mathbf{A}$ and $\mathbf{A} + (\mathbf{B} + \mathbf{C}) = (\mathbf{A} + \mathbf{B}) + \mathbf{C}$, just as in scalar algebra.

Vector Multiplication

The scalar product of two vectors with the same number of elements is a scalar found by multiplying each element of the first vector by the corresponding element in the second and adding up these products. That is, $\mathbf{x} \cdot \mathbf{y}$ (scalar product of x and y) $= x_1 y_1 + x_2 y_2 + \cdots + x_n y_n$, or $\mathbf{xy} = \sum_i x_i y_i$.

In statistical work (though not in mathematics) it is customary to think of this vector multiplication procedure as involving a row vector times a column vector. The usual form for a vector is a column, so we often write multiplication as $\mathbf{y'x}$. That indicates that we take the row vector $\mathbf{y'}$ (that's the transpose of y) and multiply it by x. The scalar product is sometimes called the dot product, the minor product, or the cross product.

One of the common quantities encountered in statistics is the sum of the cross products of two variables: Σxy. We can represent this as the scalar product of two vectors. Let us think about the x and y values as x and y vectors:

$$x = \begin{matrix} x_1 \\ x_2 \\ . \\ . \\ . \end{matrix} \qquad y = \begin{matrix} y_1 \\ y_2 \\ . \\ . \\ . \end{matrix}$$

where the subscript stands for a case number (x_1 is the value for x on case 1 and similarly for y). Then

$$\sum_i x_i y_i = \mathbf{x'y} = \mathbf{y'x}$$

Matrix Multiplication

Suppose we want to find $\mathbf{P}$, the product of $\mathbf{X}$ and $\mathbf{Y}$, where $\mathbf{X}$ and $\mathbf{Y}$ are matrices of more than one row and column. The elements p_{ij} of $\mathbf{P}$ are defined as follows:

$$p_{ij} = \sum_{g=1}^{n} x_{ig} Y_{gj}$$

where n is the number of columns in the first matrix and the number of rows in the second matrix.

To find the entry in the second row and third column of $\mathbf{P}$, multiply each element in the second row of $\mathbf{X}$ by each corresponding element in the third column of $\mathbf{Y}$ and add these products. For example,

$$\begin{pmatrix} 1 & 2 & 3 \\ 4 & 7 & 8 \\ 9 & 1 & 0 \end{pmatrix} \cdot \begin{pmatrix} 4 & 8 & 0 \\ 2 & 1 & 2 \\ 7 & 1 & 4 \end{pmatrix} = \begin{pmatrix} 29 & 13 & 16 \\ 86 & 47 & 46 \\ 38 & 73 & 2 \end{pmatrix}$$

The prefactor (the first of the two matrices we are multiplying) must have the same number of columns as there are rows in the post factor (the second of the two matrices; the reader should verify that this is necessary). The product will have the same number of rows as the prefactor and the same number of columns as the post factor (again, the reader should verify this). The associative law holds for matrix multiplication but the commutative law does not. That is, $(\mathbf{XY})\mathbf{Z}$ is equal to $\mathbf{X}(\mathbf{YZ})$; but $\mathbf{XY}$ is not always equal to $\mathbf{YX}$. In fact, sometimes $\mathbf{YX}$ will not be defined when $\mathbf{XY}$ is (because of the need for the numbers of columns and rows to "conform"). The distributive law also holds for matrices. That is $\mathbf{A}(\mathbf{B} + \mathbf{C}) = \mathbf{AB} + \mathbf{AC}$.

The transpose of a product of two matrices is equal to the product of their transposes, in reverse order. That is, $(\mathbf{AB})' = \mathbf{B}'\mathbf{A}'$. Finally, multiplication of a matrix by the identity matrix leaves the matrix unchanged. That is, $\mathbf{IA} = \mathbf{A}$ and $\mathbf{AI} = \mathbf{A}$.

Product of a Matrix and a Scalar

To multiply a matrix by a scalar we simply multiply each element of the matrix by the scalar:

$$c\begin{pmatrix} a_{11} & a_{12} & a_{13} \\ a_{21} & a_{22} & a_{23} \\ a_{31} & a_{32} & a_{33} \end{pmatrix} = \begin{pmatrix} ca_{11} & ca_{12} & ca_{13} \\ ca_{21} & ca_{22} & ca_{23} \\ ca_{31} & ca_{32} & ca_{33} \end{pmatrix}$$

Scalar multiplication is commutative, that is, $c\mathbf{A} = \mathbf{A}c$.

Another Way of Thinking About Matrix Multiplication

Notice that each entry of a product matrix is equal to the scalar product of a row vector from the first factor times a column vector from the second factor. Thus, in the first example of matrix multiplication above the value in the first row and first column of the product matrix is equal to

$$(1 \quad 2 \quad 3)\begin{pmatrix} 4 \\ 2 \\ 7 \end{pmatrix} = 29$$

Sometimes it is useful in working with matrix expressions to write the dimensions of the matrix under the matrix like this:

$$\underset{p \times n}{\mathbf{X}'} \; \underset{n \times p}{\mathbf{X}} \; \underset{p \times 1}{\mathbf{a}} \; - \; \underset{1 \times 1}{c} \; \underset{p \times 1}{\mathbf{a}}$$

Then it is possible to verify that the matrices conform, that is, that the arithmetic operations are possible. For example, in a product of several matrices,

$$\underset{p \times n}{\mathbf{X}'} \; \underset{n \times p}{\mathbf{X}} \; \underset{p \times 1}{\mathbf{a}}$$

the dimensions that are next to each other must be the same. The product matrix will have order equal to the outside dimensions. In the above example, the product matrix will be of order $p \times 1$, a column vector.

Matrix Equations as Sets of Ordinary Equations

Matrix equations can be thought of as sets of ordinary equations. We will frequently encounter this situation when both sides of a matrix equation are really vectors. For example,

$$\underset{p \times p}{\mathbf{C}} \; \underset{p \times 1}{\mathbf{x}} \; - \; \underset{1 \times 1}{c} \; \underset{p \times 1}{\mathbf{x}} \; = \; \underset{p \times 1}{\mathbf{0}}$$

The left side of the equation is a $p \times 1$ column vector; the right is a column vector of p zeros.

For example, if we plug in a matrix for $\mathbf{C}$ and a value for c,

$$\mathbf{Cx} - c\mathbf{x} = \begin{pmatrix} 1 & 2 \\ 2 & 7 \end{pmatrix}\begin{pmatrix} x_1 \\ x_2 \end{pmatrix} - 5\begin{pmatrix} x_1 \\ x_2 \end{pmatrix} = \begin{pmatrix} 0 \\ 0 \end{pmatrix}$$

Multiplying out the matrix-vector product we have,

$$\begin{pmatrix} x_1 + 2x_2 \\ 2x_1 + 7x_2 \end{pmatrix} - \begin{pmatrix} 5x_1 \\ 5x_2 \end{pmatrix} = \begin{pmatrix} 0 \\ 0 \end{pmatrix}$$

Then performing the subtraction,

$$\begin{pmatrix} x_1 + 2x_2 - 5x_1 \\ 2x_1 + 7x_2 - 5x_2 \end{pmatrix} = \begin{pmatrix} 0 \\ 0 \end{pmatrix}$$

This is the same as two ordinary equations:

$$x_1 + 2x_2 - 5x_1 = 0$$
$$2x_1 + 7x_2 - 5x_2 = 0$$

Some Matrices We Will Encounter

We now introduce a few matrices we will use extensively in the sequel. First, we recall two ideas from elementary statistics. The *sum of squares* of a variable is equal to

$$\sum_{i=1}^{n} (x_i - \bar{x})^2$$

that is, the sum of the squares of the deviations of the values from the mean of the values. Dividing this sum by $n - 1$ gives us the estimated variance in the population (s^2). The sum of the cross products of two variables x_1 and x_2 is equal to $\Sigma_i(x_{i1} - \bar{x}_1)(x_{i2} - \bar{x}_2)$, that is, the sum of the products of the deviation of the values of x_1 for each case times the deviation of x_2 for the same case. Dividing this by $n - 1$ gives us the estimated covariance of the two variables in the population. The covariance and the variance are used together to find the correlation.

In nearly all the kinds of analyses that we discuss in this book we will assume that the data have been converted to deviation score form, that is, that each value has had the mean of that variable subtracted from it. We will represent the collection of all such deviation score values for a set of variables by a matrix X. Thus, the means of the columns of X will all be 0 since the mean (and sum) of deviations from the mean of a variable is always 0. We are now going to start playing around with our deviation score matrix **X**.

The *sum of squares and cross products* matrix (sometimes abbreviated SSCP) will be

$$S = X'X$$

This is a square $p \times p$ matrix (where p is the number of variables).

Let's take a simple example of three cases and two variables. Suppose the original data are:

Case No.	Variable 1	2
1	3	2
2	5	6
3	4	1

The deviation score matrix is

$$\begin{pmatrix} -1 & -1 \\ +1 & +3 \\ 0 & -2 \end{pmatrix}$$

The **S** matrix then is

$$S = \begin{pmatrix} -1 & +1 & 0 \\ -1 & +3 & -2 \end{pmatrix} \begin{pmatrix} -1 & -1 \\ +1 & +3 \\ 0 & -2 \end{pmatrix} = \begin{pmatrix} 2 & 4 \\ 4 & 14 \end{pmatrix}$$

The diagonal elements are the sums of squares of the variables and the off-diagonal elements are the sums of cross products of the various pairs of variables. The **S** matrix is symmetric, thus each cross product appears twice.

The *variance-covariance* matrix is defined as

$$C = \left(\frac{1}{n-1}\right)S = \left(\frac{1}{n-1}\right)X'X$$

where n is the number of cases (the number of rows in **X**). That is, we divide each element in **S** by $n - 1$.

For the above data,

$$C = \left(\frac{1}{3-1}\right)\begin{pmatrix} 2 & 4 \\ 4 & 14 \end{pmatrix} = \begin{pmatrix} 1 & 2 \\ 2 & 7 \end{pmatrix}$$

The **C** matrix is symmetric. Its diagonal consists of the estimated variances of the variables x_i and its off diagonal elements are the estimated covariances of each pair of variables. In our example the variable x_1 has a variance of 1 and variable x_2 a variance of 7. Their covariance is 2.

We will now define the *correlation* matrix. The correlation is a measure of association between variables, and the correlation matrix contains the correlations of each pair of variables in the **X** matrix (sometimes called the *zero-order* correlations). First we define the diagonal matrix **D** which has as diagonal elements the reciprocals of the standard deviations of the variables:

$$\frac{1}{\sqrt{\Sigma_i (x_{ij} - \bar{x}_j)^2/(n-1)}}$$

then the correlation matrix is defined as

$$\mathbf{R} = \mathbf{D'CD}$$

For our example, the standard deviations of the variables are $\sqrt{1}$ and $\sqrt{7}$. So the **D** matrix is

$$\begin{pmatrix} 1/\sqrt{1} & 0 \\ 0 & 1/\sqrt{7} \end{pmatrix}$$

The correlation matrix is:

$$\mathbf{R} = \begin{pmatrix} 1/\sqrt{1} & 0 \\ 0 & 1/\sqrt{7} \end{pmatrix} \begin{pmatrix} 1 & 2 \\ 2 & 7 \end{pmatrix} \begin{pmatrix} 1/\sqrt{1} & 0 \\ 0 & 1/\sqrt{7} \end{pmatrix} = \begin{pmatrix} 1 & 2/\sqrt{7} \\ 2/\sqrt{7} & 1 \end{pmatrix}$$

There are two facts that are important about correlation matrices.

1. The diagonal elements are all ones, that is, the correlation of a variable with itself. Each diagonal element is the variance of a variable divided by the square of its standard deviation. Since the square of the standard deviation is the variance, we wind up with one.
2. The matrix **R** is symmetric, the off diagonal elements are the correlations of various pairs of variables (which can be represented as r_{ij}), and since the correlation of x_i with x_j is the same as the correlation of x_j with x_i, we have $r_{ij} = r_{ji}$.

One other fact that we will use in the following is that the covariance matrix of variables in standard score form is the same as the correlation matrix of the variables.

Singularity of Matrices and Determinants

A square matrix is said to be *singular* if one of its rows is equal to a linear combination of some of its other rows. It is not easy to see this except in small matrices. For example,

$$\begin{pmatrix} 1 & 2 \\ 2 & 4 \end{pmatrix}$$

is singular. Its second row is twice the first row. Also,

$$\begin{pmatrix} 1 & 2 & 3 \\ 5 & 6 & 7 \\ 7 & 10 & 13 \end{pmatrix}$$

is singular, the third row is twice the first row plus the second row. However,

$$\begin{pmatrix} 1 & 2 \\ 3 & 4 \end{pmatrix}$$

is not singular.

A *determinant* is a scalar that is derived from a square matrix. The determinant of the 2×2 matrix:

$$\begin{pmatrix} a & b \\ c & d \end{pmatrix}$$

equals $ad - bc$. Determinants are denoted by vertical rules around the matrix:

$$\begin{vmatrix} a & b \\ c & d \end{vmatrix}$$

The determinant of 3×3 matrix

$$\begin{pmatrix} a_1 & b_1 & c_1 \\ a_2 & b_2 & c_2 \\ a_3 & b_3 & c_3 \end{pmatrix}$$

is $a_1 b_2 c_3 - a_1 b_3 c_2 + a_2 b_3 c_1 - a_2 b_1 c_3 - a_3 b_2 c_1 + a_3 b_1 c_2$.

The determinant of a larger square matrix is more complicated to compute. Probably the easiest way to think of such "larger" determinants is in terms of the sum of products of cells in one row or one column times the determinant found by striking out the row and column in which that cell is found, such products being alternately positive or negative. It's probably easiest to do this with cells in the first column, in which case the formula is

$$\det A = \sum_j (-1)^{j+1} M_{j1} a_{j1}$$

where det $\mathbf{A}$ is the determinant of a matrix $\mathbf{A}$ (order n), M_{j1} is the determinant found by striking out the first column and jth row (M_{j1} is called the *minor* of a_{j1}) and a_{j1} is the jth value in the first column.

For the 3×3 determinant above,

$$\begin{vmatrix} a_1 & b_1 & c_1 \\ a_2 & b_2 & c_2 \\ a_3 & b_3 & c_3 \end{vmatrix} = a_1 \begin{vmatrix} b_2 & c_2 \\ b_3 & c_3 \end{vmatrix} - a_2 \begin{vmatrix} b_1 & c_1 \\ b_3 & c_3 \end{vmatrix} + a_3 \begin{vmatrix} b_1 & c_1 \\ b_2 & c_2 \end{vmatrix}$$

$$= a_1 b_2 c_3 - a_1 b_3 c_2 - a_2 b_1 c_3 + a_2 b_3 c_1$$

$$+ a_3 b_1 c_2 - a_3 b_2 c_1$$

This procedure provides a *recursive* definition of a determinant, in which the determinant can be *expanded* until 2×2 determinants are reached. When the matrix is fairly large, this way of evaluating determinants is very tedious even for computers. Computer programs utilize methods of evaluating determinants that are much faster.

A Super Important Fact: If a matrix is singular, its determinant is zero and vice versa. This is an important fact that will be frequently used in what follows.

Inverse of Matrices

If the determinant of a square matrix ($\mathbf{A}$) is not zero (that is, the matrix is non-singular), there exists another matrix called its *inverse* ($\mathbf{A}^{-1}$), which, when multiplied (either pre- or postmultiplication) by the original matrix, will yield the identity matrix ($\mathbf{AA}^{-1} = \mathbf{I}$ and $\mathbf{A}^{-1}\mathbf{A} = \mathbf{I}$). The inverse is analogous to the reciprocal of a scalar [the reciprocal of a is $1/a$ and $(a)(1/a) = 1$].

It turns out that the inverse of the product of two matrices is equal to the product of the inverses in reverse order. That is, $(\mathbf{AB})^{-1} = \mathbf{B}^{-1}\mathbf{A}^{-1}$ if $\mathbf{A}$ and $\mathbf{B}$ are square of the same order, and can be inverted.

In statistical work it is often necessary to find the inverse of a matrix. Unfortunately, computing inverses is very tedious. Fortunately, computers can do it quickly. One way to compute inverses is given in appendix E. The inverse of a diagonal matrix is easy, it is a diagonal matrix containing the reciprocals of the diagonal cells. For example,

$$\begin{pmatrix} 2 & 0 & 0 \\ 0 & 3 & 0 \\ 0 & 0 & 4 \end{pmatrix}^{-1} = \begin{pmatrix} 1/2 & 0 & 0 \\ 0 & 1/3 & 0 \\ 0 & 0 & 1/4 \end{pmatrix}$$

Problems

1. Make up a 3 × 3 symmetric matrix and a 3 × 3 diagonal matrix.

2. Make up a 3 × 4 matrix and then write its transpose.

3. Find the scalar product of the two vectors $\mathbf{x}$ and $\mathbf{y}$ ($\mathbf{x'y} = \mathbf{y'x}$) where $\mathbf{x'} = (2, 4, 6, 7)$ and $\mathbf{y'} = (3, 9, 5, 9)$.

4. Suppose that we have three matrices $\mathbf{A}$, $\mathbf{B}$, and $\mathbf{C}$, where

$$\mathbf{A} = \begin{pmatrix} 2 & 3 & 6 \\ 4 & 1 & 5 \\ 7 & 3 & 4 \end{pmatrix} \quad \mathbf{B} = \begin{pmatrix} 7 & 5 \\ 2 & 1 \\ 8 & 0 \end{pmatrix} \quad \mathbf{C} = \begin{pmatrix} 3 & 0 \\ 2 & 1 \\ 5 & 6 \end{pmatrix}$$

a. Find $\mathbf{AB}$.

b. Why is it not possible to perform the multiplication $\mathbf{BA}$? Is it possible to perform the multiplication $\mathbf{B'A}$?

c. Show that the distributive law holds for these matrices by computing both sides of the equation $\mathbf{A(B + C)} = \mathbf{AB} + \mathbf{AC}$.

5. Define three other matrices as follows:

$$\mathbf{D} = \begin{pmatrix} 4 & 1 \\ 6 & 3 \end{pmatrix} \quad \mathbf{E} = \begin{pmatrix} 5 & 0 \\ 2 & 8 \end{pmatrix} \quad \mathbf{F} = \begin{pmatrix} 3 & 2 \\ 1 & 0 \end{pmatrix}$$

a. Show that the associative law for multiplication holds for these matrices by computing both sides of the equation: $\mathbf{(DE)F} = \mathbf{D(EF)}$.

b. Show that the commutative law does not hold by computing both $\mathbf{DE}$ and $\mathbf{ED}$.

6. Let

$$\mathbf{G} = \begin{pmatrix} 2 & 3 \\ 6 & 1 \\ 4 & 5 \end{pmatrix} \quad \mathbf{F} = \begin{pmatrix} 7 & 1 & 3 \\ 4 & 2 & 8 \end{pmatrix}$$

Show that the transpose of products is equal to the products of transposes in the reverse order by computing both sides of the equation $\mathbf{(GF)'} = \mathbf{F'G'}$.

7. Suppose we have observed four cases on three variables. We transform the variables by subtracting from each value the mean of that variable. We have a matrix of deviation scores $\mathbf{X}$:

$$\mathbf{X} = \begin{pmatrix} -4 & 0 & 1 \\ 2 & -1 & -2 \\ 1 & 3 & -3 \\ 1 & -2 & 4 \end{pmatrix}$$

a. Compute the sum of squares and cross products matrix (SSCP) $\mathbf{S} = \mathbf{X'X}$.

b. Compute the variance-covariance matrix $\mathbf{C} = [1/(n - 1)]\,\mathbf{S}$.

c. Compute the **D** matrix (the matrix with the reciprocals of the standard deviations in the diagonal).

d. Compute **R** = **DCD**. This also can be computed as

$$[1/(n-1)]\,\textbf{DSD} = [1/(n-1)]\,\textbf{D}'\textbf{X}'\textbf{XD}$$

e. Find **R** in another way by finding the covariance matrix of the standard scores of the variables.

8. Find the determinant of the matrix

$$\begin{pmatrix} 2 & 4 & 3 \\ 1 & 3 & 6 \\ 7 & 5 & 4 \end{pmatrix}$$

9. What is the inverse of an identity matrix?

3 MULTIPLE REGRESSION I

In this chapter we will apply the matrix algebra of the previous chapter to multiple regression. We assume that the reader has had at least a beginning exposure to the idea of multiple regression. In multiple regression we explore the relationship of a single dependent variable to a set of p independent variables. The reasons for exploring this relationship may be to predict future or unknown values of the dependent variable from known or assumed values of the independent variables or to explain variations in the dependent variable. Explanation proceeds by specifying how each independent variable affects the dependent variable. Sometimes we are interested in specifying which of the independent variables are more important than the others.

We could look at the relationship of each independent variable to the dependent variable separately, by, for example, examining their correlations. However, if the independent variables are correlated among themselves, this approach is not satisfactory. The reason for this is that the various correlation coefficients are not independent, they will overlap. For example, if age and work experience are two independent variables they are probably correlated. The correlation of work experience with a dependent variable will reflect some of the relationship between age and the dependent variable.

We assume a particular kind of relationship between the independent variables and the dependent variable, a *linear* relationship; and we will talk about that assumption as a *linear model*. We let y_i represent the value of the dependent variable for case i and x_{ij} represent the value of independent variable x_j for case i. The model then is

$$y_i = \beta_0 + \beta_i x_{i1} + \beta_2 x_{i2} + \cdots + \beta_p x_{ip} + \epsilon_i$$

where we have p independent variables. The β_j's are coefficients that can be thought of as indicating the relative contribution of x_j to y, and β_0 is a *constant* term. This is a linear combination of the x's.

The term ϵ_i is called the *residual* of y_i. It is that part of the value y_i that is not accounted for by the independent variables. In the population as a whole there will be many cases at any particular combination of values for the independent variables. Although these cases have the same values for the independent variables they will not all have the same value for the dependent variable. We assume that there are many factors that make for these differences. Statisticians further assume that these factors (factors other than the independent variables in our analysis) combine in random ways to produce the residual for any given case. The residuals, therefore, are thought to be random. Although the residuals are thought of as random in any particular analysis, it might be possible in another analysis to take into account some of these other factors, if we had variables to represent them.

We assume that we have a sample of several cases (more than the number of independent variables) in which we have observed the values of the y variable and the x variables. Our task is to use the information in the sample to estimate the values of the β_j's. We will not be able to determine the values of the β_j's exactly from a sample, unless the sample contains all of the cases in the universe. We will designate the estimates of the β_j's as b_j.

In this chapter, as elsewhere in this book, we will use as an example data from a study of a new approach to the teaching of research in a school of social work. In 1978 the School of Social Service Administration at the University of Chicago instituted a program in which the teaching of research was to be done in close relationship to the teaching of practice of social work. It was thought that in this way students would come to appreciate the value of "empirically based practice" (EBP), that is, practice grounded in proven relationships among variables.

To study the effects of this change in curriculum, a questionnaire was administered to students at the beginning and at the end of the school year. The questionnaire tapped atttitudes toward research and empirically based practice and measured students' knowledge of research and statistics. The questionnaire administered at the end of the year also asked about the nature of the research course. The Statistical Package for the Social Sciences (SPSS) computer system was used for the analysis of the data. We will present some of the computer output for this study.[1]

In this chapter we will consider one of the dependent variables of this study, attitudes toward research at the end of the year (known to the computer as TOTALAT2). The independent variables we will use to explain this dependent variable are student's age (VAR007), amount of previous employment in social work (VAR013), whether or not research reports had an influence on students before coming to school (VAR060), the student's perceptions of the emphasis of the instructor on empirically based practice (EBPINCRS), and the student's attitude toward research at the beginning of the year (TOTALATT).

With one independent variable, it is easy to visualize the relationship between dependent and independent variables in a two-dimensional *scatterplot* with y and x as the coordinate axes. Table 3-1 is a scatterplot of attitudes toward research (vertical axis) and the orientation of the course to empirically based practice (horizontal axis). The scatterplot was produced on the SPSS computer system with the following commands:

Col. 1   Col. 16
SCATTERGRAM   TOTALAT2 WITH EBPINCRS
OPTIONS   4,7

The stars represent individuals located according to their values on the variables. The numbers 2 and 3 represent two or three cases at that point. (Actually these cases may not have exactly the same values on the variables, the computer has only so many print positions, so cases with values that are too close together to be represented separately are shown at the same place). In this scattergram there is evidently a slight tendency for high scores on TOTALAT2 to be related to high scores on EBPINCRS and for low scores on the two variables to go together.

The model for one independent variable is:

$$y_i = \beta_0 + \beta_1 x_{i1} + \epsilon_i$$

In our example, y_i is the score for individual i on TOTALAT2 and x_{i1} the score of that individual for EBPINCRS. We can imagine an equation like this for each case in the population, although of course we will never try to write them all out. In a way, the example equation for case i represents them all.

The equation $\hat{y}_i = b_0 + b_1 x_{i1}$ represents the best prediction of y_i knowing x_{i1} (assuming a linear model), the prediction being based on the estimates of β_0 and β_1 (b_0 and b_1) derived from the sample. The symbol $\hat{y}_i$ represents the predicted value of y for the ith case. Once we computed b_0 and b_1, we can plug in the value of x_1 for case i and find $\hat{y}_i$. This equation is represented by a straight line as in figure 3-1.

Table 3-1. Scatterplot

TOTALAT2

Attitudes toward research (vertical axis): 80.00, 75.00, 70.00, 65.00, 60.00, 55.00, 50.00, 45.00, 40.00, 35.00

EBPINCRS (horizontal axis): 45.00, 51.00, 57.00, 63.00, 69.00, 75.00, 81.00, 87.00, 93.00, 99.00

Orientation of course to empirically based practice

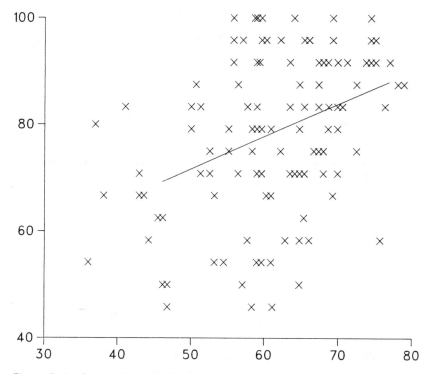

Figure 3-1. Scatterplot with Prediction Line.

In figure 3-1, e_i is the y distance from the point representing the ith case to the line, it is that part of the dependent variable value for the ith case that is not explained by the independent variable. The e_i is an estimate of ϵ_i. Clearly $e_i = y_i - \hat{y}_i$.

The Model in Matrix Terms

Let us now set up the model for more than one independent variable in matrix terms. It will simplify matters if we assume that all variables have been transformed into deviation score form. When we do that we eliminate the constant term b_0 from the equation.

We have a set of n y_i's (the values for the dependent variable for the n cases), which we stack up in a column vector we will call $\mathbf{y}$:

$$\mathbf{y} = \begin{matrix} y_1 \\ y_2 \\ . \\ . \\ . \\ y_n \end{matrix}$$

We will arrange the independent variables in an $\mathbf{X}$ matrix like that of chapter 2, that is, each row will represent the deviation score values for all the independent variables for a given case.

The coefficients β_j form a column vector β of length p:

$$\beta = \begin{matrix} \beta_1 \\ \beta_2 \\ . \\ . \\ . \\ \beta_p \end{matrix}$$

Finally, the ϵ_i's will be arranged in a column vector ϵ of length n.

Using the ideas of matrix multiplication and addition we can write our model like this:

$$\mathbf{y} = \mathbf{X}\beta + \bar{\epsilon} \quad \text{or} \quad \epsilon = \mathbf{y} - \mathbf{X}\beta$$

This matrix equation represents the whole set of equations for all the cases in the population. For the cases in the sample, we can represent the equations for the predicted values $(\hat{y}_i = b_1 x_{i1} + b_2 x_{i2} + \cdots + b_p x_{ip})$ in matrix form as $\mathbf{y} = \mathbf{Xb}$. Further, we can write the equations for the sample residuals $(e_i = y_i - \hat{y}_i)$ as $\mathbf{e} = \mathbf{y} - \hat{\mathbf{y}} = \mathbf{y} - \mathbf{Xb}$.

Solving for the Regression Coefficients

Lots of different numbers could be tried out for the b_i's and so we need some criterion for which ones to choose. The criterion that has been found to work particularly well is that of *least squares*. In this procedure, we estimate the β_j's so that the sum of the squared residuals is a minimum (i.e., $\Sigma e_i^2 = \Sigma(y_i - \hat{y}_i)^2$ should be minimized). When we have one independent variable this means we locate the line so that the sum of squares of the y distances of the points to the regression line is a minimum.

Recall that the sum of squares of a vector is equal to the scalar product of the vector with itself. This is the same thing as writing its transpose times itself. So the sum of squares of the e_i's can be written

$$e'e = (y - Xb)'(y - Xb)$$

Let us call this expression L. L can be thought of as a function of the vector b (that is, as a function of the b_i's). The y vector and X matrix are fixed (they are given by the data). Thus, the problem is to find the vector b which estimates β such that L is a minimum.

First, we have to expand L:

$$L = (y - Xb)'(y - Xb) = y'y - y'Xb - b'X'y + (Xb)'Xb$$

The terms $y'Xb$ and $b'X'y$ are transposes of each other. But when they are multiplied out they are really scalars. The transpose of a scalar is the scalar itself so these two terms are the same. So we have

$$L = y'y - 2b'X'y + b'X'Xb$$

We want to minimize this. Finding the vector b which minimizes this expression is a problem for the differential calculus. Details may be found in appendix C. Briefly, we take the derivative of L with respect to the vector b:

$$\frac{\partial L}{\partial b} = -2X'y + 2X'Xb$$

We then set this equal to zero and divide through by 2:

$$X'Xb = X'y$$

X', X and y are known, they are given by the data, but b is unknown.

$X'X$ is the SSCP matrix of the independent variables. $X'y$ is the vector of the crossproducts of the dependent variable with each of the independent variables. Multiplied out, this matrix-vector equation is really p equations in p unknowns, the p b's. These equations are called the *normal* equations. We want to solve for the b's, that is, we want to solve for the vector b. If $X'X$ is nonsingular, it has an inverse. We thus multiply both sides of this equation by $(X'X)^{-1}$ to get

$$b = (X'X)^{-1}X'y$$

The only situation in which $X'X$ is singular is when one or more of the original variables is a linear combination of the other variables (i.e., the columns of X are not independent). In this case the b vector cannot be found until the dependencies are removed by deleting variables from the analysis. If the columns of X are independent, $X'X$ will be nonsingular. (The problem of dependent columns of the X matrix is sometimes called the problem of *multicollinearity*.) At times we have $X'X$ matrices that are almost singular (they are said to be *ill conditioned*). In that case we (or rather the computer) will have difficulty in computing the inverse and the results may be inaccurate.[2]

To illustrate these ideas let us consider the construction of a regression equation involving TOTALAT2 as the dependent variable and age, previous experience, whether research reports had an impact, and TOTALATT as independent variables. These independent variables were chosen on the basis of preliminary analysis indicating that they were related to TOTALAT2.

In this study there were 121 cases, so the X matrix has 121 rows and 4 columns. We will not show the full X matrix. The SSCP matrix $(X'X)$ is

	Age	Experience	Reports	TOTALATT
Age	4296.793	223.744	-30.851	-524.875
Experience	223.744	445.322	9.264	136.317
Reports	-30.851	9.264	29.653	169.946
TOTALATT	-524.875	136.317	169.946	10162.684

The inverse of this matrix is:

.00024	-.00013	.00023	.00001
-.00013	.00233	-.00071	-.00003
.00023	-.00071	.03768	-.00061
.00001	-.00003	-.00061	.00011

The vector $X'y$ (the sum of the crossproducts of the independent variables with the dependent variable) is

$$-1680.601$$
$$231.773$$
$$181.061$$
$$5113.257$$

And

b =			
-.34229	Age	(b_1)
.49642	Experience	(b_2)
3.15286	Reports	(b_3)
.42608	TOTALATT	(b_4)

The b_j's are called *partial regression coefficients* or simply *regression coefficients*. Often we are not interested in finding b_0 (the estimate of β_0 is called the *intercept* or *constant*). However, b_0 may be found from the following formula:

$$b_0 = \bar{Y} - \sum_j b_j \bar{X}_j$$

where $\bar{Y}$ is the mean of the original dependent variable values (before finding the deviations) and $\bar{X}_j$ is the mean of the jth independent variable (before finding the deviations). For our example, $b_0 = 61.264 - [(-.34229)(26.959) + (.49642)(1.149) + (3.15286)(.430) + (.42608)(66.556)] = 40.208$.

Since we have found the vector **b**, we could, if we wanted, find the predicted values of y ($\hat{y}$) by multiplying **X** times **b**.

Review of Analysis of Variance

The analysis of variance is an extensive set of techniques in which the variation in a dependent variable is decomposed into components that are attributed to one or more independent variables. The variation in a variable is represented by the sum of squares of the variable. We begin with the total or original score sum of squares, Σx_i^2. We first break this original sum of squares down into two components—one the sum of squares around the mean $(\Sigma(x_i - \bar{x})^2$ sometimes called the *sum of the squared deviations* and the second a sum of squares due to the mean $(n\bar{x}^2)$. So $\Sigma x_i^2 = \Sigma(x_i - \bar{x})^2 + n\bar{x}^2$. Except in the last chapter, we are primarily concerned with analyzing the sum of squares around the mean and when we use the term "sum of squares" we will mean this sum of squared deviations. One of the reasons for our particular interest in the sum of the squared deviations is that it is the numerator of the variance and most research is concerned with exploring the variance in dependent variables. Having separated out the sum of squares due to the mean we are interested in dividing up the sum of squared deviations into portions that are due to one or more independent variables. After that dividing up, there will always be a part of this sum of squares that is left over which we call the *error* or *residual* sum of squares.

The simplest kind of analysis of variance is one that involves one independent variable where the independent variable is categorical. This is called a *one-way* analysis of variance. In that circumstance the sample is made up of a series of groups, one group for each category of the independent variable. Each group is thought of as a sample from a population. The independent variable is often called a *factor*. We use the analysis of variance to test the null hypothesis that the means of the populations from which these sample groups have been drawn are equal. Suppose we have k groups (k categories or levels in the independent variable or factor). Then the null hypothesis may be written as: H_0: $\mu_1 = \mu_2 = \cdots = \mu_k$. (Actually, the null hypothesis is that there is no "contrast" of the means equal to zero, where a contrast is a linear combination of the means, $\Sigma a_i\mu_i$ in which $\Sigma a_i = 0$). Even if the null hypothesis is true we would not expect the means of our sample groups to be exactly equal because of sampling variability.

Before we proceed, we need a little notation. The symbol x_{ji} means the value of the ith case in the jth group; $\bar{x}_{j.}$ represents the mean of the jth sample group; $\bar{x}_{..}$ represents the grand mean, that is the mean of all the cases, without regard to group membership; n_j is the number of cases in the jth group; and N is the total number of cases ($\Sigma n_j = N$).

To test the hypothesis we partition the sum of squares (the sum of the squared deviations) into two parts, one due to variations among the means of the groups (the *between groups sum of squares*) and the other due to variations within the groups (the *within groups sum of squares*). The between groups sum of squares is computed by subtracting the grand mean from each group mean, squaring this difference, multiplying this square by the number of cases in the group, then adding these quantities up for all the groups. This is symbolized by $\Sigma_j n_j (\bar{x}_{j.} - \bar{x}_{..})^2$. The within groups sum of squares is computed by first calculating the sum of squares within each group. We subtract the group mean from each observation; square this difference; add these squared differences up over all the cases in the group; then pool these group sums of squares over all groups, that is, we simply add them up. This may be symbolized as $\Sigma_j\Sigma_i(x_{ji} - \bar{x}_{j.})^2$. The sum of the within and between sum of squares is equal to the total deviation sum of squares.

Using the sums of squares we calculate quantities called the *mean squares*. The mean squares are the sums of squares divided by their *degrees of freedom*. The degrees of freedom for the between groups sum of squares is $k - 1$ and for within groups, $N - k$. These degrees of freedom add up to the degrees of freedom for the total sum of squares, $N - 1$. These numbers are often summarized in an analysis of variance table like this:

Source of Variation	Sum of Squares	d.f.	Mean Squares	F
Between	$\Sigma_j n_j(\bar{x}_{j.} - \bar{x}_{..})^2$	$k - 1$	s.s.$_{BET}/(k - 1)$	m.s.$_{BET}$/m.s.$_{WITHIN}$
Within	$\Sigma_j\Sigma_i(x_{ji} - \bar{x}_{j.})^2$	$N - k$	s.s.$_{WITHIN}/(N - k)$	
Total	$\Sigma_j\Sigma_i(x_{ji} - \bar{x}_{..})^2$	$N - 1$		

To test the hypothesis we must make some assumptions about our data. The assumptions are that the populations from which our samples were drawn are normally distributed and all have the same variances. If we have large enough sample sizes, violations of these assumptions will not seriously affect our results. Under these assumptions, if the null hypothesis is true the samples essentially come from the same population (all the populations are normal, have the same variance and mean so they are all the same). It can be shown that under these assumptions the between groups mean square and the within groups mean square are both estimates of the single population variance. Hence, they should be relatively close in size. However, if the null hypothesis is not true, that is, the population means are not all equal, the between groups mean square will tend to be larger than the within groups mean square. The test of the hypothesis is performed by computing the *F ratio* which is the between groups mean square divided by the within groups mean square. If the *F* ratio is large enough we reject the null hypothesis. To determine whether it is large enough we look up the *critical value* of the *F* in a table of the *F* statistic. There is a different critical value for each possible pair of values for the degrees of freedom ($k - 1$, the numerator degrees of freedom; and $N - k$, the denominator degrees of freedom) and for each probability level. Tables, however, include critical values for only certain probabilities and for certain combinations of degrees of freedom. If the calculated *F* exceeds the critical value for a particular probability (α) we can reject the null hypothesis with $1 - \alpha$ confidence.

Effects

In the analysis of variance we often talk about *effects*. In one-way analysis of variance the effect of being in a particular group is the difference between that group's mean and the mean of the means of all the groups. The mean of the means will usually not be equal to the grand mean except when we have the same number of cases in all our groups.

Two-Way Analysis of Variance

Two-way analysis of variance involves a single dependent variable and two categorical independent variables (two factors). It may be schematized as follows:

	Factor A
Factor B	$A_1 \, A_2 \ldots A_c$
B_1	
B_2	
.	
.	
.	
B_r	

Each cell in the above table has n cases. In this discussion we will assume that all cells have the same number of cases although that is not a necessary condition. Factor A (the columns factor) has c categories or levels while factor B (the rows factor) has r levels. Which factor appears in the rows and which in the columns is arbitrary.

Two-way analysis of variance usually arises in one of two ways. First, both factors might represent treatments, for example, factor A might be brief vs. extended treatment while factor B might be individual vs. family treatment. In that case, the design would have four cells representing the four possible combinations of the two factors. Alternatively, one factor could be a treatment while the other represented a characteristic of individuals such as gender. In that case, men and women would be separately assigned to the treatment conditions.

Again we need some notation. The symbol x_{jli} represents a value for a particular case. The first subscript is the number of the row; the second, the number of the column; and the third, the number of the case in the cell. The symbols $\bar{x}_{j..}$ and $\bar{x}_{.l.}$ represent the mean of the jth row and the lth column respectively, while $\bar{x}_{jl.}$ is the mean of the jlth cell. The grand mean of the observations is $\bar{x}_{...}$, while means in the populations are represented by μ's with subscripts.

In a two-way analysis of variance it is possible to divide up the deviations sum of squares into four parts, the variation due to rows, to columns, to interaction, and within groups. Rows, columns, and within groups sums of squares are computed in the same way as in one-way analysis of variance. For rows, we subtract the grand mean from each row mean, square this difference, multiply by the number of cases in the row, and add over all rows. This is symbolized as $\Sigma_j cn(\bar{x}_{j..} - \bar{x}_{...})^2$, where cn is the number of cases in each row. The degrees of freedom for this sum of squares is $r - 1$. For columns, the sum of squares is $\Sigma_l rn(\bar{x}_{.l.} - \bar{x}_{...})^2$ and the degrees of freedom is $c - 1$. For within groups, the sum of squares is found by subtracting the cell mean from each observation, squaring this difference, and adding over all cases. This is symbolized as $\Sigma_j \Sigma_l \Sigma_i (x_{jli} - \bar{x}_{jl.})^2$. The degrees of freedom for within cells is the sum of the degrees of freedom within each cell. Within each cell, we have degrees of freedom of $n - 1$ so the degrees of freedom for the within cells sum of squares is $N - rc$.

Interaction

In two-way analysis of variance we encounter a new source of variation, that due to the interaction between the independent variables. If the independent variables have a relationship to the dependent variable this relationship may occur in one of two ways, either it is *additive* or it is *interactive*.

To explain an additive situation we recall the idea of an *effect*. The effect of being in a particular row is equal to the row mean minus the grand mean. Similarly for column effects. The effect of being in a particular cell is equal to the cell mean minus the grand mean. The situation is said to be additive if for all cells the cell effect is equal to the sum of the row and the column effects for the cell. We can symbolize this as

$$(\bar{x}_{jl.} - \bar{x}_{...}) = (\bar{x}_{j..} - \bar{x}_{...}) + (\bar{x}_{.l.} - \bar{x}_{...})$$

If the cell effect is not equal to the sum of the row and column effects for any cell the situation is said to be interactive. The extent to which interaction exists in a cell is equal to the difference between the two sides of the above equation:

$$d_{jl} = (\bar{x}_{jl.} - \bar{x}_{...}) - [(\bar{x}_{j..} - \bar{x}_{...}) + (\bar{x}_{.l.} - \bar{x}_{...})]$$
$$= \bar{x}_{jl.} - \bar{x}_{j..} - \bar{x}_{.l.} + \bar{x}_{...}$$

These ideas lead to the null hypothesis that there is no interaction in the population. As with all things involving sampling variation, we may have no interaction in the population and yet observe some interaction in the sample. In fact, in real life we will nearly always have at least some interaction in the sample. The question is whether there is enough to cast doubt on the null hypothesis of no interaction in the population.

We use the d_{jl}'s to compute a sum of squares for interaction. We square each d_{jl}, multiply by n and add up over all cells: $\Sigma_j\Sigma_l n(\bar{x}_{jl.} - \bar{x}_{j..} - \bar{x}_{.l.} + \bar{x}_{...})^2$. The degrees of freedom for interaction is the product of the degrees of freedom for rows times the degrees of freedom for columns: $(r - 1)(c - 1)$. Again, the calculations are summarized in an analysis of variance table:

	Sum of Squares	d.f.	Mean Squares
Rows	$\Sigma_j cn(\bar{x}_{j..} - \bar{x}_{...})^2$	$r - 1$	s.s.$_{ROWS}/(r - 1)$
Columns	$\Sigma_l rn(\bar{x}_{.l.} - \bar{x}_{...})^2$	$c - 1$	s.s.$_{COL}/(c - 1)$
Interaction	$\Sigma_j\Sigma_l n(\bar{x}_{jl.} - \bar{x}_{j..} - \bar{x}_{.l.} + \bar{x}_{...})^2$	$(r - 1)(c - 1)$	s.s.$_{INT}/(r - 1)(c - 1)$
Within	$\Sigma_j\Sigma_l\Sigma_i(x_{jli} - \bar{x}_{jl.})^2$	$N - rc$	s.s.$_{WITHIN}/(N - rc)$
Total	$\Sigma_j\Sigma_l\Sigma_i(x_{jli} - \bar{x}_{...})^2$	$N - 1$	

The figures in the table are used to test three null hypotheses about the population:

1. The row means are equal, that is, there is no differential effect of the B treatments, $\mu_{1.} = \mu_{2.} = \cdots = \mu_{r.}$
2. The column means are equal, i.e., $\mu_{.1} = \mu_{.2} = \cdots = \mu_{.c}$
3. There is no interaction, that is, for all j and l, $\mu_{jl} - \mu_{j.} - \mu_{.l} + \mu_{..} = 0$

In practice, the interaction test is performed first. If it is not significant, we go on to test for rows and columns effects. If the interaction is significant, technically we should not pay attention to the significance of rows or columns but should merely describe how the various combinations of levels of A with levels of B are related to the dependent variable.[3]

Contrasts

If we have more than two groups for a factor and we find that the main or interaction effects are significant, we will want to know which of the groups are most contributing to the differences. This leads to the topic of contrasts among groups. The analysis of contrasts will not be dealt with in this book. Several texts deal with contrasts (see, for example, Hinkle, Wiersma and Jurs, 1979; for a discussion of contrasts in multivariate analysis see Harris, 1975).

The Analysis of Variance of Regression

It is often useful to apply the ideas of the analysis of variance to regression. To do so, we divide the variation in the dependent variable values into two parts, one due to the variation in the residuals and the other due to regression. That is, we divide up (or "partial") the sum of squares of y. The total sum of squares of y is given in vector terms as $\mathbf{y'y}$. The sum of squares due to regression is $\mathbf{\hat{y}'\hat{y}} = (\mathbf{Xb})'(\mathbf{Xb}) = \mathbf{b'X'Xb}$. The residual sum of squares $\mathbf{e'e}$ is the difference between these two terms: $\mathbf{e'e} = \mathbf{y'y} - \mathbf{b'X'Xb}$. The results can be summarized in an analysis of variance table as follows:

Source of Variation	Sum of Squares	d.f.	Mean Squares
Regression	$\mathbf{b'X'Xb}$	p	$\mathbf{b'X'Xb}/p$
Residual	$\mathbf{y'y} - \mathbf{b'X'Xb}$	$n - p - 1$	$(\mathbf{y'y} - \mathbf{b'X'Xb})/(n - p - 1)$
Total	$\mathbf{y'y}$	$n - 1$	

where the degrees of freedom (d.f.) for regression is the number of independent variables (p), degrees of freedom for residual is total number of cases minus the number of independent variables minus one. The mean squares are found by dividing each sum of squares by its degrees of freedom. If the linear model is correct, the mean square for residual is an unbiased estimate of σ^2, the variance of the ϵ's.

For our example, $p = 4$, $n = 121$, and the sum of squares for the dependent variable $(\mathbf{y'y})$ is 10318.59779. The quantity $\mathbf{b'X'Xb}$ is

$$(-.34 \;\; .50 \;\; 3.15 \;\; .43)\begin{pmatrix} 4296.79 & 223.74 & -30.85 & -524.88 \\ 223.74 & 445.32 & 9.26 & 136.32 \\ -30.85 & 9.26 & 29.65 & 169.95 \\ -524.77 & 136.32 & 169.95 & 10162.68 \end{pmatrix}\begin{pmatrix} -.34 \\ .50 \\ 3.15 \\ .43 \end{pmatrix} = 3439.83$$

The filled-in table looks like this:

Source of Variation	Sum of Squares	d.f.	Mean Squares
Regression	3439.82852	4	859.95713
Residual	6878.76928	116	59.29974
Total	10318.59780	120	

A quantity that may be quickly derived from the analysis of variance table is the square of the multiple correlation coefficient (R^2). It may be thought of as the proportion of variance "explained" or "accounted for" by the regression equation. It is the ratio of the sum of squares for regression to the total sum of squares. So we have

$$R^2 = \frac{\mathbf{b'X'Xb}}{\mathbf{y'y}}$$

The square root of this value (R) is the simple correlation between y_i and $\hat{y}_i$. In our example R^2 is $3439.8/10318.6 = .33$.

Tests of Significance

Since we have assumed that we have taken a sample from a larger population, we will want to know whether we can generalize our sample results to the population as a whole. This is done through tests of significance. The usual procedure is to test the significance of the regression as a whole and of regression coefficients individually. In order to proceed with significance testing, it is necessary to make some assumptions about our data.

The assumptions are stated in terms of the residuals in the original model, the ϵ's. We imagine that it is possible to take several observations of y at each possible combination of the x_j variables. The values of y for a particular combination of values of the independent variables will differ, because they have different residuals. These values of y and of the residuals for those y's will have a distribution. For one independent variable the situation can be visualized as in figure 3-2.

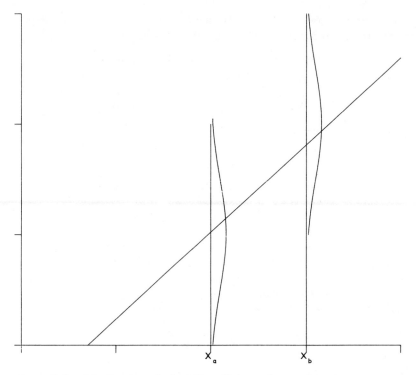

Figure 3-2.   Distribution of y's at Two Values of x.

where the vertical curves at x_a and x_b represent the distributions of the y values
when x equals x_a or x_b. The assumption of linearity is the same as saying that
the population regression line goes through the means of those distributions, so
the first assumption is that the mean of the possible ϵ's at each value of x will
be zero.

The second assumption is that the variances of the ϵ's are the same at all of
the possible combinations of values of the independent variables. A third assumption is that the ϵ's at a particular combination of x values are normally distributed. These assumptions are sometimes written like this:

$$\epsilon_i \sim N(0,\sigma^2)$$

which means that ϵ_i has a normal distribution with a mean of zero and a variance
of σ^2 which is the same at every combination of the values of the independent
variables.

A fourth assumption is that the residuals of various y values are unrelated to each other, that is they are independent of each other. This is the same thing as saying that the covariance of the residuals will be zero. This assumption would be violated if, for example, large y's tended to have large residuals as compared to small y's.

Statisticians pull all four of these assumptions together in a single expression involving matrices and vectors. This expression is

$$e \sim N(\mathbf{0}, \sigma^2 \mathbf{I})$$

where N stands for a multivariate normal distribution, $\mathbf{0}$ is a vector of zeros of length n, the number of cases, σ^2 is the common variance of the residuals, $\mathbf{I}$ is an identity matrix of order n and $\sigma^2\mathbf{I}$ is the variance-covariance matrix of the e_i's (it is a diagonal matrix with a common value σ^2 in all the diagonal cells and zeros in the off-diagonal cells, indicating zero covariance among the residuals). To understand this expression, we imagine a large number of samples, in each of which we look at the same set of combinations of values of the independent variables, and we find the residuals (the vector e) for each sample. Those residuals will have a multivariate normal distribution in which the expected values (the means) of the residuals will be zero for each combination of dependent variable values. Furthermore, the variance-covariance matrix of the residuals will have the constant σ^2 in all of the diagonal cells and zeros elsewhere, the zeros indicating zero covariance among the residuals.

It may seem that this set of assumptions is rather formidable, and it is. There are ways of handling the situation if these assumptions are not met. The techniques are rather complicated, however, and will not be dealt with here (see Press, 1972).

Under the foregoing assumptions we can test for the significance of the regression as a whole by constructing the ratio of the regression mean square to the residual mean square. Under the null hypothesis that in the population the independent variables do not predict the dependent variable these two mean squares are both estimates of the variance of y. Thus if the null hypothesis is true, the ratio will be close to one. If the null hypothesis is false (the independent variables do predict the dependent variable) the ratio will tend to be larger than one. This ratio is an F statistic with p degrees of freedom in the numerator and $n - p - 1$ degrees of freedom in the denominator. We find the probability of our obtained F by looking it up in a table of the F distribution. For our example, the obtained F is 14.502, the probability of which is less than .0001. This means that if the null hypothesis is true the probability of getting the sample results we got is less than .0001. Since this is small, and since we did get the results, we reject the null hypothesis and conclude that in the population the independent variables as a whole are likely to be related to the dependent variable. The test can be thought of as a test of the null hypothesis that the multiple correlation coefficient (R) is zero. Equivalently, it is a test of the hypothesis that all of the β_j's are zero ($\beta = 0$).

If the total regression is significant, interest will focus on particular independent variables; that is, we are usually concerned with whether particular b's are significant since the b coefficient indicates the importance of a variable in predicting the dependent variable. The hypothesis can be written H_0: $\beta_j = 0$. The b's are subject to sampling variation—that is, in different samples they will be different—so we can talk about their standard deviations or standard errors. Furthermore, since the independent variables are related to each other, the b's will be related to each other and so will, in general have nonzero covariance. Therefore, we can think about the variance-covariance matrix of the **b** vector which turns out to be:

$$V(\mathbf{b}) = (\mathbf{X'X})^{-1}\sigma^2$$

that is, we take the inverse of the SSCP matrix of the x's and multiply each value in the matrix by the residual variance. If the linear model is correct, this residual variance is estimated by the residual mean square found in the analysis of variance table. We can then write

$$\mathbf{b} \sim N[\beta,(\mathbf{X'X})^{-1}\sigma^2]$$

which means that the vector **b** is multivariate normally distributed with means of β and a variance-covariance matrix $(\mathbf{X'X})^{-1}\sigma^2$. In practice, the estimated variances of the b's will be found in the diagonal of the matrix $(\mathbf{X'X})^{-1}s^2$. Hence, the test of significance of a particular b_j (that is, H_0: $\beta_j = 0$) is computed as the ratio of b_j to the square root of its variance. This ratio is a t statistic with $n - p - 1$ degrees of freedom.

For our example, σ^2 is estimated by the mean square for residual, 59.29974. So the variance-covariance matrix of the b's is estimated as

$$\begin{pmatrix} .00024 & -.00013 & .00023 & .00001 \\ -.00013 & .00233 & -.00071 & -.00003 \\ .00023 & -.00071 & .03768 & .00061 \\ .00001 & -.00003 & -.00061 & .00011 \end{pmatrix}(59.29974)$$

which is equal to

	Age	Experience	Reports	TOTALATT
Age	.01438	-.00770	.01384	.00061
Experience	-.00770	.13838	-.04239	-.00154
Reports	.01384	-.04239	2.23421	-.03608
TOTALATT	.00061	-.00154	-.03608	.00649

The t statistic for age is

$$t = \frac{-.34229}{\sqrt{.01438}} = -2.855$$

with 116 degrees of freedom. This statistic has a probability of .0051, so we can conclude that age is significantly related to TOTALAT2. The relationship is inverse (as shown by the negative sign on the b for age) which means that as age increases attitudes toward research decrease. The significance of the other variables can be determined in a similar way.

In practice, regression analysis is almost always performed by a computer. Table 3-2 shows the output of the above analysis produced by the SPSS computer system. The program used was NEW REGRESSION, which is a part of Version 9 of the SPSS system.[4] The output was produced by the following cards:

NEW REGRESSION VARIABLES=VAR007,VAR013,VAR060,TOTALATT,
               TOTALAT2/DEPENDENT TOTALAT2/
               ENTER VAR007,VAR013,VAR060,TOTALATT/

The following aspects of the output have not been discussed above:

METHOD: ENTER. SPSS has available several methods for constructing regression equations. These methods are used to select a small set of independent variables from a larger set. These methods are discussed in the next chapter. The method used here was ENTER, which means that all independent variables named are included in the equation.

ADJUSTED R SQUARE. The interpretation of the R square is complicated by the fact that it is dependent in part on the number of independent variables in the equation. If we have a large number of variables relative to the size of the sample the R^2 will tend to be an overestimate of the R^2 in the population. The reason for this is that, in a sample, some of the association between the dependent and independent variables is due to sampling error (random errors due to sampling). In fact, if the number of independent variables is exactly one less than the number of cases and none of the independent variables are linear combinations of each other, the R^2 will be a perfect 1.0 in the sample even if the independent variables have nothing to do with the dependent variable in the population. To take care of this problem, an adjusted R^2 is computed that is an estimate of the R^2 in the population.

STANDARD ERROR. This is the *standard error of estimate.* It is the square root of the mean square of the residuals. It is an estimate of the standard devia-

Table 3-2. Regression Analysis Produced by the SPSS Computer System

FILE NEWFIL17 (CREATION DATE = 07/28/81)

```
                * * * *   M U L T I P L E   R E G R E S S I O N   * * * *

EQUATION NUMBER  1.

DEPENDENT VARIABLE..   TOTALAT2    POSTEST-ATTITS ABT RES-TOTAL SCORE

BEGINNING BLOCK NUMBER  1.   METHOD:  ENTER   VAR007   VAR013   VAR060   TOTALATT

VARIABLE(S) ENTERED ON STEP NUMBER
  1..   TOTALATT   ATTITS ABT RES - TOTAL SCORE
  2..   VAR013     NO.YRS.OF FULL TIME SW EMPLOYMENT
  3..   VAR007     AGE
  4..   VAR060     HAVE RES REPRTS MADE IMPACT ON YR THKG?

                              ANALYSIS OF VARIANCE
MULTIPLE R          0.57738                        DF      SUM OF SQUARES    MEAN SQUARE
R SQUARE            0.33336     REGRESSION          4         3439.82852      859.95713
ADJUSTED R SQUARE   0.31037     RESIDUAL          116         6878.76928       59.29974
STANDARD ERROR      7.70063

                         F =   14.50187      SIGNIF F = 0.0000

------------------------ VARIABLES IN THE EQUATION ------------------------

VARIABLE            B          SE B        BETA         T      SIG T

TOTALATT        0.42608      0.08057     0.42285      5.289   0.0000
VAR013          0.49642      0.37200     0.10313      1.334   0.1847
VAR007         -0.34229      0.11990    -0.22088     -2.855   0.0051
VAR060          3.15286      1.49473     0.16902      2.109   0.0371
(CONSTANT)     40.20845      6.32395                  6.358   0.0000
```

tion of the residuals. The standard error of estimate is a measure of the accuracy of the prediction equation. If the inferential assumptions hold, about 95% of the actual y values will be within two times the standard error of estimate on either side of the $\hat{y}$'s.

BETA. These are the standardized regression coefficients discussed below. They are not the population regression coefficients (β) discussed above.

SE B. These are the standard errors (the estimated standard deviations) of the b's.

(CONSTANT). The first number in this line is the b_0 as computed above. As with the other b's b_0 is subject to sampling variability, so the SE B for the constant is its standard error. The figures in the T and SIG T columns are used to test the null hypothesis that this constant is 0 in the population. In practice, we usually have little interest in this line. It should be noted that the probability is not exactly 0, although it is very small. Unfortunately, the SPSS system prints out very small probabilities as zero. They should be reported as $p < .001$ or $p < .0001$.

Note that in the analysis of variance table the "total" line is not shown and the F statistic and its significance are shown below the table. F and SIGNIF F refer to the entire equation.

The computer output indicates that the four variables taken together are significantly related to TOTALAT2 ($R^2 = .33$, $F = 14.502$, $p < .0001$). The variables for age, impact of research reports, and TOTALATT are highly significant ($p < .01$). The variable for experience is not significant ($p = .18$). When a variable is insignificant, it is often dropped and a new equation is computed without it. If that is done the b coefficients for the other variables will change (usually they will increase, but not always). The multiple R will be smaller.

If we test the significance of several b_j's at once, we run the usual risks encountered when several null hypotheses are tested at once. That is, if we test several H_0's each at a certain significance level (say .05) the probability that we will reject at least one true null hypothesis will be higher than the selected level. We say that the "overall" or "experiment wise" type one error rate is greater than .05. This is because of *sampling error*, the fact that sample characteristics differ from those of the population. In the case of regression coefficients, even if all the β's are zero, the probability that we will declare at least one of the β's to be different from zero will be higher than .05. The problem is complicated by the fact that the b's are related to each other, so the test of one is not independent of the test of another. One way out of this is to construct simultaneous confidence intervals (see Draper and Smith, 1981). In chapter 9 we consider another approach to this problem.

Another way of thinking about the test of significance of a particular b_j that yields equivalent results is in terms of the sequential addition of variables to the multiple regression equation. We first construct a regression equation with all the variables except x_j. This regression equation has a certain sum of squares for regression. We then construct the regression equation for all the variables including x_j. This new equation has a new sum of squares for regression that is almost always larger than the previous one (never smaller). The difference between these two sums of squares is the sum of squares due to the term $b_j x_j$ after all of the other independent variables have been entered. We can call this the *partial sum of squares* due to b_j. It has one degree of freedom so its mean square is the same. We call this the *partial mean square.*

The ratio of the partial mean square to the residual mean square (the residual after all variables, including b_j are in) can be considered a partial F. Under the assumptions, it has an F distribution with 1 and $n - p - 1$ degrees of freedom. This F provides a test for the significance of b_j and in fact is equal to the square of the t statistic found earlier.

Extending our example, we added to the above model the variable EBPINCRS, the student's assessment of the extent to which the instructor was oriented to empirically based practice. That is, we recalculated the equation with the four independent variables included above plus EBPINCRS. The resulting b values and their t statistics are as follows:

	b	t	p
TOTALATT	.41135	5.462	.0001
Experience	.21271	.601	.5488
Age	-.26997	-2.384	.0188
EBPINCRS	.19353	4.247	.0001
Reports	2.87061	2.054	.0422

and the analysis of variance table for this equation is

	Sum of Squares	d.f.	Mean Squares	F
Regression	4372.51456	5	874.50291	16.9
Residual	5946.08324	115	51.70507	
Total	10318.59779	120		

The partial S.S. is found by subtracting the S.S. for regression found in the earlier equation from that above: $4372.51 - 3439.83 = 932.72$. The F statistic for this is 18.04. This F is also the square of the t for EBPINCRS in the above table. It is significant at $p < .0001$. Hence we can conclude that EBPINCRS is related to TOTALAT2, taking into account the other independent variables. The variable "experience" is now quite insignificant and might well be dropped from the analysis.

This approach to increments in the regression sum of squares can be extended to sets of variables that might be entered into the equation all at one time. In this case the degrees of freedom for the partial sum of squares is equal to the number of variables in the set.

Interpretation of Regression Coefficients

What do the partial regression coefficients mean? A partial regression coefficient indicates how much of a change is expected in the dependent variable (y) for an increment of one unit in the independent variable, provided that there is no change in any of the other independent variables. For example, if we increase EBPINCRS by one unit, we expect an increase in TOTALAT2 of .194. In the proviso that no other variables change lies one of the significant difficulties in multiple regression analysis. The independent variables are usually correlated— that is, they vary together—and it is thus difficult to talk about varying one while holding the others constant.

Another difficulty with the regression coefficients is more readily overcome. We often want to compare the effects of two independent variables in a regression equation. This suggests that we compare their regression coefficients. However, these coefficients will usually not be directly comparable because the variables will have been measured on different kinds of scales and will have different variability. It would not make sense to compare the effects on social status of an increase of one dollar in income to the effects of an increase of one year in education.

The way out of this problem is to make use of standardized regression coefficients. *Standardized coefficients* are the regression coefficients obtained by putting all of the variables (both dependent and independent) into standard score form before performing the analysis. In practice, nobody performs two regressions, one on deviation scores and the other on standard scores, because there is a simple way to transform unstandardized regression coefficients into standardized ones. If we designate standardized coefficients as $b_j{}^*$ then:

$$b_j{}^* = \frac{s_j}{s_y} b_j$$

where b_j is the unstandardized coefficient, s_j is the standard deviation of the jth independent variable and s_y is the standard deviation of the dependent variable. Computer programs for regression usually provide both the unstandardized and standardized coefficients. In the above output, the standardized coefficients are found in the column labeled BETA.

Standardized regression coefficients are sometimes called *beta weights* and symbolized β_j, thus creating monumental confusion with the meaning we gave β_j (the population regression coefficients) earlier in this section.

Since standard scores represent numbers of standard deviations from the mean, $b_j{}^*$ represents the number of standard deviations y is expected to change for an increment of one standard deviation in x_j. Because all of the variables now have the same variance, their regression coefficients are usually considered to be comparable, and thus we can talk about one as "having more effect" than another.

The use of standardized regression coefficients is not without problems. First, in some contexts ignoring the original units of the measurement does violence to the data. Some variables may be more variable than others, and standardizing them treats them as if they are all similar. In addition, the variance of our independent variables may depend on the sample we have at hand. Samples with different variances will have quite different regression coefficients. Nonetheless, in social science research standardized coefficients are those that are usually interpreted.

Bias

The interpretation of multiple regression equations may also be affected by bias in the estimation of the regression coefficients. In technical terms, if the model used does not fit, then the b_j's or $b_j{}^*$'s will not be unbiased estimators of the true effects of the independent variables on the dependent variable. Since there are lots of components to the model (including the assumptions), there are lots of places to go wrong.

If an important variable has been left out of the regression equation, the regression coefficients of the other variables will be affected. This is because the deleted variable is correlated with the variables that are included and the regression coefficients will therefore reflect some of the contribution of the deleted variable (see Draper and Smith, 1981, and Snedecor and Cochran, 1967). Hence, it is often recommended that all variables that might be important should be included in the regression equation, even those variables that are of little interest to the analyst. However, this recommendation conflicts with the fact that models with large numbers of terms have other problems, in particular, they violate the principle of parsimony, the idea that explanations ought to be as simple as possible.

A second source of bias is errors in measurement. Random errors of measurement in the dependent variable do not bias the regression coefficients. They are included in the ϵ_i term of the model if such errors have the same variance for all $\hat{y}_i$. But errors in measuring the independent variables are more problematic. The model as we have presented it assumes that the independent variables are measured without error. In many situations, this is an untenable assumption. If the errors of measurement are independent, the result is usually an underestimate of the b_j's (i.e., the b_j and $b_j{}^*$ will be too small, see Draper and Smith, 1981, Anderson, 1958).

Still another source of bias is failure to include in the model higher order polynomial or interaction terms. Sometimes, the relationship between the dependent and independent variables is nonlinear, but can be represented by including terms that are powers of one or more independent variables or products of two or more independent variables. For example, a regression involving one independent variable, in which a squared term was required would be represented by a model such as:

$$y = \beta_0 + \beta_1 x_1 + \beta_{12} x_1^2 + \epsilon$$

A regression involving two independent variables which had interactive effects on the dependent variables (that is, effects of one differed for differing levels of the other) would have a term in which the two variables are multiplied together:

$$y = \beta_0 + \beta_1 x_1 + \beta_2 x_2 + \beta_{12} x_1 x_2 + \epsilon$$

If models such as these are the correct ones for the particular situation but the polynomial or cross-product terms are left out of the computations, the obtained b's will usually be an underestimate of the true effects of the variables. Computer programs usually allow for the generation of new variables that are powers or products of original variables, which can then be used in the regression models.

Unfortunately, this procedure often produces estimates of the b's that will be uninterpretable. Squared terms and cross-product terms are usually highly correlated with their components (that is, x_1^2 and $x_1 x_2$ are usually highly correlated with x_1). The standardized b's for these highly correlated variables will be quite large in absolute value and of opposite signs. In addition, they will be very unstable (that is, their standard errors will be quite large). However, the analysis of variance of the increment in variance explained by x_1^2 or $x_1 x_2$ will be accurate. Hence, one can ignore the obtained b's and simply interpret the significance of the additional variance explained by the polynomial and interaction terms.

For polynomial regressions, orthogonal polynomials can be used to produce interpretable b's (see Cohen and Cohen, 1975).

Residuals

Since the assumptions are intimately tied up with the residuals, it is obviously instructive to examine the residuals from the equation.

First, with regard to the assumption of normality, although you usually can not look at several e_i's for the same combination of x values to see if they are normally distributed, the e_i's taken as a whole should be normal.

There are ways by which one can explore whether or not a set of residuals seems to come from a normal distribution:

1. Plot the frequency distribution of the residuals and see if it looks right. For even moderately large samples, it probably will not look normal even if it comes from a normal distribution. What you look for is a drastic deviation, usually marked skewness.
2. Plot the cumulative distribution to see if it conforms to the cumulative normal distribution. This plot shows the proportion of cases below each value of e. If the e's are normally distributed, the cumulative normal will look like figure 3-3.

Computer programs produce the plot shown in figure 3-3 in a slightly modified form, called a normal probability plot (or P-P plot). Ideally, this plot of the cumulative distribution should produce a straight line as in figure 3-4.

There is a general problem in all of the above as to how much of a deviation from normality should be tolerated. A useful and practical discussion can be found in Roberts and Ling (1982).

The assumption of equal variance is usually examined by looking at the residuals, plotted against one or more independent variables, the dependent variable, or the predicted dependent variable $\hat{y}_i$, or some other variable like the time sequence of the observations. The predicted values $\hat{y}_i$ are most frequently used.

In general, if the ϵ_i have equal variances such plots will look like figure 3-5.

If they look like figures 3-6 or 3-7 you probably do not have equal variances.

Other Uses of Residual Plots

Residual plots may have various other appearances. One other outcome that is instructive is a curved pattern as in figure 3-8. This usually indicates that a linear model will not do and that a quadratic (squared) or higher term of some independent variable is required.

The SPSS system provides for an analysis of residuals. From the last equation above, we dropped experience and recalculated the regression equation. The

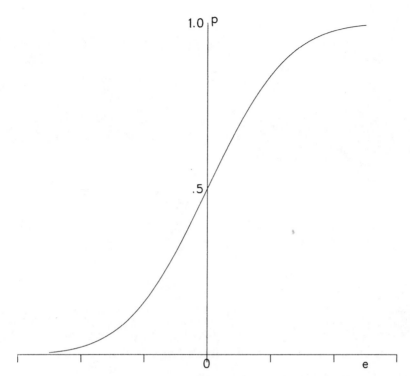

Figure 3-3. Cumulative Normal Distribution.

plots shown in figures 3-3 to 3-5 concern the residuals from that equation. They
were produced by the following control cards:

```
NEW REGRESSION VARIABLES=VAR007,VAR060,TOTALATT,
              EBPINCRS,TOTALAT2/DEPENDENT TOTALAT2/
              ENTER VAR007,VAR060,TOTALATT,
              EBPINCRS/RESIDUALS/
              SCATTERPLOT=LARGE(*PRED,*RESID)/
```

The histogram for the standardized residuals is shown in table 3-3. It is
printed vertically on the page rather than horizontally as in most textbooks. In
addition, if one turns the page on its side, the values go from positive to negative
rather than the other way around as we are accustomed. Stars and colons represent cases and form the bars of the histogram.

For purposes of plotting on this chart, the scale of standardized residuals is
divided into categories that are either .12 or .13 wide. The numbers in the third

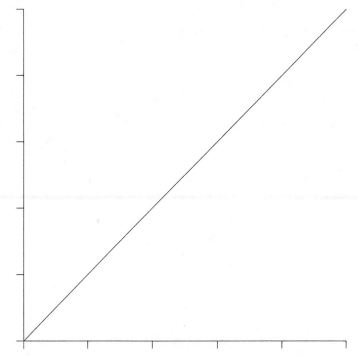

Figure 3-4. Normal Probability Plot.

column are the upper limits of these categories. Thus the star opposite the value 2.62 represents the residual of one case that lies in the interval 2.5 to 2.62 standard deviations from the mean of the residuals (the mean of the residuals is always 0). The categories labeled OUT at the top and bottom of the picture are categories for residuals that lie above 3.0 or below –3.0 standard deviations.

The second column, labeled EXP N, gives the number of cases that would be in each category if the residuals were normally distributed. These expected numbers are shown on the plot as dots and colons. Notice that the dots and colons form a normal-shaped curve.

The first column gives the actual number of residuals in each category.

The histogram in table 3-3 is somewhat ragged and clearly does not conform exactly to a normal shape. For a relatively small sample, such as this one, that is not unusual and is not necessarily a cause for alarm. Of some concern is the fact that there is a relatively large number of small residuals (residuals with large negative values). The distribution is said to be negatively *skewed* or skewed to the left.

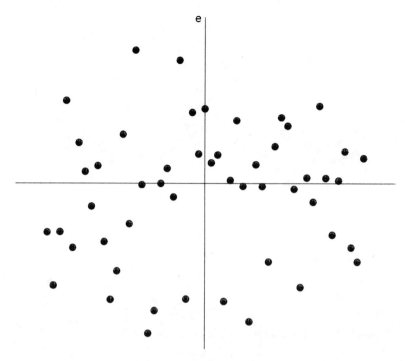

Figure 3-5. Residual Plot with Equal Variance.

Next we look at the normal probability (*P-P*) plot (table 3-4). This plot is constructed in the following way. The cases are ranked according to their standardized residuals (it does not matter that the residuals are standardized; unstandardized values would do for this purpose). For each case, two values are then determined from this ranking: the proportion of cases that actually lie at or below the case and the proportion that would be expected to lie at or below the case if the residuals were exactly normally distributed. These two values are then plotted against each other. If the residuals are exactly normally distributed, the plot will lie on the diagonal line. Let us take as an example the star that is circled on the graph. It is opposite the .25 mark on the vertical axis, indicating that one fourth of the cases lie at or below this value. The star is above the value .275 on the horizontal axis indicating that if the residuals were distributed normally, 27.5% of them would be at or below this value.

This plot confirms the negative skew of the residuals. That is, it starts out above the line, then bows below the line before crossing the line again at a relatively high value. This shape is characteristic of a negative skew. A distribution

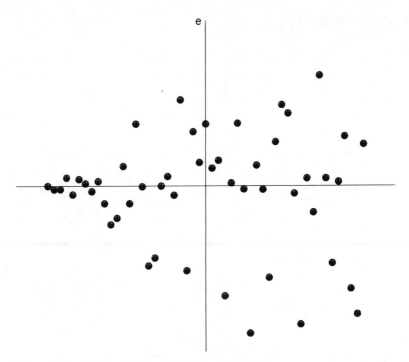

Figure 3-6. Residual Plot without Equal Variance.

that is skewed in the other direction (positively) has a reverse bow, that is, it starts and ends below the line. Distributions that are platykurtic or leptokurtic (that is that are flatter or taller than a normal curve) cross the diagonal line near the middle of the graph.

Despite some skewness in this distribution we judged that the deviation from normal was not enough to seriously threaten our conclusions.

Next we examine the scatterplot of the residuals and the predicted scores (table 3-5). The star in front of RESID and PRED is the SPSS system way of representing temporary variables, that is, variables that are computed only for purposes of analysis of residuals and are not kept. On this plot, a single dot represents one case while a colon represents two cases with about the same values on both variables. There is no apparent relationship between the two variables in this plot, and no evidence that the variances of the residuals differ for different values of $\hat{y}$. Hence this diagnostic looks good.

On the Source of Unequal Variances

Sometimes the source of unequal variances is that you shouldn't have expected equality in the first place. As an example, let us take an analysis of variance

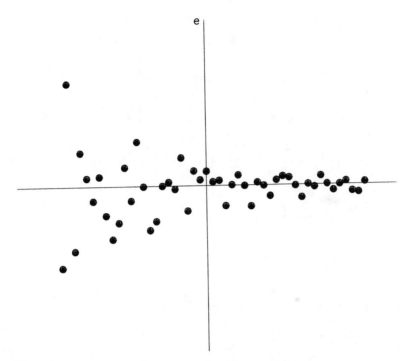

Figure 3-7. Residual Plot without Equal Variance.

situation (the analysis of variance can be reduced to regression) in which the dependent variable is a proportion. My example involves the proportion of days patients spent in the community during one year following discharge from a psychiatric hospital. Suppose I am interested in examining the differences in the means of this proportion in two hospitals. Suppose that the (unknown) truth is that patients from hospital A spend an average of 80% of the days in the community while patients from hospital B average 50% of the days. I take samples from each hospital and examine the data. According to elementary probability theory (the binomial distribution), the variances in each sample will be approximately:

$$P(1 - P)/365$$

where P is equal to proportion of days in the community for that hospital. For hospital A, then, the variance of the proportions will be $(.8)(.2)/365$, while for hospital B the variance will be $(.5)(.5)/365$. We cannot expect variances to be equal in this situation.

When one is dealing with data in the form of proportions, this will always be the situation. That is, the assumption of equal variances will generally not be met, unless the null hypothesis is true. If what you hope is true is true, that is,

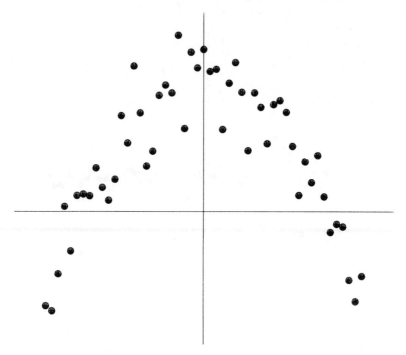

Figure 3-8. Curved Residual Plot.

that H_0 is false, you won't be able to prove it because the assumptions are not met. (The general problem is that the variance is dependent on the mean of the distribution; here the mean is the proportion .8 or .5.)

Luckily, there is a way out of this dilemma—through transformations—by changing each of the proportions observed into something else that behaves better. One of three transformations is usually chosen for this purpose. The first is the *arcsin* transformation. Its formula is: $y = 2 \arcsin \sqrt{x}$. (Arcsin$\sqrt{x}$ means the angle whose sine is $\sqrt{x}$; see the appendix on trigonometry). The resulting (transformed) values will have almost equal variances. Other transformations that are sometimes used for such data are the *probit* and *logit* transformations (see Cohen and Cohen, 1975).

It turns out that when one applies transformations for the propose of equalizing variances, the data is also often made to be more normal, thereby killing two assumptions with one stone.

Other Transformations

If the data arise out of counts of events occurring within a set time period (e.g., number of violations by a juvenile during a year period) or in areas of particular

56

Table 3-3. Histogram of Standardized Residuals

```
HISTOGRAM - STANDARDIZED RESIDUAL
 N EXP N      ( * = 1 CASES,    . : = NORMAL CURVE)
 O  0.13   OUT
 O  0.07   3.00
 O  0.10   2.87
 O  0.14   2.75
 1  0.19   2.62 *
 O  0.27   2.50
 O  0.36   2.37
 O  0.49   2.25
 O  0.64   2.12 .
 1  0.82   2.00 :
 O  1.05   1.87 .
 O  1.32   1.75 .
 1  1.63   1.62 *.
 2  1.98   1.50 *:
 3  2.37   1.37 *:*
 3  2.79   1.25 **:
 1  3.23   1.12 *  .
 9  3.69   1.00 ***:*****
 3  4.15   0.87 ***.
 4  4.59   0.75 ****.
 9  5.00   0.62 ****:****
 9  5.37   0.50 ****:****
 5  5.67   0.37 *****.
 7  5.89   0.25 *****:*
 7  6.03   0.12 *****:*
 3  6.08   0.00 ***  .
10  6.03  -0.12 *****:****
 4  5.89  -0.25 ****  .
 4  5.67  -0.37 ****  .
 3  5.37  -0.50 ***  .
 7  5.00  -0.62 ****:**
 3  4.59  -0.75 ***  .
 2  4.15  -0.87 ** .
 5  3.69  -1.00 ***:*
 1  3.23  -1.12 *  .
 O  2.79  -1.25     .
 1  2.37  -1.37 *.
 3  1.98  -1.50 *:*
 2  1.63  -1.62 *:
 O  1.32  -1.75 .
 2  1.05  -1.87 :*
 3  0.82  -2.00 :**
 2  0.64  -2.12 :*
 1  0.49  -2.25 *
 O  0.36  -2.37
 1  0.27  -2.50 *
 O  0.19  -2.62
 O  0.14  -2.75
 O  0.10  -2.87
 O  0.07  -3.00
 O  0.13   OUT
```

Table 3-4. Normal Probability Plot of Standardized Residuals

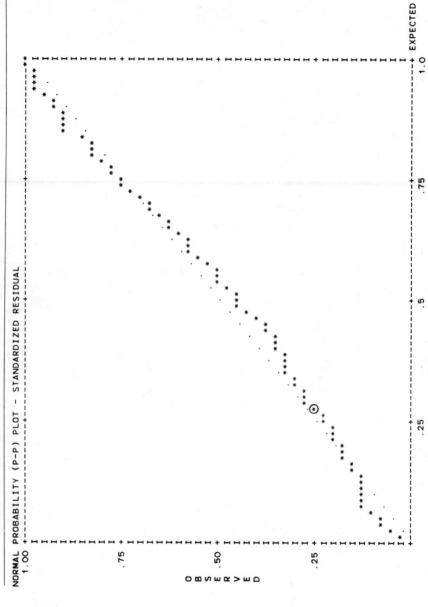

Table 3-5. Scatterplot of Standardized Residuals

size, and the occurrences are relatively rare, the data will probably be in the form of a *Poisson* distribution. The Poisson is similar to the binomial. Variance stabilization and approximate normality may often be achieved by applying the square root transformation. That is, square roots of all observations are taken and entered into the analysis.

If the data are in the form of length of time between events (e.g., number of days between violations) the distribution is usually of a *negative exponential* type. The transformation to be used in this situation is the natural logarithm of the observations. The natural logarithm is also used when variables are related multiplicatively rather than additively.

The Assumption of Uncorrelated Residuals

The assumption that the residuals are independent (or uncorrelated) is the assumption that is most obscure, and sometimes the most difficult to deal with. The technical way of expressing it is that the variance-covariance matrix of the e's is diagonal. If this assumption is violated, this means that the size of the e's are related to each other. For example, the e's for two y's that are both very far from the mean are both quite large, while those y's that are close to the mean have e's that are quite small. The assumption can be checked in some circumstances by estimating the variance-covariance matrix with the product ee'. In practice, one usually hopes that by dealing with the other assumptions this one will also be taken care of.

Testing for Linearity

Testing for linearity is also called testing for *lack of fit*. Graphical methods of examining linearity are:

1. Plot the dependent variable against the independent variable. If a clear curvature shows up, a linear model will not work. Unfortunately, sometimes a nonlinear trend doesn't show up clearly in such a graph.
2. Plot the residuals against the dependent variable or $\hat{y}$ and/or one or more of the independent variables. This was discussed above.

Another way of determining the possible existence of a nonlinear term is to do a sequential multiple regression. Start with only the linear term then introduce a squared term. Determine whether the additional variance explained is significant (look at the partial F). If it is, the association is nonlinear and the squared term is needed in the model. If the additional variance is not significant, the situation is somewhat ambiguous since a higher order term (like x^3) might be needed even if x^2 is not needed. However, in practice one usually ignores that subtlety. If x^2 is significant, then one sometimes goes on to try x^3.

Notes

1. This study is reported in Deborah H. Siegel, *A Study of the Integration of Research and Practice in Social Work Education,* Unpublished Doctoral Dissertation, The School of Social Service Administration, The University of Chicago, March 1982.)

2. A necessary but not sufficient condition for independence is having at least one more case than there are independent variables.

3. If the numbers of cases in the various columns of the design are proportional to each other, that is, if the numbers of cases in column two are a constant multiple of the numbers of cases in the same rows in column one, and similarly for all the columns, we have an *orthogonal* design. In that case, the four sums of squares add to the total sum of squares and the tests of the rows and columns effects are independent. If we do not have an orthogonal design, the test of the rows and columns effects are not statistically independent.

4. In SPSS-X NEW REGRESSION is called simply REGRESSION.

4 MULTIPLE REGRESSION II

Building a Regression Equation

In the social sciences we often have a large number of variables that we think might have some importance in explaining a dependent variable. We could compute a regression equation involving all of the variables (assuming that we have more cases than variables, which is not always the case). However that course of action is problematic for at least two reasons:

1. The use of a large number of variables will spuriously inflate the R^2 as described in chapter 3.
2. Using large numbers of variables violates the principal of parsimony, which says that we should keep our explanations as simple as possible.

Hence, researchers often want to have a way to select a subset of independent variables that will be relatively small and yet do a good job of predicting the dependent variable. There are a number of ways this can be done.

1. Compute separate regression equations for every possible subset of the independent variables. That is, variables are taken one at a time, then two at a time, three at a time, etc. until we get to the entire set. Out of this large number

of regression equations we select that equation that best maximizes the two conflicting criteria of parsimony and large explanatory power. That is, we select an equation that has a large R^2 and relatively few variables.

Unfortunately this procedure is very cumbersome if we have very many variables, because of the large number of equations to be computed. The number of equations will be $2^p - 1$ where p is the number of independent variables. For 10 independent variables we would have to compute 1023 equations. If we have very many variables, the task of computing all those equations is time consuming even for a computer, so this approach is rarely used.

2. Look at the ordinary correlations of each independent variable with the dependent variable (called the *zero order correlations*) and select those that have relatively high correlations. Unfortunately, this simple approach fails to take into account the fact that these correlations overlap as discussed earlier.

3. Adopt forward inclusion. In this method an equation is built up in a number of steps in which one variable at a time is chosen to add to the equation. This is usually done on a computer. In the first step the variable with the largest zero order correlation with the dependent variable is chosen and a regression equation with just that variable is computed. Next, all of the other variables are checked to see which one would add the greatest amount to the regression sum of squares. That variable is then added and a new regression equation is computed. It should be remembered that the regression coefficient for the first variable, and its significance, will change when the second variable is entered. The process continues until none of the remaining variables would add significantly to the prediction equation.

4. Use backward elimination. This method is essentially the reverse of the previous one. First, an equation is computed with all of the variables entered. If any variables are insignificant, the least significant variable is removed and a new equation computed. The process continues until all of the remaining variables are significant.

5. The stepwise method is a refinement of the forward inclusion method. It is possible that a variable that enters at one step will become insignificant at a later step, when other variables are entered. Hence, in the stepwise method all the variables already in the equation are checked when a new variable enters and if a variable has become insignificant it is removed.

These five methods for selecting variables to explain a dependent variable in a regression equation have become very popular in social science research. The forward inclusion technique has become particularly ubiquitous. Unfortunately, there are serious drawbacks to the use of any statistical approach to the selection of a small set of predictors from a larger set. The problem comes about because of the sampling errors already mentioned. Sample associations are rarely exactly equal to the associations in the population. Hence, in any given sample, some of the correlations of independent variables will be larger than they should be (either positively or negatively), simply because of random sampling variation. The selection procedures outlined above will tend to select those variables. In a way the procedures inappropriately capitalize on random sampling fluctuations. Errors of measurement will further aggravate the situation. The more variables one starts with the worse the problem is.

If the sample is large it is possible to investigate this problem by dividing the sample into two parts. One part is used to construct the regression equation and the other is used as a *replication* sample. The b_j's obtained from the first sample are used to compute $\hat{y}$'s for the other sample. The correlation of these $\hat{y}$'s with the observed y's is then obtained. We then compare this correlation with the multiple R found in the first sample. Remember that the multiple R is simply the ordinary correlation of $\hat{y}$ with y. The second R is almost always less than the first. If a small set of independent variables has been selected from a large set of candidates, the second R will usually be very much lower, thereby demonstrating the hazards in using selection techniques.

Rather than selecting variables statistically, it is far better to begin the study with firm hypotheses about exactly how a small number of variables are related. Selection procedures should be used only in highly exploratory studies and the results viewed with great suspicion until they are replicated.

Number of Cases

In any regression analysis, *the number of cases should exceed the number of independent variables by a wide margin.* Harris (1975) suggests that the number of cases should exceed the number of independent variables by at least 50. In selection procedures, this rule should be applied to the total number of variables that are candidates for inclusion in the model.

Coding of Categorical Variables for Regression Analysis

Frequently we would like to utilize categorical variables as independent variables in regression analysis. Regression analysis as we have presented it assumes that all the variables are interval. However, it is possible to employ categorical independent variables by recoding them. We will discuss two methods for coding categorical variables. In both methods it is necessary to construct $k - 1$ new variables (where k is the number of categories in the categorical variable) to contain the information in the categorical variable.

Dummy Variable Analysis

In dummy variable analysis we construct a set of dichotomous variables, that is, variables with only two values. Theoretically, any two values could be chosen, but it is convenient to use zero and one. Cases in the first category are given the value one for the first dummy variable and all other cases are given the value of zero. Cases in the second category are coded one for the second dummy variable, all others are coded zero and so forth. We have only $k - 1$ dummy variables, so the last category is coded zero on all of the dummy variables. If we try to use k dummy variables, we will encounter a serious problem: the kth variable will be a linear combination of the previous variables (the reader should demonstrate this) and when we plug the variables into a regression equation it will be impossible to invert the $X'X$ matrix since it is singular.

For a three category variable the values of the dummy variables can be schematized like this:

| | *Dummy Variables* | |
Category	d_1	d_2
A	1	0
B	0	1
C	0	0

The two dummy variables taken together capture all of the information contained in the original three-category variable. The category coded zero on all dummy variables is called the *reference* category.

Once we have coded the variables, we can perform a regression analysis. Suppose that we did a regression analysis using only one categorical variable (with two dummy variables). The regression equation would look like this:

$$\hat{y}_i = b_0 + b_1 d_{1i} + b_2 d_{2i}$$

The regression coefficients can be interpreted as follows: b_0 is the mean of the reference category; b_1 is the difference between the mean of the first category and the mean of the reference category; and b_2 is the difference between the mean of the second category and the mean of the reference category.

An analysis of variance of the regression will be identical to an ordinary one-way analysis of variance of the original categories. Thus, it is possible to do an analysis of variance by doing a regression analysis of dummy variables. In fact, we can introduce two or more categorical variables into the regression by dummying all of them, create interaction terms by computing products of the dummy variables, and thereby conduct higher order analyses of variance through regression. In this sense the analysis of variance can be thought of as a subcategory of regression analysis.

Effects Coding

In effects coding we construct $k - 1$ trichotomous variables for our k category variable. Again we select one of the categories as a reference category. This time we give the reference category a value of minus one on all of the new variables. We code the other categories exactly as we did in dummy variable coding. For our three-category variable, the codes would be as follows:

Category	Effects Variables	
	d_1	d_2
A	1	0
B	0	1
C	-1	-1

In effects coding the regression coefficients have these meanings: b_0 is the mean of the means of the categories (usually this will not be equal to the grand mean unless the categories have the same numbers of cases). The b_j's are the differences between the mean of the jth category and the mean of means. This is the *effect* of category j. The effect of the last category is minus the sum of the effects of categories one through $k - 1$ (the effects of all k categories must add to zero). Obviously it is possible to convert b coefficients produced in dummy variable analysis to those produced by effects coding and vice versa; but sometimes it is more convenient to use effects coding in the first place, particularly when we want to compare categories with the mean of means rather than with some particular category.

The analysis of variance of regression using effects coding will be identical to that of dummy variable coding.

Part and Partial Correlation—Statistical Control

The simple, zero-order correlation between two variables is an index of the extent to which the two variables vary together. Another way to put this is that it indicates the accuracy of predictions of one variable knowing the other and using the regression equation for the predictions. A more precise formulation of the correlation coefficient is that its square represents the amount of *shared* variance in the two variables; that is, it is the proportion of the variance in one that is *explained* by the variance in the other. We have discussed briefly one extension of the idea of correlation—the multiple correlation coefficient. The square of the multiple R is the proportion of the variance of a dependent variable accounted for by a set of independent variables.

Often we have a situation in which we have two independent variables, but these independent variables play different roles. That is, one of these variables is the one we are really interested in, while the other variable represents sources of variation that we want to control or remove. For example, we might be studying the outcome of some service program and be interested in examining the relationship of amount of service to outcome. However, we might believe that motivation of the client also contributes to variation in outcome. We would be interested, then, in examining the relationship between amount of service and outcome controlling for motivation. More generally, if we have a set of several independent variables, we may want to divide that set into two subsets, one a series of control variables and the other a set that we might term *primary independent variables*. In the example used earlier, we might want to know the association between EBPINCRS and TOTALAT2, controlling for the other independent variables. There are two indices of association involving control variables, the *partial correlation* and the *part* or *semipartial* correlation. We will present two different ways of viewing each of these coefficients.

When we were dealing with multiple regression, we made no assumptions about the distributions of the independent variables; that is, tests of the significance of R or of the b's only require assumptions about the distribution of the ϵ's. When we come to partial correlation, the assumption is usually made that all variables are multinormally distributed.

The partial correlation coefficient is defined as the correlation of two sets of residuals from two regression equations. For the simplest case, involving three variables, the partial correlation of variables y and x, holding z constant (written $r_{xy \cdot z}$) is found by finding the regression of y on z (the regression equation predicting y from z) and the regression of x on z, and then finding the ordinary correlation coefficient between the residuals for the two equations. Thus, the effect of z is removed from both y and x and what is left is correlated. The partial correlation coefficient controlling for several variables ($z_1, z_2, \ldots, z_p$) is found by obtaining the residuals from the two multiple regression equations predicting y and x respectively from the set of z_i's. This coefficient is denoted $r_{yx \cdot 12 \cdots p}$.

While the foregoing is a conceptual definition of the partial correlation coefficient, it is possible to compute the coefficient directly from the simple correlations among the variables, without going through the step of finding the regressions and the residuals. For the three-variable problem, the computing formula is

$$r_{yx \cdot z} = \frac{r_{xy} - r_{yz}r_{xz}}{\sqrt{1 - r_{yz}^2}\ \sqrt{1 - r_{xz}^2}}$$

The formula for higher order partials is

$$r_{yx \cdot 12 \cdots p} = \frac{r_{xy \cdot 12 \cdots p-1} - r_{xp \cdot 12 \cdots p-1}r_{yp \cdot 12 \cdots p-1}}{(1 - r_{xp \cdot 12 \cdots p-1}^2)^{1/2}\,(1 - r_{yp \cdot 12 \cdots p-1}^2)^{1/2}}$$

where $1, 2, \ldots, p$ represent the z_i variables.

Actual application of the latter formula is tedious because it requires the building up of a series of lower order partials to reach the one we want.

Another formula, which is somewhat easier, involves the square of the partial:

$$r_{yx \cdot 12 \cdots p}^2 = \frac{R_{y \cdot x12 \cdots p}^2 - R_{y \cdot 12 \cdots p}^2}{1 - R_{y \cdot 12 \cdots p}^2}$$

where the R^2's are squares of multiple correlation coefficients involving y as the dependent variable. In our example, the partial correlation of EBPINCRS with TOTALAT2, controlling for the other four independent variables, is .368 (the zero-order correlation, not controlling for any other variables is .389).

The formula just above leads to another, quite useful, interpretation of the partial correlation coefficient. The numerator of this index consists of two R^2 each of which may be interpreted as indicating percentages of variance explained. $R_{y \cdot x12 \cdots p}^2$ is the percentage of the variance of y explained by x and all the p control variables. $R_{y \cdot 12 \cdots p}^2$ is the percentage of variance explained by the control variables alone. The difference between these two R^2's represents the increment in variance explained when we add x to the regression equation. (This difference will always be positive or zero and rarely will it be zero.) The denominator of this fraction is the proportion of the variance in y that is not explained by the control variables. Thus the fraction may be thought of as:

$$\text{partial correlation coefficient squared} = \frac{\begin{array}{c}\text{increment in proportion of}\\\text{variance explained by } x \text{ over}\\\text{and above that explained by}\\\text{control variables}\end{array}}{\begin{array}{c}\text{proportion of variance not}\\\text{explained by control variables}\end{array}}$$

A pictorial representation of this is presented after the discussion of part correlation.

Part Correlation

The part correlation coefficient (also called the *semipartial* and symbolized $r_{y(x \cdot 12 \cdots p)}$) is defined as the ordinary correlation between the variable y and the residuals of the regression of x on the control variables. Thus, in the case of the partial correlation, the effects of the control variables have been removed from both x and y, while in part correlation the effects of control variables are removed only from x. For the three-variable situation the computing formula is

$$r_{y(x \cdot z)} = \frac{r_{yx} - r_{yz}r_{xz}}{\sqrt{1 - r_{xz}^2}}$$

Another view of the part correlation recalls the notion of increments of variance explained discussed earlier. The square of the part correlation of y with x controlling for variables $z_1, z_2, \ldots, x_p$ is the difference between the proportion of the variance of y explained by x and the control variables minus the proportion of variance explained by the control variables alone:

$$r_{y(x \cdot 12 \cdots p)}^2 = R_{y \cdot x 12 \cdots p}^2 - R_{y \cdot 12 \cdots p}^2$$

The part correlation squared therefore is the ratio of the increment in variance explained by x over and above that explained by the control variables to the total variance of y. To put that in the terms that we used earlier, the part correlation squared is equal to the partial sum of squares due to x (after $z_1, z_2, \ldots, z_p$ have been accounted for) divided by the total sum of squares for y. There is thus a close connection between the part correlation and the test of significance for b; and, in fact, a test of significance for b provides also a test of significance of the corresponding part correlation.

The distinction between the partial and the part correlation may be helped by a picture. See figure 4-1. In this picture the entire bar represents the variance of y. It has an area of one so that portions of the bar represent proportions of the variance of y. The area marked with northeast to southwest diagonals represents the proportion of variance explained by the control variables; while the area marked with northwest to southeast diagonals represents the proportion of variance explained by x. The proportion of variance explained by both the control variables and x is represented by the cross-hatched area. The area A represents the square of the part correlation, the proportion of variance explained by x over and above that explained by the control variables. The square of the partial correlation is the ratio of the area A to the area B, where the area B is the proportion of variance not explained by the control variables.

It is possible that the relationship between x and y will be different at different levels of a control variable z, that is, that there is an interaction between x and z in their relationship to y. When that happens, the partial and part correla-

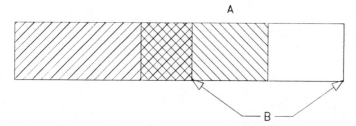

Figure 4-1.   Distinction between the Partial and the Part Correlation

tions will be a kind of average of the different relationships. In this situation, the part and partial correlations can be quite misleading; and the interactions should be explored, rather than trying to interpret the part or partial correlations. If all of our variables are multivariate normally distributed, such interactions will not occur.

5 MORE ON MATRICES

Before we go on to other techniques, we need to develop some more ideas in matrix algebra. Again, patience is in order.

Vectors

We defined vectors as matrices of one row or one column. Actually the idea of vectors is somewhat more elementary than that of matrices and is a critical idea in much of mathematics and statistics. We will introduce here a geometric representation of vectors. In what follows, we will think of vectors both as points in space and as *directed line segments*.

Let us begin by imagining a two-dimensional space, that is, a plane, with coordinate axes x_1 and x_2 as in figure 5-1. Every point in this two-dimensional space can be specified or located in reference to the two coordinate axes x_1 and x_2. Thus the point v has the x_1 value of x_{1v} and the x_2 value of x_{2v}.

We can represent the location of the point v by its x_1 and x_2 coordinates as follows:

$$\mathbf{v} = \begin{matrix} x_{1v} \\ x_{2v} \end{matrix}$$

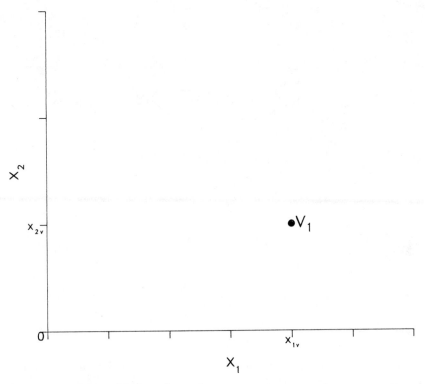

Figure 5-1. Plane with Coordinate Axes.

This is a vector of order 2. In three-dimensional space, a point could be located by its three coordinates and this could be represented by a vector of order 3, and so on for higher dimensional space.

Another way of thinking about vectors is as *directed line segments*. By this we mean simply the line going out from the origin to the point we located earlier. See figure 5-2. When vectors are represented this way, we sometimes put arrows at their ends. When thought of this way vectors have two characteristics that will be of interest to us. First of all, they have a direction (some aim one way and others aim another) and they have a length. By length we mean the distance from the end of the vector to the origin of the space (the place the coordinate axes intersect).

Vector Length

Vector length is determined as follows. Consider the diagram of figure 5-3. I have drawn a triangle with a right angle in which the hypotenuse is the vector **v**.

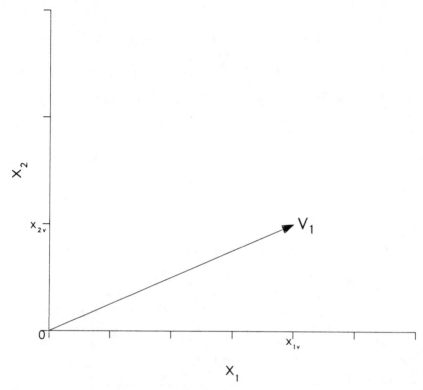

Figure 5-2. Vectors as Directed Line Segment.

By the Pythagorean theorem, the length of the vector $\mathbf{v} = \sqrt{x_{1v}^2 + x_{2v}^2}$.

Now if I jump to the idea of a vector in p dimensions, with p coordinates, the length of that vector can be expressed in a similar way. The length of a vector is symbolized as $\|\mathbf{v}\|$, so

$$\|\mathbf{v}\| = (x_{1v}^2 + x_{2v}^2 + \cdots + x_{pv}^2)^{1/2}$$

That is, the length of a vector is the square root of the sum of squares of the coordinates of the vector. This can be written in terms of the scalar product as $\|\mathbf{v}\| = (\mathbf{v}'\mathbf{v})^{1/2}$.

Angles Between Vectors

Now going back to two dimensions, suppose that I have two vectors as in figure 5-4. We will be interested in the angle between these two vectors α. It turns out

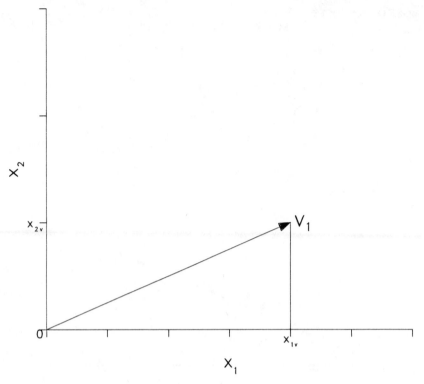

Figure 5-3. Determination of Vector Length.

that a function of the angle α called the cosine of α has the following relationship to the vectors $\mathbf{v}_1$ and $\mathbf{v}_2$:

$$\cos\alpha = \frac{\mathbf{v}_1{}'\mathbf{v}_2}{\|\mathbf{v}_1\|\,\|\mathbf{v}_2\|}$$

That is, the cosine of the angle between $\mathbf{v}_1$ and $\mathbf{v}_2$ is equal to the scalar product of the vectors $\mathbf{v}_1$ and $\mathbf{v}_2$ divided by the product of the lengths of $\mathbf{v}_1$ and $\mathbf{v}_2$. Although this idea has been developed in just two dimensions, it holds in any number of dimensions.

Our knowledge of the definitions of the scalar product of two vectors and the lengths of two vectors allows us to write the cosine of α as

$$\cos\alpha = \frac{\sqrt{\sum_i x_{i1}x_{i2}}}{\sqrt{\sum_i x_{i1}^2}\sqrt{\sum_i x_{i2}^2}}$$

76

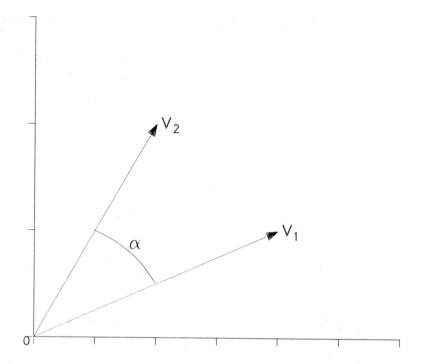

Figure 5-4. Two Vectors and Their Angle.

This looks suspiciously like the formula for the correlation between two variables, and in fact, if v_1 and v_2 are made to represent two variables, and if we plot them properly, the cosine of the angle between them will be equal to the correlation of the two variables.

Two vectors will be said to be *orthogonal* if their scalar product is equal to zero. Geometrically, this is the same thing as saying that they are perpendicular or at right angles to each other. If we are thinking about the vectors as representing variables, then orthogonal variable-vectors will have scalar products equal to zero, the cosine of the angle between them will be equal to zero and their sum of cross products, covariance and correlation will all be equal to zero.

Vector Sums

Recall that to add two vectors we simply add the corresponding elements. For example,

$$\underset{\mathbf{v}_1}{\begin{pmatrix} 2 \\ 1 \end{pmatrix}} + \underset{\mathbf{v}_2}{\begin{pmatrix} 1 \\ 3 \end{pmatrix}} = \underset{\mathbf{v}_{1+2}}{\begin{pmatrix} 3 \\ 4 \end{pmatrix}}$$

77

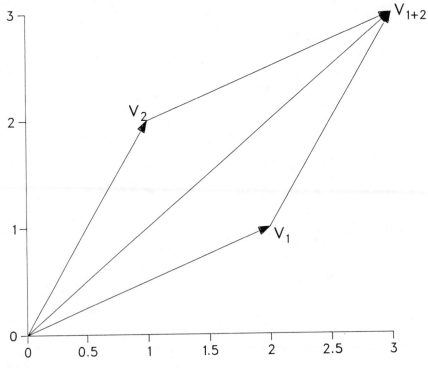

Figure 5-5. Sum of Two Vectors.

This may be represented geometrically as in figure 5-5. Notice that by connecting v_1 and v_{1+2} and v_2 and v_{1+2}, I have constructed a parallelogram the diagonal of which is v_{1+2}.

Product of a Scalar and Vector

The product of a vector and a scalar is found by simply multiplying each element of the vector by the scalar. (Again, this is like multiplying a matrix by a scalar.) For example,

$$2\underbrace{\begin{pmatrix} 3 \\ 2 \end{pmatrix}}_{v_1} = \underbrace{\begin{pmatrix} 6 \\ 4 \end{pmatrix}}_{v_2}$$

This is shown geometrically in figure 5-6. So the product vector is in the same direction, but twice as long. Sometimes we will multiply by scalars that are less

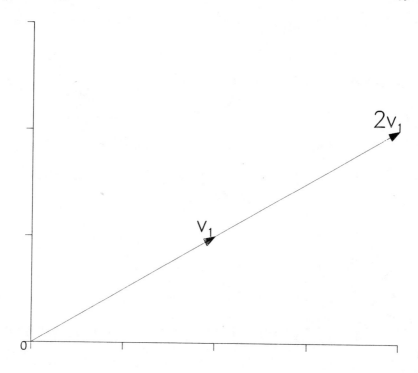

Figure 5-6. Product of a Vector and a Scalar.

than one so the resulting vector will be in the same direction but shorter than the original vector. For example, $.5v_1$ would look like figure 5-7. Multiplying by a negative number reverses the direction of the vector as in figure 5-8. The ideas of vector addition and multiplication by a scalar can be put together to give us the idea of linear combinations of vectors.

A linear combination of two vectors is an expression of the form $t = a_1 v_1 + a_2 v_2$, where v_1 and v_2 are vectors and t is a new vector defined by the equation. More generally, for more than two vectors we can write a linear combination as

$$t = \sum_i a_i v_i$$

Our use of the idea of vectors in statistics will usually involve more than one vector. A set of vectors is said to be independent if none of them are linear com-

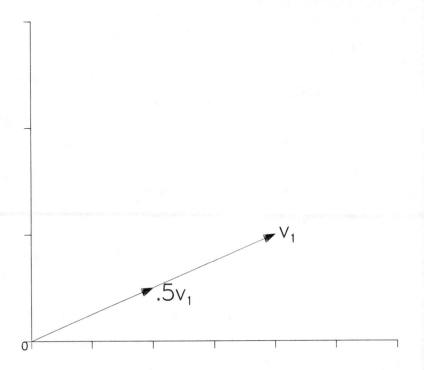

Figure 5-7. Product of a Vector and a Scalar When Scalar Is Less Than One.

binations of the others. Thus, a set of vectors $\mathbf{v}_i$ are dependent if there exist coefficients a_i such that

$$\mathbf{v}_k = \sum_i a_i \mathbf{v}_i \qquad \text{for } i \text{ not equal to } k$$

for one or more of the vectors $\mathbf{v}_k$.

Decomposing Vectors

These ideas can be used in reverse to *decompose* a vector into the sum of two other vectors. For example, we might want to decompose our $\mathbf{v}_1$ like this:

$$\mathbf{v}_1 = a_1 \mathbf{f}_1 + a_2 \mathbf{f}_2$$

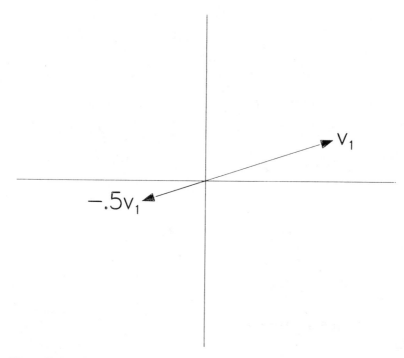

Figure 5-8.   Product of a Vector and a Scalar When Scalar Is a Negative
Number.

where $\mathbf{f}_1$ and $\mathbf{f}_2$ are two vectors that go in a particular direction and a_1 and a_2
are coefficients chosen to multiply by $\mathbf{f}_1$ and $\mathbf{f}_2$ so that the above equation is true.
   We can visualize this as in Figure 5-9, where we have drawn in a parallelogram,
so that $a_1\mathbf{f}_1 + a_2\mathbf{f}_2 = \mathbf{v}_1$. We want to find a_1 and a_2. If we know the angles θ and
ϕ this is easily done with trigonometry.

Vector Spaces

Consider the two-dimensional (plane) space with a couple of vectors in it. Choose
any two, as long as they do not fall on the same line, that is, they have to aim in
different directions. It should be obvious that any other point (or vector) in the
plane space (say $\mathbf{t}$) can be represented by a linear combination of the two vectors:

$$\mathbf{t} = a_1\mathbf{v}_1 + a_2\mathbf{v}_2$$

We need only choose a_1 and a_2 properly. Sometimes a_1 and/or a_2 will have to

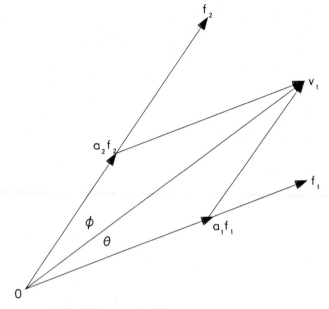

Figure 5-9.   Decomposing Vectors.

be negative in order to be able to construct a parallelogram with the desired vector in the diagonal.

The idea can be easily extended to three-dimensional space. If we have three vectors, not all of which lie in the same plane, we can generate any other point (vector) in the space by a linear combination of the first three vectors:

$$t = a_1 v_1 + a_2 v_2 + a_3 v_3$$

The ideas we are developing are important to mathematicians and statisticians, so there are lots of terms surrounding these ideas. A set of vectors is said to *span* a space if all the points in the space can be represented as linear combinations of the set. Thus, the vectors v_1 and v_2 in our plane above span the two-dimensional space. However, a spanning set can have more vectors than are absolutely necessary to generate the particular space (for example, if we want to generate a plane, three vectors in the plane could span it, but only two are necessary). So a set of vectors is called a *basis* of a space if it spans the space but has no more vectors than are necessary to generate the space. A space of p dimensions requires p vectors for a basis. Our sets of v_i vectors above are bases for their spaces of two and three dimensions.

We required that two vectors in a plane not be on the same line and that three

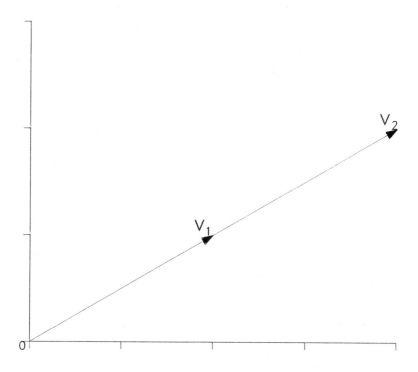

Figure 5-10.   Two Vectors on the Same Line of a Plane.

vectors in the three-dimensional space not all be in the same plane in order for us
to generate all the vectors in those spaces. These qualifications are important and
should be examined further. Suppose, in the plane I choose two vectors that are
on the same line as in figure 5-10. The reader should verify that only points on
that line can be generated by linear combinations of these two vectors. Similarly,
if three vectors all lie in the same plane, only points on that plane can be generated by them (unless all three are on the same line, in which case they only
generate that line). Thus, a set of two vectors on the same line spans a space of
only one dimension and a set of three vectors in the same plane spans a space of
only two dimensions.

It turns out that a set of p vectors will span a space of p dimensions only if
the vectors are independent. We can readily see this in a plane. In a plane, if two
vectors are dependent they lie on the same line. Consider the two vectors $(2,1)$
and $(4,2)$ in figure 5-11. The two vectors lie on a straight line and are dependent
since $2(2,1) = (4,2)$.

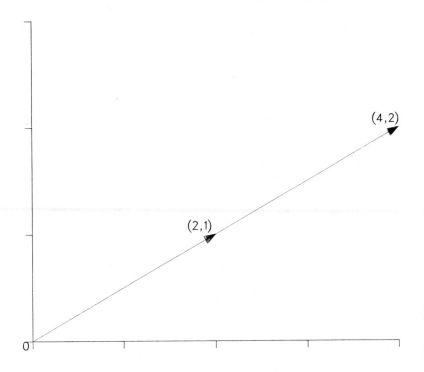

Figure 5-11. Two Dependent Vectors.

We are now ready to bring together the ideas of vectors and matrices and our algebraic and geometric ideas. First, note that if we are dealing with a space of p dimensions we need p coordinates to locate any point. Thus each vector will have p elements:

$$\mathbf{v} = (x_1, x_2, \ldots, x_p)$$

If I have a set of vectors, I can arrange these vectors in a matrix by either stacking them on top of each other or by lining them up vertically next to each other. The dimensionality of the space spanned by the vectors will be the number of independent vectors in the set of vectors. This is called the *rank* of the set of vectors. If the vectors in a set of vectors form the columns of a matrix, the number of independent vectors is said to be the *column rank* of the matrix. *Row rank* can be similarly defined. The row rank and column rank of a matrix are equal.

If I have p vectors in a space of p dimensions, I will have a square $p \times p$ matrix.

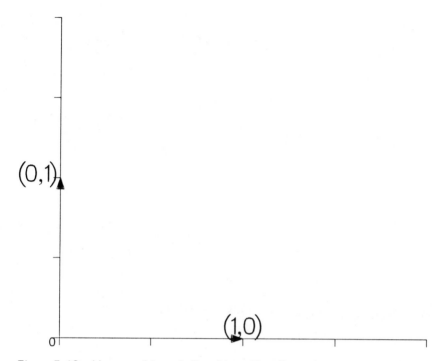

Figure 5-12.   Vectors of Length One Along Coordinate Axes.

If the vectors are independent (that is, if they span the space of p dimensions, and are a basis for the space), the determinant of the matrix will be nonzero and the matrix will be nonsingular. If, on the other hand, the vectors are dependent, the determinant will be zero; and if the determinant is zero, the vectors will be dependent. In this case, the vectors will be confined to a space of less than p dimensions. A square matrix is said to be of *full rank* if its rank is equal to its order. A full rank matrix is nonsingular.

If a square matrix is singular (not of full rank), the rank is the size of the largest submatrix whose determinant is not zero (submatrices are formed by crossing out the same number of rows and columns).

Although the vectors in a basis set (p vectors spanning a space of p dimensions) do not have to be at right angles to each other, for some purposes mathematicians like bases that are made up of orthogonal vectors. Even better are orthogonal vectors of length one. Of all possible bases made up of orthogonal vectors of length one, one is particularly simple. It is the one composed of vectors of length one along the coordinate axes. In two-dimensional space these vectors are (1,0) and (0,1) (they are called unit vectors). See figure 5-12. These basis vectors can be stacked in a matrix which would look like this:

$$\begin{pmatrix} 1 & 0 \\ 0 & 1 \end{pmatrix}$$

In p-dimensional space a similar set of basis vectors would look like this if arranged in a matrix:

$$\begin{matrix} 1 & 0 & 0 & \ldots\ldots 0 \\ 0 & 1 & 0 & \ldots\ldots 0 \\ \cdot & \cdot & \cdot & \cdot \\ \cdot & \cdot & \cdot & \cdot \\ \cdot & \cdot & \cdot & \cdot \\ \cdot & \cdot & \cdot & \cdot \\ 0 & 0 & 0 & \ldots\ldots 1 \end{matrix}$$

which is, of course, the identity matrix.

The reason that unit vectors are desirable is that any vector can be written as the linear combination of unit vectors, in which the coefficients of the linear combination are simply the coordinates of the vector.

Product of Matrices of Different Ranks

The rank of the product of matrices is less than or equal to the smallest of the ranks of the matrices being multiplied. Of course, the rank of an inverse is the same as the rank of the original matrix since they must both be of full rank.

Transformation of a Vector by a Matrix

We will now develop a geometric representation of the product of a vector and a matrix.

Suppose that I have the following product of a matrix times a column vector:

$$\underset{\textbf{A}}{\begin{pmatrix} 2 & 1 \\ -1 & 3 \end{pmatrix}} \underset{\textbf{v}_1}{\begin{pmatrix} 2 \\ 1 \end{pmatrix}} = \underset{\textbf{v}_2}{\begin{pmatrix} 5 \\ 1 \end{pmatrix}}$$

Sometimes we will talk about the matrix $\textbf{A}$ as *transforming* $\textbf{v}_1$ into $\textbf{v}_2$ (other terminology for this is that $\textbf{A}$ *maps* $\textbf{v}_1$ into $\textbf{v}_2$ or that $\textbf{v}_1$ is *carried into* $\textbf{v}_2$ by $\textbf{A}$). $\textbf{A}$ could be multiplied by any vector in the plane, of course, and thus $\textbf{A}$ is thought of as a *transformation* of the plane, that is, it carries any vector in the plane into another vector in the plane. Transformations do not have to be represented by premultiplication by A; we could post multiply, that is,

$$(2, \ 1) \begin{pmatrix} 2 & 1 \\ -1 & 3 \end{pmatrix} = (3, \ 5)$$

but then we get a different transformed vector.

We can transform two or more vectors at once by lining them up in a matrix and multiplying by A:

$$\underset{A}{\begin{pmatrix} 2 & 1 \\ -1 & 3 \end{pmatrix}} \underset{v_1 \ v_2}{\begin{pmatrix} 2 & 3 \\ 1 & 4 \end{pmatrix}} = \underset{v_1^* \ v_2^*}{\begin{pmatrix} 5 & 10 \\ 1 & 9 \end{pmatrix}}$$

where v_1^* and v_2^* are the transformations of v_1 and v_2. Of course, here it may be hard to tell which of the matrices being multiplied is the transformation matrix and which is a matrix of vectors, but in what follows we will try to keep that straight.

If a two-by-two transformation matrix A has dependent vectors (so that its determinant is zero), it will carry all vectors in the plane into vectors that all lie on the same straight line. (The reader should verify this in an example.) In p dimensions a transformation matrix with determinant equal to zero (with dependent vectors) will carry all vectors in the p dimensional space into a space of less than p dimensions, in fact, into a space of dimensionality equal to the rank of the matrix.

Some kinds of transformation matrices are particularly useful. One is a matrix that does not alter the lengths of vectors multiplied by them. (Length is said to be *preserved*.) For example, consider the matrix

$$A = \begin{pmatrix} .6 & .8 \\ -.8 & .6 \end{pmatrix}$$

and the product

$$\underset{A}{\begin{pmatrix} .6 & .8 \\ -.8 & .6 \end{pmatrix}} \underset{v_1}{\begin{pmatrix} 2 \\ 1 \end{pmatrix}} = \underset{v_2}{\begin{pmatrix} 2 \\ -1 \end{pmatrix}}$$

Obviously, v_1 and v_2 have the same length.

Even better is a transformation matrix that carries vectors into vectors of the same length and also preserves the angles between vectors. The matrix A, just above, is such a matrix. Such matrices are called orthonormal transformations. The reader should carry out the following matrix multiplication to verify that

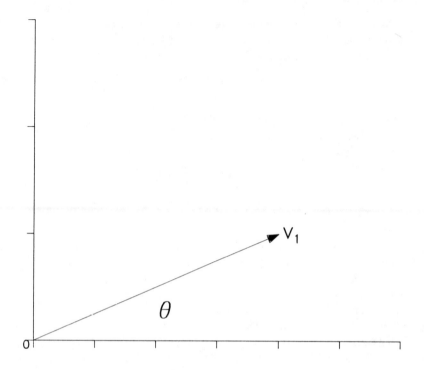

Figure 5-13. A Simple One Vector Situation.

the transformed vectors have the same length and the same angle as before (by showing that the cosines of the angles are the same):

$$\begin{pmatrix} .6 & .8 \\ -.8 & .6 \end{pmatrix} \begin{pmatrix} 2 & 3 \\ 1 & 4 \end{pmatrix} = \begin{pmatrix} v^*_{11} & v^*_{12} \\ v^*_{21} & v^*_{22} \end{pmatrix}$$
$$\quad\ \ \mathbf{A} \qquad\ \ \mathbf{v}_1\ \mathbf{v}_2 \qquad\ \ \mathbf{v}^*_1\ \ \mathbf{v}^*_2$$

There are several interesting facts about orthonormal transformation matrices. Two are given here. First, the determinant of such a matrix is 1 (this should be verified on $\mathbf{A}$ above). Second, the transpose of an orthonormal matrix $\mathbf{A}$ is the same as its inverse $(\mathbf{A}' = \mathbf{A}^{-1})$. Thus,

$$\mathbf{A}'\mathbf{A} = \mathbf{I}$$

The reader should verify that this is true for the example above. In geometric terms, this is the same thing as saying that orthonormal matrices are composed

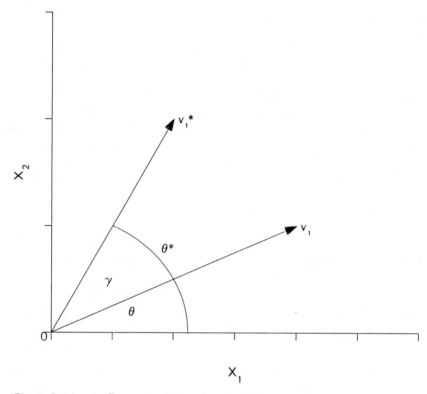

Figure 5-14. An Example of Transforming Vectors.

of orthogonal vectors (ortho-) of length one (-normal). It is also the same thing as saying that orthonormal matrices are composed of vectors of length one whose scalar products with each other are zero.

An orthonormal transformation is sometimes thought of as a *rigid rotation* because it simply rotates sets of vectors through some angle in space.

Do We Transform Vectors or Coordinate Axes?

The transformations we will be performing will often be rigid orthonormal transforms. Consider again a simple one-vector situation, as in figure 5-13. Here the vector v_1 makes the angle θ with the x_1 axis. Suppose that for some reason we want to change things so that v_1 makes a different angle θ^* with x_1, as in figure 5-14. One way to think about this is in terms of transforming v_1 into v_1^* by finding an orthonormal transformation matrix **A** which will rotate $\mathbf{v}_1$ by the angle $\gamma = \theta^* - \theta$.

However, another way to get things the way we want them is to leave $\mathbf{v}_1$ where it is and rotate the axes, as in figure 5-15. Here I have rotated the axes to new positions x_1^* and x_2^*, such that the angle between x_1^* and $\mathbf{v}_1$ is θ^*. The angle between x_1^* and x_1 is the same γ as above.

Either way of thinking about orthonormal transformations gets one to essentially the same place. In the sequel we will usually think about transformations in terms of rotations of the axes. Thought of this way, when we multiply a vector by a transformation matrix, the result will be a vector of the coordinates of the old vector in the new coordinate axis system.

Projections

In the following, we will talk occasionally about the "projection" of a vector onto a space. The projection is found by dropping a line from the vector to the

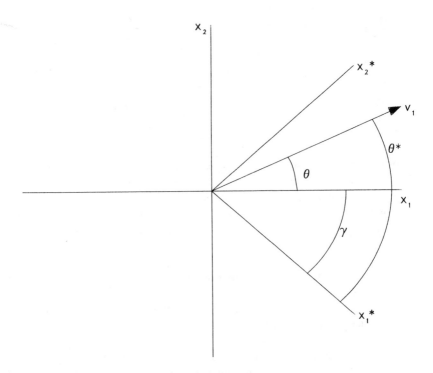

Figure 5-15. An Example of Rotating Axes.

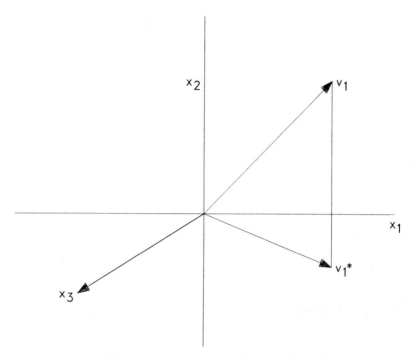

Figure 5-16.   Example of Projection of a Vector.

space, such that the line is perpendicular to the space. The *projection* is the intersection of the perpendicular and the space. This can only be visualized when the space on which we are projecting is a plane or a line. An example is shown in figure 5-16 where v_1^* is the projection of v_1 on the x_1, x_3 plane. Another example is shown in figure 5-17.

A vector's projection is shorter than the vector, unless the vector is already in the space on which it is being projected, in which case the vector and its projection are the same. We will frequently project vectors on coordinate axes. If we have orthogonal axes, the lengths of the projections on the axes will be the coordinates of the vector.

Problems

1. Find $a_1 v_1 + a_2 v_2$ where $a_1 = 4, a_2 = 2, v_1' = (5,3)$, and $v_2' = (2,1)$.
2. Find the length of the vector $v_1' = (3,2,3)$.

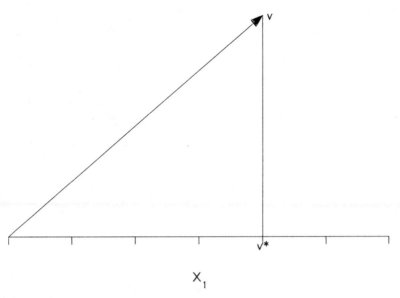

Figure 5-17. Example of Projection of a Vector.

3. Find the cosine of the angle θ between the vectors $\mathbf{v}_1$ and $\mathbf{v}_2$ where $\mathbf{v}_1' =$ (3,2) and $\mathbf{v}_2' = (4,5)$.

4. The matrix

$$\begin{array}{cc} 2 & 1 \\ 4 & 2 \end{array}$$

is singular. If we use it as a transformation matrix in two-dimensional, plane space, it will carry all vectors in the plane into a straight line. Demonstrate this to yourself by multiplying this matrix by the vectors $\mathbf{v}_1' = (3,5)$ and $\mathbf{v}_2' = (7,2)$. Locate the original vectors and the transformed vectors on a plot of the two-dimensional space.

5. Under what circumstances would the transformation matrix $\mathbf{A}$ carry the vector $\mathbf{x}$ into the same vector $\mathbf{y}$ whether it is pre- or postmultiplied?

6 PRINCIPAL COMPONENTS ANALYSIS

We study principal components analysis for two reasons, first because the ideas in it are central to much of multivariate analysis and secondly as a data reduction technique. By the latter we mean that we start with a relatively large number of variables and hope to wind up with a smaller number of variables that include most of what was in the larger set of variables. It is sometimes said that principal components analysis and factor analysis reveal the *structure* of a set of observations.

Let us suppose that we have made observations of n subjects on p variables and that the variable values have been transformed into deviation score form. Our variables are not divided into dependent and independent variables, they are just variables. We arrange the data in an $n \times p$ matrix X and we assume that there are more subjects than there are variables $(n > p)$ so the matrix is longer than it is wide.

Now the variables we are dealing with probably have nonzero correlations among them. The task we set for ourselves is to find new variables y_j that are linear combinations of the old variables x_j such that the y_j's are uncorrelated. Why would we want to do this? Well, sometimes uncorrelated variables are nicer than correlated ones. For example, in multiple regression analyses, the correlations among the dependent variables cause problems in interpreting the outcome of the analysis even though one of the reasons we do it is because of these correlations.

So we want y's that look like this for case i:

$$y_{i1} = a_{11}x_{i1} + a_{21}x_{i2} + \cdots + a_{p1}x_{ip}$$
$$y_{i2} = a_{12}x_{i1} + a_{22}x_{i2} + \cdots + a_{p2}x_{ip}$$
$$.$$
$$.$$
$$.$$
$$.$$

and we want to try to choose the a's such that the y_j's are uncorrelated. For case i, we can write this series of equations in matrix terms:

$$y'_j = x'_j A$$

where y'_i is a row vector representing the values for case i on the y variables and x'_i is a row vector representing the values on the x variables. A is a matrix, each column of which contains the coefficients for one of the linear combinations.

If I want to represent the situation in terms of the values of the variables for all the cases I will need matrices in place of vectors:

$$Y = XA$$

Each entry of this matrix will be a linear combination of the form

$$y_{ij} = a_{1j}x_{i1} + a_{2j}x_{i2} + \cdots + a_{pj}x_{ip}$$

where this represents the value for case i of new variable y_j.

We established the requirement above that the y variables be uncorrelated. I now want to establish a further requirement, namely that the first new variable (y_1) have maximum variance of all the possible new variables that are linear combinations of the x_i's, that is, I want y_1 to "spread out" the cases as much as possible. Further, I want the rest of the y variables (all uncorrelated with y_1 and with each other) to be ordered so that they have decreasing variance.

Two Variables, Three Cases

Let us try to understand the situation by looking at a simple example involving three cases (v_1, v_2, v_3) and two variables (x_1, x_2). We will use the example from chapter 2. The sets of values for the three cases can be viewed as three vectors stacked in a matrix:

$$
\begin{array}{cc}
 & x_1\ x_2 \\
v_1 & 3\quad 2 \\
v_2 & 5\quad 6 \\
v_3 & 4\quad 1
\end{array}
$$

The mean of x_1 is 4 and of x_2, 3. So the deviation matrix (**X**) looks like this:

$$
\begin{array}{cc}
 & x_1\ x_2 \\
v_1 & -1\ -1 \\
v_2 & +1\ +3 \\
v_3 & \ \ 0\ -2
\end{array}
$$

These three cases (in terms of their deviation values) may be plotted as in figure 6-1. (The location of the axes for the original data is shown by dotted lines. This illustrates that using the deviation scores is the same thing as trans-

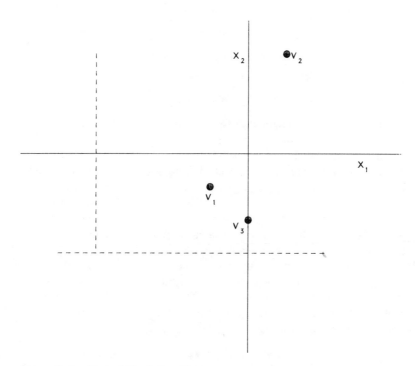

Figure 6-1. Plot of Deviation Values.

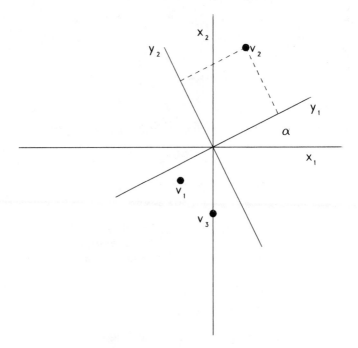

Figure 6-2.   Rotation of Coordinate Axes.

lating or moving the coordinate axes to the point representing the means of the two variables, the translation taking place without rotation. The point representing the means is called the *centroid*.)

Suppose now we rotate the coordinate axes by some angle α as in figure 6-2. In reference to the new axes y_1 and y_2, the cases v_1, v_2, and v_3 have new values, denoted by their projections on those axes. We have drawn those projections in for v_2. We are interpreting these new axes as new variables, so we can talk about the sum of squares of the values of the cases on these new variables. These sums of squares will be different from the old sum of squares on x_1 and x_2.

We will focus first on determining only the first of our new variables. Our problem is to find that rotation that will cause our first variable y_1 to have the most variance of all the possible rotations. The variable y_1 can be written as a vector $\mathbf{y}_1$ which holds the values for all cases for y_1. This vector is a linear combination of the vectors representing x_1 and x_2, that is,

$$\mathbf{y}_1 = a_{11}\mathbf{x}_1 + a_{21}\mathbf{x}_2$$

or, with p x variables (in p dimensions),

$$y_1 = \sum_j a_{j1} x_j$$

where the subscript j ranges from 1 to p.

In terms of the score of individual i on variable y_1 this would be written

$$y_{i1} = \sum_j a_{j1} x_{ij}$$

The y_1 scores for all individuals will form a vector $\mathbf{y}$, for which

$$\mathbf{y}_1 = \mathbf{X}\mathbf{a}_1$$

where $\mathbf{a}_1$ is the vector that was the first column of the matrix $\mathbf{A}$, and $\mathbf{y}_1$ is the column vector of scores on y_1. Since we will be dealing with these vectors for a while, I will drop the subscript 1 and just write $\mathbf{y}$ and $\mathbf{a}$. We want to find a's such that the variance of y is maximized. It turns out that the mean of y is zero.[1]

Since the mean of y is 0, the sum of squares of y is merely $\mathbf{y}'\mathbf{y}$. So,

$$\sum_i y_i^2 = \mathbf{y}'\mathbf{y} = (\mathbf{X}\mathbf{a})'(\mathbf{X}\mathbf{a}) = \mathbf{a}'\mathbf{X}'\mathbf{X}\mathbf{a}$$

but

$$\mathbf{X}'\mathbf{X} = \mathbf{S} \quad \text{so} \quad \sum_i y_i^2 = \mathbf{a}'\mathbf{S}\mathbf{a}$$

The variance of y is this divided by $n - 1$:

$$s_y^2 = \frac{\sum_i y_i^2}{n-1} = \frac{\mathbf{a}'\mathbf{S}\mathbf{a}}{n-1} = \mathbf{a}'\mathbf{C}\mathbf{a}$$

where $\mathbf{C}$ is the covariance matrix of the x's.

There is a problem here, however. With what has been said, it is possible to make $\Sigma_i y_i^2$ (and thus the variance) as large as we want just by making our a_j's very large. So we need another condition in order to solve the problem. The condition is easy to identify if we remember that we are trying to build a matrix $\mathbf{A}$ made up of vectors $\mathbf{a}$. The matrix $\mathbf{A}$ can be thought of as a transformation matrix on our coordinates. We would like our transformation matrix to be an orthonormal one. The reason for this is that we want to leave the points representing the cases where they are in the space, we do not want to change their relative positions, or to change their lengths (their distances from the origin). We merely want to perform a rigid rotation of the axes of the space. That means the matrix $\mathbf{A}$ must be orthonormal. Thus, we will want the length of $\mathbf{a}$ to be equal to one. So our requirement is that

$$\|\mathbf{a}\| = (\mathbf{a}'\mathbf{a})^{1/2} = 1$$

squaring both sides of this equation we get $\mathbf{a}'\mathbf{a} = 1$.

Let us now return to our example and get the $\mathbf{S}$ (SSCP) matrix $\mathbf{X}'\mathbf{X}$:

$$
\begin{array}{ccc}
\mathbf{X}' & \mathbf{X} & \begin{array}{c}\text{SSCP}\\ \text{matrix}\end{array}\\
\begin{pmatrix} -1 & +1 & 0 \\ -1 & +3 & -2 \end{pmatrix} & \begin{pmatrix} -1 & -1 \\ +1 & +3 \\ 0 & -2 \end{pmatrix} = & \begin{pmatrix} 2 & 4 \\ 4 & 14 \end{pmatrix}
\end{array}
$$

And the $\mathbf{C}$ matrix [the covariance matrix, $\mathbf{X}'\mathbf{X}/(n-1)$] is

$$\frac{1}{3-1}\begin{pmatrix} 2 & 4 \\ 4 & 14 \end{pmatrix} = \begin{pmatrix} 1 & 2 \\ 2 & 7 \end{pmatrix}$$

We want to rigidly rotate the coordinate axes, which is the same thing as finding a new variable $y_1 = a_{11}x_1 + a_{21}x_2$ such that:

1. the variance of y_1 is maximized. Since the variance of y_1 is $\mathbf{a}'\mathbf{Ca}$, this means that we want to choose the a_{j1}'s such that $\mathbf{a}'\mathbf{Ca}$ is maximized; and
2. the "length" of $\mathbf{a}$ must be equal to 1. That is, we require that $\mathbf{a}'\mathbf{a} = 1$ or $\mathbf{a}'\mathbf{a} - 1 = 0$.

We can write these conditions succinctly as follows.

Find the vector $\mathbf{a}$ which maximizes $F = \mathbf{a}'\mathbf{Ca}$ subject to $\mathbf{a}'\mathbf{a} - 1 = 0$.

For our example, we want to find a_{11} and a_{21} such that

$$(a_{11} \quad a_{21})\begin{pmatrix} 1 & 2 \\ 2 & 7 \end{pmatrix}\begin{pmatrix} a_{11} \\ a_{21} \end{pmatrix}$$

is maximized, while

$$(a_{11} \quad a_{21})\begin{pmatrix} a_{11} \\ a_{21} \end{pmatrix} - 1 = a_{11}^2 + a_{21}^2 - 1 = 0$$

This is not an uncommon problem in mathematics and mathematicians have discovered that the best way to solve it is to make use of a new variable called a *Lagrange multiplier.* This allows us to set up a single equation (with matrices and vectors) like this

$$G = a'Ca - \lambda(a'a - 1)$$

where λ is a Lagrange multiplier.

In this way we have gotten our two conditions into one function. If all the matrices and vectors in this equation are multiplied out we have a single scalar equation. Before there were only p unknowns (the p a's), now one more unknown, λ has been added; so the problem now is to find the λ and the a's such that this single function is maximized. (Appendix C attempts to provide some understanding of how this function is developed.)

In order the find the values of the a's and λ which maximize this function, we take the partial derivatives of G with respect to the a's and λ and set those equal to 0 (again, see appendix C).

The partial derivatives of G with respect to all the a's at once may be found by differentiating G with respect to the vector a:

$$\frac{\partial G}{\partial a} = 2Ca - 2\lambda a$$

Set this equal to zero, divide through by 2, and we have

$$Ca - \lambda a = 0$$

This vector and matrix equation actually contains p scalar equations. The partial derivative of G with respect to λ is

$$\frac{\partial G}{\partial \lambda} = -(a'a - 1)$$

Setting this equal to zero we have

$$a'a = 1$$

(Here, we are back to an equation that is the same as one of our original conditions.) Now we have $p + 1$ equations in $p + 1$ unknowns (the p a's plus the λ).

If the equations are well behaved we should be able to solve for all of the unknowns. Let us go back to the first p equations, written in matrix-vector terms as

$$Ca - \lambda a = 0$$

Inserting an identity matrix in the second term does not change anything so I can write

$$Ca - \lambda I a = 0$$

Now factor out the a vector:

$$(C - \lambda I)a = 0$$

I could make this equation true by making the a vector the null vector (the vector with all zeros), but that is not a very good solution (it is called a *degenerate* solution). It would make my y's all zero and thus they would have zero variance which wouldn't maximize anything.

Instead of focusing on **a**, let's pay attention to the matrix $C - \lambda I$ (this is a $p \times p$ square matrix). Think for a moment about this matrix as a transformation matrix operating on **a**. $C - \lambda I$ must be such that it will transform **a** into a null vector, in other words, send **a** into a space of zero dimension. In order for a transformation matrix to do that it must be singular and thus its determinant must be equal to 0. Hence, our problem is to choose λ such that $|C - \lambda I| = 0$.

Now to return to our example, let's set up the matrix $C - \lambda I$:

$$\overset{\textbf{C}}{\begin{pmatrix} 1 & 2 \\ 2 & 7 \end{pmatrix}} - \overset{\lambda \textbf{I}}{\begin{pmatrix} \lambda & 0 \\ 0 & \lambda \end{pmatrix}} = \begin{pmatrix} 1 - \lambda & 2 \\ 2 & 7 - \lambda \end{pmatrix}$$

The determinant of this matrix is

$$\begin{vmatrix} 1 - \lambda & 2 \\ 2 & 7 - \lambda \end{vmatrix} = (1 - \lambda)(7 - \lambda) - 4 = \lambda^2 - 8\lambda + 3$$

We set that equal to 0 and solve for λ, that is,

$$\lambda^2 - 8\lambda + 3 = 0$$

$$\lambda = 7.6 \text{ or } .4$$

—since the solution for a quadratic equation $ax^2 + bx + c = 0$ is

$$x = \frac{-b \pm \sqrt{b^2 - 4ac}}{2a}$$

We have two values for λ satisfying the equation. The one we want right now is the largest. We will deal with the other one a bit later. These λ's are called *eigenvalues* of the matrix **C**.

Returning to our original equations,

$$\textbf{Ca} - \lambda \textbf{a} = 0$$

can be written in our problem as

$$\begin{pmatrix} 1 & 2 \\ 2 & 7 \end{pmatrix} \begin{pmatrix} a_{11} \\ a_{21} \end{pmatrix} - \lambda \begin{pmatrix} a_{11} \\ a_{21} \end{pmatrix} = \begin{pmatrix} 0 \\ 0 \end{pmatrix}$$

Multiplying through, we get two scalar equations:

$$a_{11} + 2a_{21} - \lambda a_{11} = 0 \tag{6.1}$$

$$2a_{11} + 7a_{21} - \lambda a_{21} = 0 \tag{6.2}$$

and our third equation for length,

$$a_{11}^2 + a_{21}^2 = 1 \tag{6.3}$$

We know that $\lambda = 7.6$, so we plug that in and get

$$a_{11} + 2a_{21} - 7.6a_{11} = 0 \quad \text{or} \quad -6.6a_{11} + 2a_{21} = 0 \tag{6.1a}$$

$$2a_{11} + 7a_{21} - 7.6a_{21} = 0 \quad \text{or} \quad 2a_{11} - .6a_{21} = 0 \tag{6.2a}$$

$$a_{11}^2 + a_{21}^2 = 1 \tag{6.3a}$$

Now we need to solve these three equations for the two unknowns a_{11} and a_{21}. Having more equations than unknowns is generally a problem (values of the two unknowns that fit two equations will generally not fit the third). However, in this case it turns out that the first two equations are redundant. They say essentially the same thing. This is because the first is -3.3 times the second (within rounding error). Hence one of those equations is not necessary. We discard the first, leaving us two to solve,

$$2a_{11} - .6a_{21} = 0 \quad \text{and} \quad a_{11}^2 + a_{21}^2 = 1$$

We solve the first of these for a_{11} in terms of a_{21}:

$$a_{11} = \frac{.6a_{21}}{2} = .3a_{21}$$

and plug this value into the second:

$$(.3a_{21})^2 + a_{21}^2 = 1$$

$$.09a_{21}^2 + a_{21}^2 = 1$$

$$1.09a_{21}^2 = 1$$

$$a_{21}^2 = 1/1.09$$

$$a_{21} = .96$$

Plug this value back into the first equation to find a_{11}:

$$2a_{11} - (.6)(.96) = 0$$

$$a_{11} = .29$$

Hence, the vector **a** is

$$\mathbf{a} = \begin{pmatrix} a_{11} \\ a_{21} \end{pmatrix} = \begin{pmatrix} .29 \\ .96 \end{pmatrix}$$

To go back to where we started, we wanted to find a new variable y_1 that would be a linear combination of the old variables x, such that the variance of y_1 was maximized (subject to the condition of a rigid rotation). The new y_1 is

$$y_1 = .29x_1 + .96x_2$$

(*Note*: The solutions found here for λ and the a's were determined by setting the partial derivatives of G equal to zero. Solutions to such equations could produce minima or points of inflection as well as maxima. It can be shown that the first eigenvalue is associated with a maximum and the last with a minimum.)

This equation can be interpreted as an equation involving vectors. Think of x_1 and x_2 as vectors of length one lying on the x_1 and x_2 axes. Then y_1 is the sum of the vectors $.29x_1$ and $.96x_2$. We can diagram this as in figure 6-3. The vector y_1 has length one (it is the hypotenuse of a right triangle whose bases have length .29 and .96 and $(.29)^2 + (.96)^2 = 1$). This vector locates the new coordinate axis y_1.

Obviously, in this two-dimensional space, the second new axis has to be perpendicular to the first, so I have drawn it in in the diagram. When I get to more than two dimensions, the situation is a little more complicated, as we shall

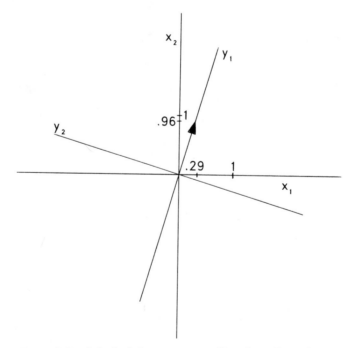

Figure 6-3. Principal Components as New Coordinate Axes.

see a bit further on. For now, simply accept that I have located the second axis y_2 (representing a second new variable). It turns out that $a_{21} = -.96$ and $a_{22} = .29$. So $y_2 = -.96x_1 + .29x_2$.

The full transformation matrix $\mathbf{A}$ is then

$$\mathbf{A} = \begin{pmatrix} .29 & -.96 \\ .96 & .29 \end{pmatrix}$$

(The reader should verify that this is an orthonormal transformation matrix. I could, of course, now find the values of y_1 and y_2 for the three cases by solving for the matrix $\mathbf{Y}$ in the expression $\mathbf{Y} = \mathbf{XA}$.)

The values of λ are called the eigenvalues (or characteristic roots or latent roots) of $\mathbf{C}$. The vectors of $\mathbf{A}$ are called the eigenvectors of $\mathbf{C}$.

Since y_1 was chosen so as to maximize its variance, it is of interest to ask what its variance is. The variance of y_1 is $\mathbf{a'Ca}$:

$$(.29 \quad .96) \begin{pmatrix} 1 & 2 \\ 2 & 7 \end{pmatrix} \begin{pmatrix} .29 \\ .96 \end{pmatrix} = 7.6$$

This is equal to the first λ found above. It turns out that the variance of y_2 is equal to the second λ (.4). The reader may verify this. The sum of these λ's (or variances) equals 8, the sum of the variances of the original variables $(1 + 7)$. The two variables (coordinate axes) y_1 and y_2 are called the *principal components* of the variables x_1 and x_2.

Two Variables, n Cases

Our example has dealt with a situation in which we have just three cases measured on two variables. Now we need to generalize things somewhat. First, let's stick with two variables but consider lots more cases. Let's assume, for the moment, that the variables have a bivariate normal distribution. In this situation the plot of the cases would look like figure 6-4 (I assume the values are in deviation form). The assumption of bivariate normality assures that the plot will have a shape like an ellipse, with more of the cases near the center (represented on the drawing by a darker shading).

In this case, the first principal component (y_1) will be the principal axis of the ellipse and y_2 (the second principal component) will be perpendicular to y_1, as in figure 6-5. If you turn this figure so that y_1 is horizontal, you will see a scatter plot like figure 6-6. Using this plot, it is possible to explore the association between y_1 and y_2. One way to do this is through regression analysis. If we construct the regression line $y_2 = b_0 + b_1 y_1$, it turns out that $b_0 = 0$ and $b_1 = 0$ so the regression line is $y_2 = 0$, the y_1 axis. It is clear also that the correlation r_{12} is equal to 0.

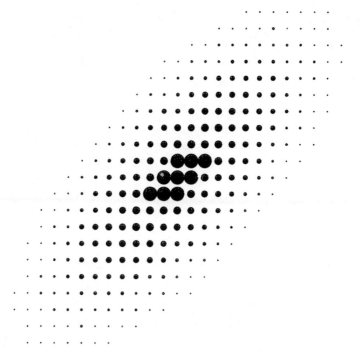

Figure 6–4. Plot of Bivariate Normal Distribution.

What all of this tells us is that principal components analysis produces new variables that are uncorrelated in the case of a bivariate normal distribution.

We began this discussion with the assumption that the two variables were bivariate normally distributed. If they are not, their scatter plot will not be the nice neat ellipse of figure 6-4, it will be some other, perhaps indescribable shape. But most of what has been said in this section still holds. That is, the first principal component will, in some sense, be the major axis of the distribution (that is, it will go through the "center" of the distribution) and the principal components will be uncorrelated.

One final point before we leave the case of two variables. This has to do with the relationship between the regression lines and the first principal component. The reader will recall that in dealing with two variables, x_1 and x_2, we can think either about predicting x_1 from x_2 or we could predict x_2 from x_1. Thus, we could construct two equations, $x_1 = b_{12}x_2$ and $x_2 = b_{21}x_1$. Unless the variables are perfectly correlated, the lines representing these two equations will not be in the same place. The first principal component will lie between these two

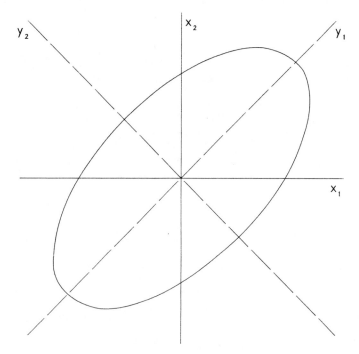

Figure 6-5. Principal Components of Bivariate Normal Distribution.

lines. The situation can be diagramed as in figure 6-7 (again we assume bi-variate normality).

Three Variables

We want to reach the point where we can deal with any number of variables with this procedure (say p variables), but let's take it slowly and now consider three. Suppose we have measured a number of cases (say n) on three variables x_1, x_2, and x_3. We want to find three new variables y_1, y_2, and y_3 (the principal components) that are linear combinations of the x variables, that are uncorrelated with each other, and that are such that the first has maximum variance.

Let's first try to visualize the scatter plot of values on these three variables. It will be a plot in three dimensions. We will assume that we are dealing with deviation scores so the center of the plot will be at the intersection of the three coordinate axes. Matters are a little easier if we assume the three variables are

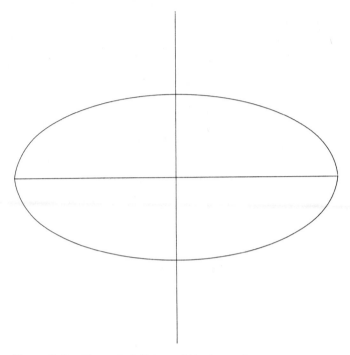

Figure 6-6. Figure 6-5 Oriented Horizontally.

multivariate normally distributed. In that case, the plot would look something like a squashed football as in figure 6-8. The center of this football is relatively dense and it gets less dense as we move out from the center. This figure (the football) is called an ellipsoid. The first principal component is the principal axis of the ellipsoid (the longest line through the center of the shape).

What is the second principal component? We require that it be orthogonal to the first, but in three-dimensional space there are an infinite number of lines that can be orthogonal to a given line. However, we require that the line selected go through the original origin, so that confines us to lines in a particular plane. Let's turn the diagram (figure 6-8) so that y_1 is horizontal as in figure 6-9.

The middle ellipse in figure 6-9 is a cross-section of the ellipsoid pictured earlier. It is the largest cross-section of the ellipsoid perpendicular to y_1 and is in the center of the football. All lines in it are orthogonal to y_1. The second principal component, y_2, is chosen so that it is in the plane and goes through the principal axis of the ellipse. The third and final principal component (y_3) is located so that it is perpendicular to both y_1 and y_2. In three dimensions, after

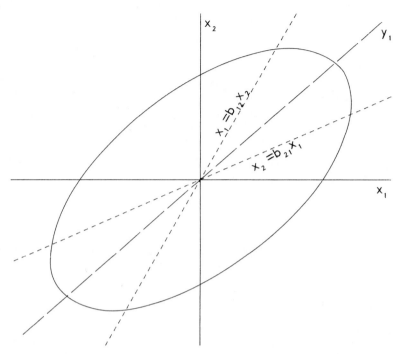

Figure 6-7. Relation between Regression Lines and First Principal Component.

we have located y_1 and y_2, there is only one place for y_3 to go. So we might visualize the location of our three principal components as in figure 6-10.

So much for the geometry of the three-dimensional case. We will not deal with the algebra of three dimensions, but rather move to the general p dimension situation.

p Variables

The basic algebra involved in extracting the principal components of p variables has been dealt with above in connection with the two-variable case. But a little discussion is needed to flesh out the picture.

Unless one of the p variables is a linear combination of the others (which would be the case if one of the columns of the $\mathbf{X}$ matrix was a linear combination of the other columns), we will require p principal components (a p dimensional space).

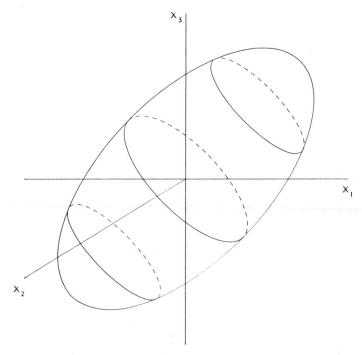

Figure 6-8.   Plot of Three Multivariate, Normally Distributed Variables.

The basic equations to be solved are (remember, they are reached after differentiating the function labeled G above and setting the results equal to 0)

$$Ca - \lambda a = 0$$

To find λ, we set the determinant $|C - \lambda I|$ equal to zero. This determinant looks like this:

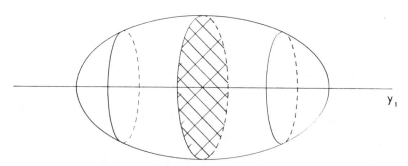

Figure 6-9.   Ellipsoid of Figure 6-8 Oriented Horizontally.

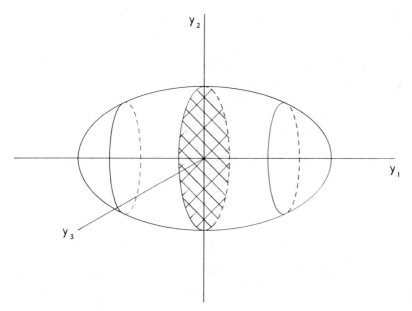

Figure 6-10. Location of Three Principal Components.

$$
\begin{vmatrix}
c_{11} - \lambda & c_{12} & \cdots & c_{1p} \\
c_{21} & c_{22} - \lambda & \cdots & c_{2p} \\
\cdot & & & \cdot \\
\cdot & & & \cdot \\
\cdot & & & \cdot \\
c_{p1} & \cdots & \cdots & c_{pp} - \lambda
\end{vmatrix} = 0
$$

Expanding this determinant will result in a polynomial in λ of degree p. A polynomial of degree p generally has p different roots. That is, there are p different values that will satisfy this equation. In the above example, we had a simple quadratic equation to solve to find the λ's. The solution of polynomial equations of degree larger than two is not easy and the reader is advised to leave that to the computer.

For nonsingular C matrices (the C matrix will be nonsingular if the x_i variables are independent), all of the λ's will be real (that is, not imaginary) and positive. If C is singular, there will be r nonzero λ_i's where r is the rank of C. Each of the nonzero λ's or eigenvalues is associated with an eigenvector (a vector of p a's). The a's in that vector are found by plugging the eigenvalue into the $p + 1$ equations and solving for the p a's. One of the equations will always be redundant and thus may be discarded. Thus, p eigenvectors (each of them a principal component) may be obtained, all orthogonal and uncorrelated with each other. If C is singular, one or more of the λ's will be zero and will not have an associated eigenvector. In this instance, the original p variables will be confined to a space of less than p dimensions.

The variance of each principal component will be the eigenvalue associated with that principal component. The sum of the eigenvalues will be the sum of the variances of the original x variables (the trace of the C matrix). The eigenvectors will form an orthonormal matrix. There are many other interesting facts about the relationships among a matrix, its eigenvalues, and its eigenvector matrix. One is that the product of the eigenvalues is equal to the determinant of the matrix.

As the above disquisition indicates, the thing that determines the outcome of the principal components analysis is the variance-covariance matrix C. It is the only known quantity in the equations we solve, the individual values of the x variables are forgotten, once having been used to find the S matrix. In a sense, this is as it should be; the principal components technique attempts to simplify the underlying structure of the variables, a structure described in the first instance by their variances and covariances. Therefore, principal components analysis is usually thought of as an analysis of the variance-covariance matrix.

Principal components analysis is very much affected by the variances of the variables involved (a variable with more variance than the others will tend to dominate the analysis), so frequently the analysis is done on variables that have been transformed into z scores (so they all have the same variance). In this case, the matrix being analyzed will be the correlation matrix R (rather than C) (see Maxwell, 1977, p. 41).

If the variables are measured using quite different scales (or *metrics*), for example, dollars and years, it is usually preferable to use the R matrix. If the variables are all of the same kind (for example, if all are attitude items measured on a five-point agree–disagree scale) items that have small variances do not distinguish cases as well as items with large variances, so it may be desirable to retain these distinctions by using the covariance matrix.

Scaling of Principal Components

The requirement that our principal components vector have length one was arbitrary, enabling us to solve the problem and thus locate the axes. The vector could, however, have any length, as long as it stayed on that axis. Other vectors along the same axis as y_1 are found by multiplying all of the values in a_1 by the same constant. This may be written $a_1{}^* = ca_1$ where c is any number, other than zero. This is called *scaling* the principal components. A frequent scaling that is used is to make the lengths of a equal to the corresponding eigenvalue (this is done by multiplying by the square root of the eigenvalue). When this is done with principal components derived from standardized variables (z scores), that is, when the covariance matrix is a correlation matrix, the a's will be correlations between the principal components and the original variables. Such a scaling is often useful in interpreting the principal components, as discussed below.

Reducing the Number of Principal Components

In principal components analysis, we begin with a set of correlated variables and wind up with a set of uncorrelated variables that are linear combinations of the original variables. Uncorrelated variables are simpler than correlated variables, so that is an advantage. However, we usually end up with as many new variables (principal components) as we started with and we often want to achieve greater simplicity by reducing the number of variables (we call this *data reduction*). If things work out right, we may be able to make use of only a few of the principal components.

The principal components are arranged in order of the amount of original variable variance they account for. Thus, if the principal components analysis has really helped in the task of data reduction, only the first few principal components will account for most of the variance in the original variables. The rest of the components may be relatively unimportant.

How many principal components should be "saved"? There is no firm answer to that question, but researchers have developed several alternative criteria. Most of the criteria require us to know the amount of variance accounted for by each principal component. That may be computed by dividing the eigenvalue for each principal component by the total variance (the sum of the eigenvalues or the trace of the **C** matrix, if we began with the **R** matrix, then this is the number of variables). Some criteria are:

1. Determine arbitrarily the proportion of variance you want to capture with the principal components and take as many as are required to reach that proportion.
2. If you are using an **R** matrix to begin with, take all principal components with eigenvalues of 1.0 or greater. This is a commonly used criterion that is somewhat arbitrary but seems to work quite well.
3. Base the decision on prior expectations as to how many dimensions there are in the original variables.
4. Perform the *scree* test. Make a plot in which the number of each principal component is on the horizontal axis and the amount of variance (or the

eigenvalue) is on the vertical axis. This is shown in figure 6-11. Disregard the principal components that come after the scree in the curve (the part where the curve levels out: 5 in figure 6-11). Sometimes this doesn't work because the curve doesn't scree very dramatically, or there may be more than one scree.

Other criteria exist, including some that are more analytically based (for example, tests of the significance of principal components). However, in practical work the above criteria seem to work.

Naming the Principal Components

If we have been able to reduce a set of original variables to a smaller set of orthogonal principal components we will have accomplished something. In some

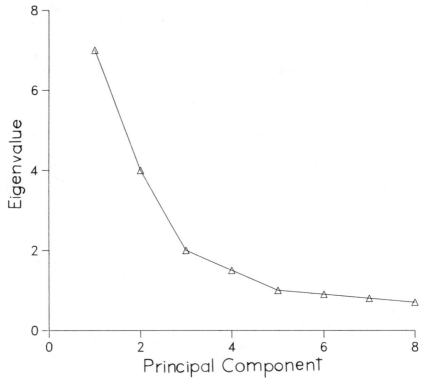

Figure 6-11. Scree Test.

studies that is the end of the analysis (we may have only wanted to explore the structure of a set of variables), in other studies, we may want to go on to use the principal components as variables in further analysis, for example in a multiple regression.

Either way, we usually want to describe in some way (to name) the new variables we have constructed. We often think of them as underlying dimensions of the original variables, perhaps as new constructs, and so we want to explicate these concepts.

The process of naming the principal components makes use of the transformation matrix A (recall that the values of the new variables are found by the matrix equation $Y = XA$). If we started out with a correlation matrix R and the components have been properly scaled, then the transformation matrix gives us the correlations of the principal components with the original variables. We name a principal component by examining those variables that are highly correlated with that component and attempting to describe what is common to those variables. Sometimes all or most of the variables are moderately correlated with the first principal component and such a component is considered to be a *general* component, common to all of the original variables. Then the other components may be describable in more specific terms. At times the process of naming principal components occurs after *rotation,* a procedure we take up in chapter 7.

Example

In the study of research teaching introduced in chapter 3 we asked a series of 26 questions designed to tap students' attitudes toward research (the Kirk-Rosenblatt Research Inventory). An abbreviated version of the wording of these questions is shown in table 6-1. Students responded to these questions on a six-point scale ranging from strongly agree (1) to strongly disagree (6). Of the 26 items, 8 are worded positively, that is, agreement indicates a positive attitude toward research while the remaining 18 are worded negatively. The authors of the items believe that most of them fall into three groups—items concerning the usefulness of research, the importance of doing research, and confidence in the validity of social work research.

Means and standard deviations for the items are shown in table 6-2. Tables 6-3 to 6-5 present the results of a principal components analysis using the FACTOR routine of SPSS. This analysis was performed on the correlation matrix of the variables (not the covariance matrix). The correlation matrix is not shown but it can be printed out as part of the FACTOR routine. This output was produced with the following control statements:

Table 6-1. Questions Designed to Tap Students' Attitudes toward Research

Variables	Labels
VAR410	RESEARCH IS NOT PARTICULARLY USEFUL TO PRACTITIONERS
VAR411	RESEARCH DOESNT GENERATE USEFUL SOCIAL WORK KNOWLEDGE
VAR412	SOCIAL WORKERS SHOULD RELY ON KNOWLEDGE FROM RESEARCH
VAR413	SOCIAL WORK SHOULD BE MORE SCIENCE THAN ART
VAR414	A MAJOR PART OF PROF EDUCATION SHOULD INCLUDE RESEARCH TRAINING
VAR415	FINDINGS HAVE LIMITED APPLICABILITY TO PRACTICE
VAR416	MEASUREMENT INSTRUMENTS ARE USUALLY RELIABLE
VAR417	RESEARCH FINDINGS ARE SLANTED FOR FUNDING SOURCES
VAR418	MUCH SOCIAL WORK RESEARCH IS NOT VALID
VAR419	THE CONCLUSIONS OF RESEARCH ARE BIASED IN FAVOR OF INITIAL HYPOTHESES
VAR420	MOST SW RESEARCHERS ARE SKILLED
VAR421	ADMINISTRATORS SHOULD BE REQUIRED TO EVALUATE PROGRAM EFFECTIVENESS
VAR422	SOCIAL WORKERS SHOULD KEEP ABREAST OF RESEARCH IN FIELD
VAR423	MOST RESEARCH IS DONE FOR PUBLIC RELATIONS
VAR424	CONTINUATION OF PROGRAMS SHOULD DEPEND ON EFFECTIVENESS
VAR425	LIMITED RESOURCES SHOULDNT GO TO EVALUATION RESEARCH
VAR426	RESEARCH OFTEN EXAMINES INSIGNIFICANT QUESTIONS
VAR427	RESEARCH TENDS TO LEGITIMATE PROGRAMS RATHER THAN PROVIDE CORRECTIVE FEEDBACK
VAR428	METHODOLOGICAL PROBLEMS ARE SO GREAT FINDINGS ARE INVALID
VAR429	RESEARCH IS NOT RELATED TO PRACTICE NEEDS
VAR430	I ONLY TAKE RESEARCH COURSES BECAUSE THEY ARE REQUIRED
VAR431	RESEARCHERS ARE NOT SELF CRITICAL ABOUT THEIR OWN STUDIES
VAR432	STATISTICS IS A SMOKESCREEN TO OBSCURE INVALID FINDINGS
VAR433	MOST IMPORTANT SOCIAL WORK QUESTIONS ARE NOT ACCESSIBLE TO RESEARCH
VAR434	MOST RESEARCH ARTICLES ARE INCOMPREHENSIBLE TO ME
VAR435	RESEARCH IS TOO TIME CONSUMING TO USE IN PRACTICE

Determinant of correlation matrix = 0.0000262(0.26228154D-04)

Table 6-2 Means and Standard Deviations for Questions
Listed in Table 6-1

VARIABLE	MEAN	STANDARD DEV	CASES
VAR410	4.8899	1.2045	109
VAR411	4.6697	1.3881	109
VAR412	2.9174	1.3819	109
VAR413	3.8257	1.2899	109
VAR414	4.0826	1.5642	109
VAR415	3.6881	1.4253	109
VAR416	3.4862	1.1354	109
VAR417	2.7523	1.2334	109
VAR418	3.5872	1.2111	109
VAR419	3.3578	1.0846	109
VAR420	3.4037	1.4150	109
VAR421	2.1835	1.2558	109
VAR422	1.8349	1.0759	109
VAR423	4.0642	1.1728	109
VAR424	4.0459	1.2648	109
VAR425	3.9817	1.2545	109
VAR426	3.6422	1.4371	109
VAR427	2.9725	1.0493	109
VAR428	3.3670	1.2521	109
VAR429	3.6972	1.2134	109
VAR430	3.7706	1.6590	109
VAR431	3.6055	1.2249	109
VAR432	3.8624	1.1094	109
VAR433	2.7339	1.3787	109
VAR434	4.5963	1.2332	109
VAR435	4.2936	1.3215	109

FACTOR   VARIABLES=VAR410 TO VAR435/
                TYPE=PA1/ROTATE=NOROTATE/
STATISTICS   1,4,5

TYPE=PA1 requests a principal components analysis. In the next chapter we will look at other factor analyses using other TYPE= commands. The statistics requested are means and standard deviations of the original variables, eigenvalues and the principal components matrix.

Table 6-3 is really two different tables. A line can be drawn between the EST COMMUNALITY and the FACTOR columns to separate the tables. There is *no* relationship between the lines in the first table and those in the second. In a principal components analysis the first table can be ignored. The second table gives the eigenvalues for each of the principal components (since the analysis is being done by a factoring program the principal components are called *factors*).

A correlation matrix is the same as a covariance matrix of standardized variables. The variance of a standardized variable is always 1.0. The ones in the diagonal of the correlation matrix may be thought of as these variances. The

Table 6-3. Eigenvalues

VARIABLE	EST COMMUNALITY	FACTOR	EIGENVALUE	PCT OF VAR	CUM PCT
VAR410	1.00000	1	6.39778	24.6	24.6
VAR411	1.00000	2	2.66526	10.3	34.9
VAR412	1.00000	3	1.73029	6.7	41.5
VAR413	1.00000	4	1.53808	5.9	47.4
VAR414	1.00000	5	1.41768	5.5	52.9
VAR415	1.00000	6	1.24371	4.8	57.7
VAR416	1.00000	7	1.16956	4.5	62.2
VAR417	1.00000	8	1.03113	4.0	66.1
VAR418	1.00000	9	0.95141	3.7	69.8
VAR419	1.00000	10	0.91955	3.5	73.3
VAR420	1.00000	11	0.76122	2.9	76.3
VAR421	1.00000	12	0.74550	2.9	79.1
VAR422	1.00000	13	0.67817	2.6	81.7
VAR423	1.00000	14	0.63308	2.4	84.2
VAR424	1.00000	15	0.59815	2.3	86.5
VAR425	1.00000	16	0.49864	1.9	88.4
VAR426	1.00000	17	0.43936	1.7	90.1
VAR427	1.00000	18	0.40656	1.6	91.6
VAR428	1.00000	19	0.37173	1.4	93.1
VAR429	1.00000	20	0.32639	1.3	94.3
VAR430	1.00000	21	0.31350	1.2	95.5
VAR431	1.00000	22	0.28740	1.1	96.6
VAR432	1.00000	23	0.25791	1.0	97.6
VAR433	1.00000	24	0.23184	0.9	98.5
VAR434	1.00000	25	0.21852	0.8	99.4
VAR435	1.00000	26	0.16758	0.6	100.0

Table 6-4. First Four Columns of Principal Components Matrix

FACTOR MATRIX USING PRINCIPAL FACTOR. NO ITERATIONS

	FACTOR 1	FACTOR 2	FACTOR 3	FACTOR 4
VAR410	0.65745	-0.24466	0.05236	-0.31457
VAR411	0.61298	0.09583	-0.04606	-0.04443
VAR412	-0.52762	0.22984	0.10258	0.11692
VAR413	-0.16297	0.21352	-0.09055	-0.13582
VAR414	-0.52734	0.44695	-0.04012	-0.12897
VAR415	0.64258	-0.20028	0.24627	0.14372
VAR416	-0.15107	-0.20326	0.69016	0.05686
VAR417	0.30472	0.49326	0.08161	-0.38559
VAR418	0.43162	0.57864	-0.08745	0.23247
VAR419	0.13668	0.42560	0.31558	-0.44772
VAR420	0.08869	-0.12195	0.54728	0.31993
VAR421	-0.44325	0.27460	0.20542	0.07456
VAR422	-0.56136	0.27178	0.29259	0.32207
VAR423	0.49911	0.47404	0.11618	-0.11630
VAR424	-0.40053	0.30898	0.41684	0.03865
VAR425	0.57464	-0.15837	0.40607	-0.06298
VAR426	0.57230	0.29368	0.00182	0.43717
VAR427	0.58865	0.43526	0.22894	-0.26373
VAR428	0.46419	0.50978	0.00078	0.33722
VAR429	0.47507	0.16486	-0.23377	0.32771
VAR430	0.64885	-0.30392	0.13930	-0.03093
VAR431	0.48892	0.05484	-0.30701	0.03232
VAR432	0.48739	0.37873	-0.15729	-0.03435
VAR433	0.37200	-0.04231	0.00965	0.48428
VAR434	0.58420	-0.15309	0.16903	-0.10546
VAR435	0.72218	-0.34808	0.02643	-0.01293

eigenvalues add up to 26, the sum of the variances of the standardized variables. This is, of course, the number of variables.

In the next column is the percentage of variance accounted for by each principal component. This is the eigenvalue divided by the sum of all the eigenvalues. The last column is the cumulative percentage. It is useful in telling us how much of the total variance in the set of variables we would account for if we paid attention to only the first k principal components. For example, if we keep only the first five principal components we will account for only 52.9% of the variance. The eight principal components with eigenvalues greater than 1.0 account for 66.1%.

Table 6-4 shows the first four columns of the principal components matrix (the machine actually printed out the first eight columns, those representing all the principal components with eigenvalues greater than one. The machine could have printed out all 26 columns of the matrix). These are standardized loadings, that is, the sum of the squared values in each column adds to the eigenvalue for that component. These numbers are the correlations of the principal components with the variables. Note that most of the variables are at least moderately associated with the first principal component.

As indicated above, a principal components analysis might be used to identify a relatively small number of new orthogonal variables that represent most of the variance of the original variables. Unfortunately, this analysis is disappointing in that regard. It takes seven principal components to capture 60% of the variance and nine to almost reach 70%. Ideally, we would like to have four or five principal components accounting for 60-70%. Of course, seven to ten new variables is an improvement over the 26 we started with.

We go on to try to describe the first few principal components from the data in table 6-4. Matters are not terribly clear. Looking first at the high loadings on the first principal component, we note that all of the positive items except for VAR420 have negative loadings. VAR420 has close to a zero loading. The negative items all have positive loadings. In addition, no positive item has a loading with an absolute value over .6. Further, four of the five items that the authors think of as reflecting "usefulness" (VAR410, VAR411, VAR415, VAR429, and VAR435) have loadings over .6. Hence, we might conclude that principal component one reflects the positive-negative dimension of the items as well as usefulness. However, the interpretation is clouded by the fact that lots of other items also have relatively high loadings.

I have even more difficulty interpreting the second principal component. Of seven items with loadings over .4 only one is a positive item. Beyond that, I am unable to see much of a pattern. Attempts to interpret the rest of the principal components appear to be fruitless.

None of the above should be taken as an indication of weakness of the instrument or as indications of problems in the analysis. Principal components analysis frequently does not produce dimensions that are naturally interpretable; when it does, that is an unexpected plus. It's primary usefulness is as a data reduction technique, reducing a large number of variables to a smaller number of uncorrelated variables that do almost as good a job of representing the variance in the original variables. At the end of the next chapter we will reanalyze these data using factor analysis and will see that that technique yields more interpretable dimensions.

Principal components analysis also has an important place pedagogically as it is the foundation for a number of multivariate techniques including factor analysis, discriminant analysis, and others.

Note

1.
$$\bar{y} = \frac{\Sigma_i y_i}{n} = \frac{\Sigma_i(a_{11}x_{i1} + a_{21}x_{i2} + \cdots + a_{p1}x_{ip})}{n}$$

$$= \frac{a_{11}\Sigma_i x_{i1}}{n} + \frac{a_{21}\Sigma_i x_{i2}}{n} + \cdots + \frac{a_{p1}\Sigma_i x_{ip}}{n}$$

$$= a_{11}\bar{x}_1 + a_{21}\bar{x}_2 + \cdots + a_{p1}\bar{x}_p$$

Since we assumed that the x's are in deviation score form, all of the $\bar{x}$'s are zero, so $\bar{y}$ is zero also.

7 FACTOR ANALYSIS

In the last chapter we suggested that one way to use principal components analysis was to pay attention to only the first few components, on the grounds that they accounted for most of the variation that is common to the variables. Factor analysis can be thought of as an extension of principal components analysis. The difference is that in factor analysis, we assume that there are only a few components (called *factors*) that are common among the variables, that is, we assume that the variables as a whole have a few common elements. In factor analysis that assumption is built in from the beginning. Hence, a further distinction between the two techniques is that principal components analysis attempts to account for variances in the variables while factor analysis accounts for covariances or correlations. We assume in factor analysis that the factors account for the covariations among the variables, an assumption that is not necessary in principal components analysis.

Points as Variables Instead of Individuals

We are accustomed to think of points in space as representing individuals. It is possible to think of points as representing variables rather than individuals. Suppose we have a measure x that we have taken on two individuals, p and q. We can locate the variable x in a space according to the scores of the individuals as in figure 7-1. Individual q received a score of 4 while individual p received a score of 3. In the diagram, the axes of the space represent individuals rather than variables. We could call this an "individual" or "subject" space as contrasted to a "variable" space in which the axes represent variables.

If we have taken the measure on n individuals, then we need a space of n dimensions to locate the point. Obviously we can locate several points in our space, representing several variables, each point placed in accordance with the scores of our subjects. In the following, we think of these points as vectors and use arrows to represent the vectors (see chapter 5). The lengths of the vectors will equal the square root of the sum of squares of the scores of the individuals on each variable (if we have z scores then the length will be $\sqrt{n-1}$), and the cosine of the angle between two vectors is equal to the correlation coefficient

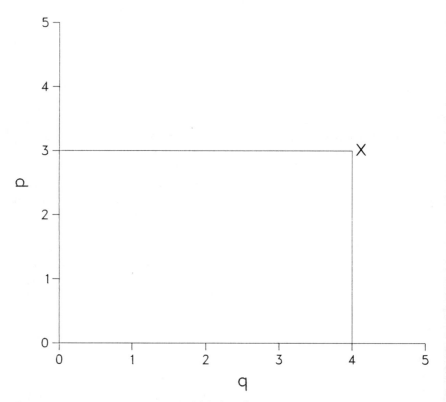

Figure 7-1. Location of One Variable in a Space.

(see chapter 5). If the correlation between the variables is 1.0, the vectors representing the variables are on the same line out from the origin. If the correlation between them is equal to 0, then the vectors will be on lines at right angles to each other.

Subspaces

When we first locate variables, we do so in spaces of dimension n, where n is equal to the number of cases. This is somewhat extravagant, and we would like to know how small a space could be used to represent our variables (where "small" refers not to distances or volumes but rather to dimensionality). Imagine, for example, two variables (x_1 and x_2) involving three individuals (p, q and r), which we locate in a three-dimensional space (one dimension for each individual) as in figure 7-2. It is possible to find a plane through the origin in which the vectors representing the variables lie, and thus it is possible to capture two variables in some two-dimensional space (a plane), and this is true even if we have lots of individuals. We will insist on having more individuals than variables, so we will never need a space of more than p dimensions to capture all of our p variables, although we start by locating them first in a space of n dimensions where n is the number of cases.

But it may be possible to reduce the dimensionality of our variable space even further. Suppose I have three variables on three individuals and locate these in space as in figure 7-3 (I am temporarily violating my rule of having more individuals than variables. I want to look at three variables, which would require at least four individuals if I followed my rule, but I can't draw pictures in four dimensions). It is possible that I will discover that all three vectors now fall in the same plane. If this happens, I will feel very good, for some parsimony will have been achieved—I need only two dimensions to capture my three variables; in fact, I will say that the three variables together reflect only two dimensions of say, personality. Of course I am left with the rather thorny problem of describing those dimensions, but that problem we will leave for later.

In the real world, we will often encounter the situation in which the three vectors almost fall in the same plane, but not quite. We will be satisfied with this situation, and will then want to describe the plane (that is, describe its axes) and describe how much the three vectors protrude from it.

We have come to the first main idea in factor analysis. In a factor analysis we begin with a large number of variables and we are first of all interested in how many underlying dimensions are necessary to represent them. That is, we imagine that the p variables can be represented by vectors lying in a space of r dimensions or almost lying in that space.

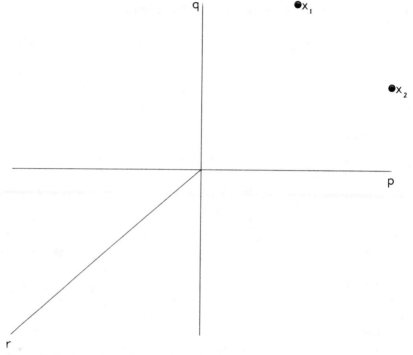

Figure 7-2.　Location of Two Variables in a Space.

We will now develop some ideas in factor analysis somewhat more formally. We will deal with variables in their standardized forms. That is, we will assume that each x variable has been transformed as follows:

$$z_i = \frac{x_i - \bar{x}}{s_x}$$

The Decomposition of Variables

We are going to think of a set of p variables as being composed of a series of factors, that is z is a linear combination of factors:

$$z_j = a_{j1}f_1 + a_{j2}f_2 + \cdots + a_{jr}f_r + a_j^*f_j^*$$

The factors f_1 through f_r are thought of as factors that all contribute, though in varying degrees, to a set of variables of which z_j is a member. Notice that here

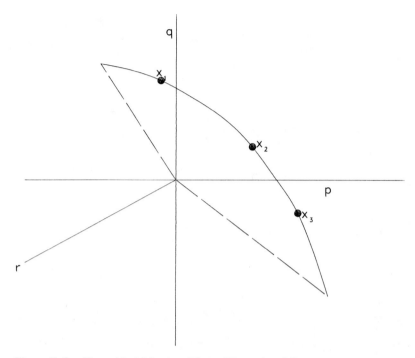

Figure 7-3.   Three Variables in a Three-Dimensional Space.

we represent the original variables as linear combinations of factors, while in our discussion of principal components we represented the principal components (analogous to factors) as linear combinations of our original variables. The factor f_j^* is a factor *specific* to z_j, that is, not shared with the other variables (it is called a *unique* factor). The factor f_j^* is usually composed of two components, one due to errors of measurement (unreliability) and the other a *valid* (nonerror) component, which is not shared with the other variables. For the time being, we will require that all of the f's and f^*'s be uncorrelated (orthogonal). In the above, the f's are variables, that is, they take on different values for each case (e.g., f_{ik} is the value of the ith individual on the f_k factor). I can arrange, by selecting proper values for the a's, for the f's and f^*'s to be variables in standard score form.

The f's are vectors along coordinate axes of the r dimensional subspace we talked about above, while the f^*'s represent that part of the variable that cannot be captured in that subspace. Figure 7-4 is a picture of one variable with two common factors. The common factors F_1 and F_2 are represented as coordinate axes in the horizontal plane while the specific factor F^* is represented in the vertical dimension.

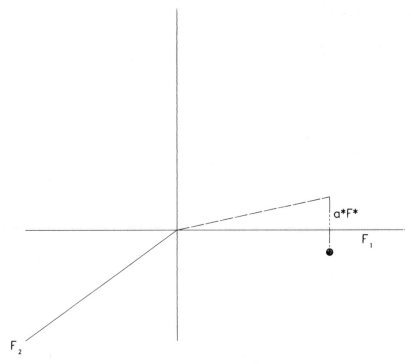

Figure 7-4. One Variable with Two Common Factors.

We want to find the values a_{jk}; they give us the weighting of each factor in the original variables.

We can write the above expression to represent the score of a given individual (i) as follows:

$$z_{ij} = a_{j1}f_{i1} + a_{j2}f_{i2} + \cdots + a_{jr}f_{ir} + a_j^* f_{ij}^*$$

where z_{ij} is the value of z_j for the ith individual, f_{i1} is the value of the ith individual on the f_1 factor, etc.

We have p variables. For each of our n individuals we could write out p equations like the above. Let us imagine what the list of p equations for one individual (the ith individual) would look like this:

$$z_{i1} = a_{11}f_{i1} + a_{12}f_{i2} + \cdots + a_{1j}f_{ij} + \cdots + a_{1r}f_{ir} + a_1^* f_{i1}^*$$
$$+ 0f_{i2}^* + \cdots + 0f_{ij}^* + \cdots + 0f_{ip}^*$$

. . . .

$$z_{ij} = a_{j1}f_{i1} + a_{j2}f_{i2} + \cdots + a_{jj}f_{ij} + \cdots + a_{jr}f_{ir} + 0f_{i1}^*$$
$$+ 0f_{i2}^* + \cdots + a_j^* f_{ij}^* + \cdots + 0f_{ip}^*$$

126

. . . .

$$z_{ip} = a_{p1}f_{i1} + a_{p2}f_{i2} + \cdots + a_{pj}f_{ij} + \cdots + a_{pr}f_{ir} + 0f_{i1}^*$$
$$+ 0f_{i2}^* + \cdots + 0f_{ij}^* + \cdots + a_p^* f_{ip}^*$$

This set of equations shows that there are r *common* factors and p *unique* factors. On the right side of each equation there are $r + p$ terms; but some of these are zero, so for any one variable there are at most only $r + 1$ nonzero terms. On the left side of the equation we have the z scores for each variable for one case, the ith case. This can be thought of as a vector, the z_i' vector.

In chapter 2 we introduced the idea of a Z matrix, the matrix of z scores from n individuals on p variables. The above column of z scores is the same as one of the rows in the Z matrix of chapter 2. That is why we designate it with a prime, even though it appears here as a column.

On the right side of this set of equations the a coefficients can be gathered together into a matrix A:

$$
\begin{array}{cccccccccc}
a_{11} & a_{12} & \cdots & \cdots & \cdots & a_{1r} & a_1^* & 0 & \cdots \; \cdots \; \cdots & 0 \\
\cdot & & & & & & & & & \\
\cdot & & & & & & & & & \\
\cdot & & & & & & & & & \\
a_{j1} & a_{j2} & \cdots & a_{jj} & \cdots & a_{jr} & 0 & 0 & \cdots \; a_j^* \; \cdots & 0 \\
\cdot & & & & & & & & & \\
\cdot & & & & & & & & & \\
\cdot & & & & & & & & & \\
a_{p1} & a_{p2} & \cdots & \cdots & \cdots & a_{pr} & 0 & 0 & \cdots \; \cdots \; \cdots & a_p^*
\end{array}
$$

This matrix has p rows and $r + p$ columns. It is composed of a $p \times r$ matrix of a's next to a $p \times p$ diagonal matrix of a^*'s. Let us now define a vector f_i', collecting the values of case i on the factors. This vector has $r + p$ values:

$$
f_i' =
\begin{array}{c}
f_{i1} \\
f_{i2} \\
\cdot \\
\cdot \\
\cdot \\
f_{ir} \\
f_{i1}^* \\
\cdot \\
\cdot \\
\cdot \\
f_{ip}^*
\end{array}
$$

The equations above may now be represented in vector-matrix form as

$$\underset{p \times 1 \quad p \times (r+p) \quad (r+p) \times 1}{\mathbf{z}_i' = \quad \mathbf{A} \ \mathbf{f}_i'}$$

(Note that $\mathbf{z}_i'$ and $\mathbf{f}_i'$ are column vectors, although they are primed.) This represents matters in terms of a single case.

Now I want to represent the situation for all cases at once. Start with the left side of the equations above. If I line up all the values for the other cases in columns I will have a matrix of z scores, the scores for each case in columns. This matrix will be the transpose of the matrix $\mathbf{Z}$ defined in chapter 2. So I will represent it as $\mathbf{Z}'$.

On the right side, $\mathbf{A}$ is a matrix of coefficients that stays the same for all cases. The vector f_i' has values for case i for all of the factors, so it will be different for each case. I can line up the vectors f_i' (for i from 1 to n) in a matrix that I will call $\mathbf{F}'$. So on the right side I have $\mathbf{AF}'$. Thus,

$$\underset{p \times n \quad p \times (r+p) \quad (r+p) \times n}{\mathbf{Z}' = \quad \mathbf{A} \ \mathbf{F}'}$$

that is, the z scores may be found by multiplying the matrix of coefficients $\mathbf{A}$ times the matrix of values on the factors $\mathbf{F}'$.

The Correlation Matrix and Its Factors

In the above matrix equation, let us postmultiply the left side by $\mathbf{Z}$ and the right side by $(\mathbf{AF}')'$. [We can do this because $(\mathbf{Z}')' = \mathbf{Z} = (\mathbf{AF}')'$, and in matrix algebra it is legal to multiply both sides of an equation by equal things, just as in scalar algebra] . Thus,

$$\mathbf{Z}'\mathbf{Z} = \mathbf{AF}'(\mathbf{AF}')' = \mathbf{AF}'\mathbf{FA}'$$

(Remember that $(\mathbf{F}')' = \mathbf{F}$). Now divide both sides of the equation by $n - 1$:

$$[1/(n-1)] \, [\mathbf{Z}'\mathbf{Z}] = [1/(n-1)] \, [\mathbf{AF}'\mathbf{FA}']$$

In chapter 2 we asserted that the covariance matrix of standardized values $[1/(n-1)] \, [\mathbf{Z}'\mathbf{Z}]$ was the correlation matrix $\mathbf{R}$, so the left side of the equation is $\mathbf{R}$.

On the right side of the equation we are multiplying by $1/(n-1)$. This multiplication is commutative so I can write the right side as

$$\mathbf{A}\{[1/(n-1)] \, [\mathbf{F}'\mathbf{F}]\}\mathbf{A}'$$

$\mathbf{F}$ is a matrix of values on factors that are like variables and, although we do not know these values, we assume they are in standard score form. Therefore, $\mathbf{F}$ is a matrix of standard scores (like $\mathbf{Z}$), so the matrix $[1/(n-1)] \, [\mathbf{F}'\mathbf{F}]$ is a matrix of the correlations among the factors. Further, we required at the beginning that the factors have zero correlations among themselves. Therefore the matrix $[1/(n-1)]$ $[\mathbf{F'F}]$ has zero values in the off-diagonal cells and 1's in the diagonal. It is the $(p+r) \times (p+r)$ identity matrix $\mathbf{I}$. Multiplying the identity matrix by another matrix leaves the other matrix unchanged so we have

$$\mathbf{R} = \mathbf{AA'}$$

Remember that a few pages back we said that we wanted to find the values a_{jk}, they give us the weightings of the factors in the original variables. Now that translates into finding a matrix $\mathbf{A}$ such that when we multiply $\mathbf{A}$ by its transpose we get the correlation matrix. We may also want to find the matrix $\mathbf{F}$ but we will leave that for later.

The matrix $\mathbf{AA'}$ is formed by performing a number of multiplications of vectors (each row of $\mathbf{A}$ is multiplied by each column of $\mathbf{A'}$). It is instructive to look at a couple of these vector multiplications.

First let's look at the product of the jth row of $\mathbf{A}$ times the jth column of $\mathbf{A'}$. On the left side of the equation this will be the value r_{jj}, which will be 1.0, the correlation of variable j with itself. On the right side we have

$$a_{j1}^2 + a_{j2}^2 + \cdots + a_{jr}^2 + 0 + \cdots + a_j^{*2} + \cdots + 0$$

Each of these terms can be thought of as representing proportions of the variance of z_j. That is, a_{jk}^2 is the proportion of the variance of z_j accounted for by f_k.

The value a_j^{*2} is the proportion of variance contributed by the unique factor. The sum of the other a_{jk}^2's is the proportion of the variance of z_j contributed by the common factors. This quantity is called the *communality* and is represented by h_j^2. Note that

$$a_j^{*2} = 1 - \sum_k a_{jk}^2 = 1 - h_j^2$$

In the actual computations we only determine the a_{jk}'s directly, once we have those we will know the value of a_j^*.

Now look at the product of the ith row and the jth column. On the left side of the equation this is r_{ij}, the correlation of variable i with variable j. On the right side it is

$$a_{i1}a_{j1} + a_{i2}a_{j2} + \cdots + a_{ik}a_{jk} + \cdots + a_{ir}a_{jr}$$

Note that none of the a^*'s appear, not even a_i^* or a_j^*. Thus, as we would expect, the unique parts of z_i and z_j do not contribute to their correlation. The correlation between z_i and z_j is fully accounted for by the common factors.

Now suppose that we were to truncate $\mathbf{A}$ (and therefore $\mathbf{A'}$) by dropping off the columns containing the coefficients for the unique factors. Let us now look at the product AA' (A having been truncated). Call this product $R\dagger$. So $R\dagger = AA'$ (with A having only the common factor coefficients). A little thought should convince you that $R\dagger$ is the same as R except in the principal diagonal. That is, in the off-diagonal cells we find the correlations of the variables. However, in the diagonal cells of $R\dagger$ we find the communalities.

The first computational task in factor analysis is to find the truncated matrix A that satisfies this equation; that is, we must find the matrix A such that $AA' = R\dagger$. To do this we must start with $R\dagger$. However, from our data we are able to compute only the off-diagonal cells of $R\dagger$ (the correlations among the variables); we cannot determine the communalities. We must therefore make some estimates of the communalities of the variables in order to do the computations.

In theory, plugging the correct communalities into the matrix R will cause the rank of R to be reduced from p, the number of variables, to the number of common factors r. That is required in order for us to extract exactly r common factors from the data. While all of this is sound mathematically, it usually does not work out so neatly in the real world. That is because what I have described above is a model and like all statistical techniques, the model is an oversimplification of reality; that is, it usually does not fit in practice. As always, however, it is possible that the model will fit closely enough that we will gain understanding in using it.

Two sources of lack of fit are discussed below.

1. The data we are working with are usually subject to two kinds of errors, sampling errors (we usually have a sample of some universe) and measurement errors. This means that the correlation matrix that we start out with will not be a perfect representation of the relationships among the variables in the real world.

2. We often find that the matrix A that is required to perfectly reproduce the off-diagonal elements of R (that is, the matrix A such that $AA' = R\dagger$) has more columns than we would like (we can always perfectly reproduce R by having as many common factors as variables). One of the purposes of the analysis is to achieve some parsimony in description of the variables. That means we want only a few common factors. But often we need a large number of factors (sometimes as many factors as original variables) to perfectly reproduce $R\dagger$. The reasons for this may be either the errors of sampling or measurement mentioned above or the fact that our situation does require lots of factors, but some of the factors are unimportant. We get around this problem by trying to find a few factors that "almost" reproduce the correlations among the variables. That is we try to find an A matrix with only a few columns such that AA' is almost equal to $R\dagger$.

Statisticians have discovered that there are many different approaches to finding an A matrix, depending on the meaning we assign to "almost" and depending on how we think about the original data (for example, whether or not we have a sample, whether or not we want to account for measurement error, and whether or not the variables are normally distributed). These different approaches are called *methods of initial factor extraction*. We describe below several such methods.

Before going into specific methods, a couple of aspects of all methods should be mentioned. Performing a factor analysis always involves finding the eigenvalues and eigenvectors of some matrix (as was done in the last chapter). Computationally, that means that an equation like $|\mathbf{Q} - \lambda\mathbf{I}| = 0$ must first be solved for the λ's. The various extraction methods differ in the matrix $\mathbf{Q}$ that is plugged into this equation. It is usually some version of the correlation matrix $\mathbf{R}$. Further, as mentioned above, the computational procedures require that we make initial estimates of the communalities of the variables, that is, we must estimate what amount of each variable's variance we expect that variable to have in common with the other variables. In some techniques this estimate is critical to the solution; in others it is less critical. That is because some techniques use iterative procedures that adjust the initial estimates of communality to values that are more satisfactory. What we mean by "iterative" and "adjust" is described below.

Initial Estimates of Communality

There is no foolproof way to estimate the communality of a variable. Some of the estimates that have been suggested are:

1. The reliability of the variable, if estimates of the reliability are available. This is an upper limit on communality and is used because that part of the variance that is not reliable is theoretically due to random error, which shouldn't correlate with anything and thus cannot be common to other variables.
2. Use the highest correlation of a variable with another variable. This will usually give an estimate that is too low, since it takes into account the variable's relationship with only one other variable.
3. Use the squared multiple correlation of the variable with all the other variables in the analysis. This also will usually give an underestimate, but it seems to be better than other estimates in many situations and has become widely used.

Many computer programs use the third estimate as the "default" option for determining communalities, that is, it is used unless the program is told to use something else.

Number of Factors

Many factoring methods also require that the number of factors be specified beforehand. Obviously this is often a problem, since the analyst may not have any idea how many factors exist in his data. As indicated above, the more factors we specify, the closer we will be able to reproduce the correlation matrix, but this is at the expense of the principle of parsimony. So we need some compromises. There are several approaches:

1. Decide, on the basis of theory or prior knowledge, how many factors you think are in the variables.
2. Use only those factors that account for at least a certain average proportion of the variance of the variables, say 1% or 5%. The average proportion of variance accounted for by a factor is equal to its eigenvalue divided by the number of original variables.
3. Extract all factors that have eigenvalues greater than some number, usually one.
4. Find the eigenvalues of the original **R** matrix (as we would do if we were to perform a principal components analysis) and set the number of factors equal to the number of eigenvalues greater than some number, say one. This is sometimes called the *eigenvalue one* criteria. This criterion is different from the preceding one because here we are looking at the eigenvalues for the original correlation matrix while in criteria three we were looking at the eigenvalues of the **R**† matrix. This criteria seems to work well in practice and is the default procedure for some popular computer programs (e.g., the Statistical Package for the Social Sciences and SCSS).
5. Use the scree test as described in the last chapter.
6. The most sophisticated procedure for determining the number of factors is based on criteria of statistical significance of factors. This criteria is discussed in greater detail later on. It can be used only if we make restrictive assumptions about the data.

If you have guessed wrong on the number of factors, the analysis can always be done again using more or fewer. That is, if the model with k factors does not fit, a $k + 1$ model should be tried. In fact, some analysts suggest beginning with one factor and moving up until the model fits adequately. It is also possible that the original model had too many factors, as indicated by very small eigenvalues for the last factors. In that situation, the analysis could be done over with fewer factors.

Extraction Methods

Principal Axis Factoring

Principal axis factoring is the simplest extraction method. To use it one must begin by specifying the number of factors to be extracted and the communality estimates. Usually the squared multiple correlations are used as communalities. The eigenvalue equation $|R\dagger - \lambda I| = 0$ is then solved ($R\dagger$ is equal to R except for estimated communalities in the diagonal). If we have decided on k factors, then the eigenvectors corresponding to the k largest eigenvalues are taken as our factors and arranged in an A matrix. When we do this, we will have an A matrix that usually does not reproduce perfectly either the diagonal or off-diagonal elements of $R\dagger$. That is, the diagonal elements of AA' will not be exactly equal to our original estimated communalities, and the off-diagonal elements will not be exactly equal to the correlations among the variables. That is because we incorrectly estimated the communalities, and the number of factors we decided on at the beginning is probably not enough (there really are more common factors among the variables).

Principal Axis Factoring with Iterations

This approach is a refinement of the preceding one in that the estimates of communality we start out with are improved through a series of steps called iterations. Again, the number of factors must be determined beforehand. However, this time, after going through a principal axis solution the diagonal elements of the product AA' are used as new estimates of communality, that is, they are put into the diagonal of the R matrix. The process is then repeated over and over until two successive estimates of the communalities are close together. (By close together I mean that the sum of the differences of the successive communality estimates is very small.) Each attempt to find an A matrix is called an *iteration*.

In this author's view, principal axis factoring with iterations should usually be the method of choice for beginning factor analysts. Other methods are more complex and involve assumptions that are often problematic in real situations.

In this procedure no attention is paid to what happens to the off-diagonal elements of AA' in deciding whether or not to stop the iteration process, that is, it does not matter how closely the original correlations are reproduced (although they are reproduced as well as they can be with this number of factors and with the current estimates of communalities). A technique called *unweighted least squares* or *minres* takes into account the off-diagonal elements of AA' in deciding when to stop the iteration process.

Other Extraction Methods

The following is a brief description of some other methods of initial factor extraction.

Generalized Least Squares. In this approach (known as GLS), variables with greater communality are given greater weight in the solution on the assumption that the unique variance is like error variance and variables with much error in them should not be allowed to affect the solution too much. Again, an iterative procedure is used in which the significance of the deviation between the reproduced and observed correlations is assessed at each iteration.

Maximum Likelihood Solution. In this procedure (known as MLS), the fact that the data are a sample from a population is explicitly recognized. That is, the observed correlation matrix is assumed to be only an estimate of the correlation matrix in the population. We make the demanding assumption that the distribution of the original variables and the factors is multivariate normal. It is assumed that in some sense there exists an **A** matrix for the population (the values of which can be thought of as population parameters) and we want to estimate that **A** matrix. The estimated **A** matrix is that matrix that would be most likely to produce the observed correlation matrix. Again, an iteration procedure is used. Another approach similar to maximum likelihood is Rao's canonical factoring.

Alpha Factoring. This procedure is applicable to the psychometric situation in which we assume that we have a sample of variables from a universe of variables rather than a sample of individuals. In fact, we assume that we have the whole population of individuals. We want to find the factors that presumably exist in the population of variables. The correlation matrix is first "corrected for attenuation" on the assumption that observed correlations are depressed by errors of measurement. Again, an iteration process is used.

With a given number of factors, specified before hand, the off-diagonal elements of the original **R** matrix may or may not be well reproduced by the **AA'** matrix. Thus one of the tests of the adequacy of the analysis is the extent to which **AA'** approximates the correlations among the variables.

It is possible to look at the residual correlation matrix (the matrix $\mathbf{R}\dagger - \mathbf{AA'}$), or the differences in the squares of the entries in these matrices. The off-diagonal elements of this difference should be nearly zero. Alternatively, the matrix of partial correlations among the variables, controlling for the factors, should be nearly an identity matrix. A statistical test is available (see Lawley and Maxwell, 1971).

Other statistical tests are also available to test whether or not the data fit the model (see Kim and Mueller, 1978). All of these tests are based on the assumption that we have a multivariate normal distribution of the variables.

It should be noted that we hope that any such test will prove insignificant — since what is being tested is the fit of a model and a significant result indicates lack of fit. If the test is significant, a larger number of factors is required for adequate fit, and another solution with one more factor might be tried. However, relying on the criteria of statistical significance will usually yield a number of factors that are relatively unimportant and may be uninterpretable.

The assessment of the adequacy of the factor solution should also focus on the resulting communalities of the variables. Although the objective of factor analysis is to reproduce the correlations among the variables and not necessarily account for a large part of the variance of the variables, variables with low communalities have little in common with the rest of the set and perhaps should not be in the analysis. A cleaner analysis might be obtained by dropping them.

One other source of difficulty in factor analysis is a correlation matrix in which most of the correlations are quite small. If there is not much correlation among the variables, there is little point in performing factor analysis.

Rotation

The results of the initial factor solution are twofold: first, the determination of the number of factors necessary to almost reproduce the correlations among the variables (the determination of the dimensionality of the common factor space); and second, the identification of that common factor space by locating orthogonal axes for the space. The coordinate axes are located in terms of their positions relative to the original variables. See figure 7-5. However, the location of coordinate axes in a space is an arbitrary matter. In the above example, the axes could be located in any number of other positions, as long as they still pass through the origin and as long as they stay in the plane. In fact they do not even have to be orthogonal, that is, at right angles, they could be placed as in figure 7-6. Even with nonorthogonal axes it is possible to locate any point in the plane in terms of its perpendicular distance to the two axes.

The objective of the rotation step in factor analysis is to find a location for the coordinate axes that helps us better understand the interrelationships of the variables. The initial solution is almost always quite difficult to interpret. Interpretation usually depends on our being able to talk about what the factors mean as if they were hypothetical variables that we can name and describe. The only way we can do that is in terms of the original variables, by identifying the factors with the variables that are highly related to it. Thus, we would like each factor to be related to a few variables and not related to the others. As in principal

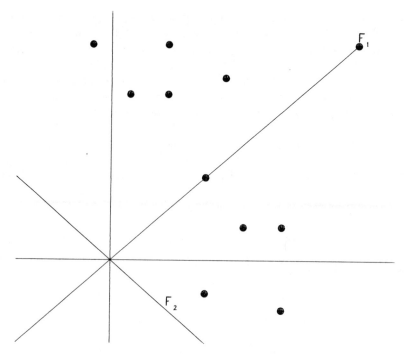

Figure 7-5.   Initial Factor Solution.

components analysis, the initial factor solution almost always produces a first factor with which most of the variables have moderately high correlations. Geometrically, this first factor goes through the middle of all of the variables, as in figure 7-5. The other factors have smaller correlations and tend to be *bipolar* (to have both positive and negative loadings). It would be desirable to rotate the factors so that they pass through clusters of variables. In the process of rotating factors we will not be changing the space in which the factors lie nor will we change the communalities of the variables. That is, we will continue to account for the same amount of variance.

As with everything in factor analysis, there are lots of ways to do rotations. The methods may be classified into two broad categories: orthogonal and oblique. In orthogonal rotations, we insist that the coordinate axes stay at right angles to each other; in oblique rotations we relax this requirement.

Before describing some of the methods of rotation, some further comments on the criteria for locating the factors are in order. The objective of rotations is to find a *simple structure*. What is meant by simple structure is not all that sim-

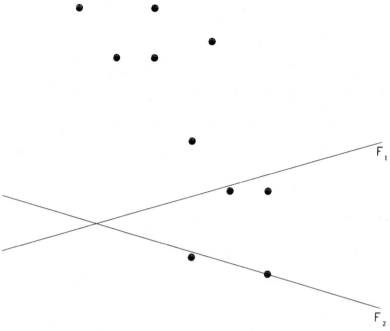

Figure 7-6. Nonorthogonal Factors.

ple. One of the aspects of simple structure is that each factor should have a small number of variables with high loadings while the rest of the variables have low loadings. Another criteria has to do with the factorial complexity of a variable. The *factorial complexity* of a variable is the number of factors with which it is highly related. Ideally, the factorial complexity of a variable should be 1.

Orthogonal Rotations

There are two basic procedures for performing orthogonal rotations, the *varimax* and the *quartimax* methods. In varimax rotations the objective is to simplify the columns of the **A** matrix, that is, to simplify the factors in accordance with the criteria of having a few high loadings and the rest small. In quartimax rotations the goal is the simplification of the rows (to achieve low factorial complexity). Sometimes these two criteria are combined, perhaps weighting one more than the other. Names for such combinations of criteria are *equimax* and *biquartimax*. The most common rotation method is the varimax.

Oblique Rotations

Often oblique rotations yield a picture that is closer to representing the real world, that is, we may have no reason to believe that the underlying factors are, in fact, uncorrelated and it would do violence to reality to force an orthogonal solution on the data. However, the price paid for greater realism is greater complexity; it is often harder to interpret the results.

To begin with, oblique solutions produce two basic factor matrices instead of one, the factor pattern matrix and the factor structure matrix. The factor pattern matrix contains the coefficients for the observed variables in terms of linear combinations of the factors. The structure matrix contains the correlations of the variables with the factors. For orthogonal factors, these matrices are the same, but not for oblique factors.

The pattern matrix may be thought of as containing regression coefficients for the observed variables as dependent variables with the factors as independent variables. When independent variables are correlated, the regression coefficients are affected by these correlations. Similarly, it is difficult to interpret the correlations of the variables and the factors (the structure matrix) since these correlations are affected by the correlations among the factors.

Another important matrix produced as a result of oblique rotations is the matrix of correlations among the factors. All three of these matrices are employed in the interpretation of the results. Computer programs for oblique rotation often allow one to control for the degree of obliqueness of the solution.

Factor Scores

The factors derived from factor analysis can be thought of as variables that take values for each case. Sometimes it is desirable to estimate those values. Sometimes we want to use the factors as independent or dependent variables in other analyses.

Values on the factors are, of course, unobserved. Since the factors have been derived out of the original variables, the only things we have to use to determine the values of the factor variables are the values for each case on the original variables.

In principal components analysis, determination of the values of the components is straightforward. The original model was stated in chapter 6 as

$$Y = XA$$

where X is the matrix of the original variable values, Y is the matrix of principal components values, and A is the transformation matrix. Usually a principal components analysis is done by a factor analysis program where the equation used is

$$\mathbf{X'} = \mathbf{BY'}$$

In order to find the matrix of the y (principal components) values, we multiply each side of the equation by $\mathbf{B}^{-1}$ to get:

$$\mathbf{B}^{-1}\mathbf{X'} = \mathbf{Y'}$$

Hence the $\mathbf{A}$ matrix we must multiply by the $\mathbf{X}$ matrix to get principal components scores is the inverse of the matrix $\mathbf{B}$ that we get from a principal components analysis done with a factor analysis program.

When we get to scores for factors, the situation is somewhat more complicated. We will not be able to obtain the factor scores exactly, they must be estimated. We want to determine factor scores using linear combinations of the original variable values; but those variables have some unique elements that will cause errors when they are used to determine scores on common factors. Again, several ways have been developed to deal with this problem. We will consider two.

The first is quite simple. It consists of constructing scales for a factor from a simple summation of variables that load highly on that factor, "highly" being arbitrarily determined. Often the variables are put into standard score form first.

The second approach uses reasoning derived from regression analysis. For the first factor, we want to produce a variable $\hat{\mathbf{f}}_1$ which is maximally correlated with the factor $\mathbf{f}_1$. That variable ($\hat{\mathbf{f}}_1$) will be a linear combination of the x's: $\hat{\mathbf{f}}_1 = \mathbf{X}\mathbf{b}_1$. Our task is to find the values in the vector $\mathbf{b}_1$. Using a least squares criteria for determining the b's in $\mathbf{b}_1$, we want b's such that $\Sigma(f_{1i} - \hat{f}_{1i})^2$ is a minimum (f_{1i} is the value of f_1 for the ith case and $\hat{f}_{1i}$ is the estimated value). From chapter 3 we know that $\mathbf{b}_1 = (\mathbf{X'X})^{-1}\mathbf{X'f}_1$. Now multiply the right side of the equation by $(n-1)/(n-1)$ like this:

$$\mathbf{b}_1 = (n-1)(\mathbf{X'X})^{-1}\mathbf{X'f}_1(1/n-1)$$

Now $[1/(n-1)]^{-1} = n-1$ so

$$\mathbf{b}_1 = \{[\mathbf{X'X}/(n-1)]^{-1}\}\{\mathbf{X'f}_1/(n-1)\}$$

If all of the variables are in standard score form, $\mathbf{X'X}/(n-1)$ is the correlation matrix of the original variables, $\mathbf{R}$, and $\mathbf{X'f}_1/(n-1)$ is the vector of correlations of $\mathbf{f}_1$ with the x variables. These correlations are given by the factor loadings (the factor structure matrix in oblique rotations). We can write this as

$$\mathbf{b}_1 = \mathbf{R}^{-1}\mathbf{a}_1$$

where $\mathbf{a}_1$ is a column of the factor loadings matrix. To get the values for $\hat{\mathbf{f}}_1$, we multiply this by the matrix of original values:

$$\hat{\mathbf{f}}_1 = \mathbf{b}_1\mathbf{X} = (\mathbf{R}^{-1}\mathbf{a}_1)\mathbf{X}$$

This represents things in terms of the first factor. To represent all of the factors at once, we replace the vectors with matrices:

$$\hat{F} = R^{-1}AX'$$

where **A** is the matrix of correlations between the factors and the variables (the factor loadings in an orthogonal rotation and the factor structure in an oblique rotation). The matrix of coefficients $R^{-1}A$ is called the *factor score coefficient* matrix.

Even for orthogonal rotations, the $\hat{f}$s will usually not be perfectly uncorrelated, because their values are estimated rather than being exact.

Of these two methods for determining factor scores, the first (summation of variables with high loadings on a factor) is clearly the simplest. Theoretically, it will produce less accurate estimates. It is often used, however, particularly in the situation in which the analyst does not want to reify the factor loadings (because they are affected by sampling and measurement error) but rather wishes to use them heuristically, to indicate relative importance of variables to factors. The regression method for estimating factor scores is used by SPSS and SCSS. These and other large scale computer programs also permit the computation of scales from variables, so that it is possible to compute factor scores that are sums of selected *x* variables.

Finally it should be noted that the factor scores depend very much on the rotation used. Different locations for the factors in the common factor space will obviously result in different scores.

Example

We present here a factor analysis of the items from the last chapter. The principal factor with iterations method was used for the initial factoring. The factoring process was stopped after four factors in the hope that that number of factors would be sufficient. (The SPSS default would have been eight, the number of principal components with eigenvalues over one). The factors were then rotated using the varimax method. The SPSS control statements were as follows:

```
FACTOR      VARIABLES=VAR410 TO VAR435/
            TYPE=PA2/NFACTORS=4/ROTATE=VARIMAX/
STATISTICS  1,4,5,6,7
```

TYPE=PA2 calls for the principal axis with iterations method. The statistics requested include means and standard deviations of the original variables, communalities, eigenvalues, initial factor matrix, rotated factor matrix and factor score coefficient matrix. Table 7–1 is composed of two separate tables. The first

Table 7-1. Beginning Communalities and Eigenvalues

VARIABLE	EST COMMUNALITY	FACTOR	EIGENVALUE	PCT OF VAR	CUM PCT
VAR410	0.61209	1	6.39778	24.6	24.6
VAR411	0.57093	2	2.66526	10.3	34.9
VAR412	0.43537	3	1.73029	6.7	41.5
VAR413	0.29332	4	1.53808	5.9	47.4
VAR414	0.61685	5	1.41768	5.5	52.9
VAR415	0.49632	6	1.24371	4.8	57.7
VAR416	0.39758	7	1.16956	4.5	62.2
VAR417	0.39016	8	1.03113	4.0	66.1
VAR418	0.54508	9	0.95141	3.7	69.8
VAR419	0.41594	10	0.91955	3.5	73.3
VAR420	0.33811	11	0.76122	2.9	76.3
VAR421	0.48663	12	0.74550	2.9	79.1
VAR422	0.57082	13	0.67817	2.6	81.7
VAR423	0.46798	14	0.63308	2.4	84.2
VAR424	0.40705	15	0.59815	2.3	86.5
VAR425	0.46803	16	0.49864	1.9	88.4
VAR426	0.57236	17	0.43936	1.7	90.1
VAR427	0.58147	18	0.40656	1.6	91.6
VAR428	0.52016	19	0.37173	1.4	93.1
VAR429	0.42269	20	0.32639	1.3	94.3
VAR430	0.60537	21	0.31350	1.2	95.5
VAR431	0.44807	22	0.28740	1.1	96.6
VAR432	0.52837	23	0.25791	1.0	97.6
VAR433	0.42397	24	0.23184	0.9	98.5
VAR434	0.44758	25	0.21852	0.8	99.4
VAR435	0.64550	26	0.16758	0.6	100.0

CONVERGENCE REQUIRED   9 ITERATIONS

Table 7-2.　Principal Factor Matrix

FACTOR MATRIX USING PRINCIPAL FACTOR WITH ITERATIONS

	FACTOR 1	FACTOR 2	FACTOR 3	FACTOR 4
VAR410	0.63566	-0.22805	0.07551	-0.20802
VAR411	0.57661	0.08491	-0.02835	-0.00383
VAR412	-0.49045	0.19069	0.06610	0.03623
VAR413	-0.14572	0.15140	-0.05584	-0.12396
VAR414	-0.50313	0.39353	-0.02532	-0.15735
VAR415	0.61801	-0.17736	0.19939	0.16275
VAR416	-0.14038	-0.16699	0.53820	0.09939
VAR417	0.28816	0.41609	0.08582	-0.31624
VAR418	0.41688	0.53227	-0.10841	0.19224
VAR419	0.12883	0.34543	0.25602	-0.28316
VAR420	0.08175	-0.09227	0.34006	0.21571
VAR421	-0.40948	0.22621	0.16839	0.09420
VAR422	-0.54386	0.26148	0.25513	0.32134
VAR423	0.47601	0.41627	0.10191	-0.08607
VAR424	-0.37385	0.25772	0.31882	0.04490
VAR425	0.54833	-0.14271	0.32964	-0.02243
VAR426	0.55901	0.29095	-0.05058	0.41642
VAR427	0.58276	0.41690	0.24600	-0.24436
VAR428	0.44750	0.46814	-0.04277	0.24946
VAR429	0.44310	0.13103	-0.21204	0.20437
VAR430	0.62411	-0.27927	0.13538	0.01377
VAR431	0.45204	0.03595	-0.23543	-0.02496
VAR432	0.45642	0.31355	-0.12660	-0.10674
VAR433	0.34023	-0.02514	-0.03007	0.28156
VAR434	0.54948	-0.14277	0.12928	-0.07705
VAR435	0.71085	-0.34172	0.00907	-0.01837

table shows the estimated communalities that were put in the diagonal of the **R** matrix at the beginning of the iterative process. These are the squared multiple correlations of each variable with all of the other variables. The second tabulation in table 7-1 is identical to that of table 6-3; it shows the eigenvalues, percent of variance, and cumulative percent for a principal components analysis of the variables. If we had not told **SPSS** how many factors to extract, the program would have used this information to decide this, and would have extracted eight factors, the number of eigenvalues over one.

Table 7-2 shows the principal factor matrix. Note that the relative sizes of the loadings here are similar to those of the last chapter, only they are generally lower. Usually we do not attempt to interpret this matrix, although it may be of some interest.

Table 7-3 is also separate tables. The first gives the "final" communalities of the variables. These are the sums of squares of the rows of the preceding factor matrix. The figures indicate proportions of variance of the variables that are accounted for by the four factors. Some of the figures are quite low; we would like them to be higher. This table may be used to suggest variables that do not have

Table 7-3. Final Communalities and Factor Eigenvalues

VARIABLE	COMMUNALITY	FACTOR	EIGENVALUE	PCT OF VAR	CUM PCT
VAR410	0.50505	1	5.83749	58.6	58.6
VAR411	0.34050	2	2.10675	21.1	79.7
VAR412	0.28259	3	1.07578	10.8	90.5
VAR413	0.06264	4	0.94162	9.5	100.0
VAR414	0.43341				
VAR415	0.47963				
VAR416	0.34712				
VAR417	0.36354				
VAR418	0.50581				
VAR419	0.28164				
VAR420	0.17737				
VAR421	0.25608				
VAR422	0.53250				
VAR423	0.41766				
VAR424	0.30984				
VAR425	0.43020				
VAR426	0.57311				
VAR427	0.63364				
VAR428	0.48346				
VAR429	0.30023				
VAR430	0.48602				
VAR431	0.26168				
VAR432	0.33405				
VAR433	0.19657				
VAR434	0.34496				
VAR435	0.62249				

Table 7-4. Varimax Rotated Factor Matrix

VARIMAX ROTATED FACTOR MATRIX

	FACTOR 1	FACTOR 2	FACTOR 3	FACTOR 4
VAR410	0.67034	0.04764	0.23039	0.01859
VAR411	0.40983	0.33521	0.24234	-0.03803
VAR412	-0.50874	-0.14036	-0.04721	0.04292
VAR413	-0.18218	-0.06693	0.09575	-0.12572
VAR414	-0.60282	-0.15324	0.15390	-0.15118
VAR415	0.56212	0.28379	0.08258	0.27622
VAR416	-0.04522	-0.20942	-0.00477	0.54882
VAR417	0.03569	0.12311	0.57712	-0.11848
VAR418	-0.00846	0.62920	0.31663	-0.09794
VAR419	-0.05975	-0.00853	0.52405	0.05810
VAR420	0.07385	0.06172	-0.02708	0.40911
VAR421	-0.47756	-0.06636	0.00726	0.15350
VAR422	-0.64476	0.01613	-0.11905	0.31993
VAR423	0.14637	0.36724	0.51119	-0.00744
VAR424	-0.46367	-0.09953	0.12583	0.26290
VAR425	0.51350	0.11335	0.23992	0.31002
VAR426	0.20679	0.71553	0.10526	0.08529
VAR427	0.25294	0.28283	0.69753	0.05589
VAR428	0.04207	0.63564	0.27863	-0.00523
VAR429	0.24756	0.47199	0.03087	-0.12336
VAR430	0.65283	0.15061	0.08580	0.17260
VAR431	0.34868	0.28086	0.10258	-0.22516
VAR432	0.20053	0.34354	0.36587	-0.20484
VAR433	0.23931	0.35238	-0.07733	0.09564
VAR434	0.52899	0.12267	0.19612	0.10781
VAR435	0.76699	0.16968	0.04786	0.05608

TRANSFORMATION MATRIX

		FACTOR 1	FACTOR 2	FACTOR 3	FACTOR 4
FACTOR	1	0.79431	0.50062	0.34415	0.00369
FACTOR	2	-0.58403	0.50299	0.61795	-0.15509
FACTOR	3	-0.02759	-0.22572	0.38243	0.89556
FACTOR	4	-0.16499	0.66741	-0.59451	0.41701

much in common with the rest of the variables and therefore might be dropped. In this case we might want to drop VAR413, VAR420, and VAR433.

The second part of table 7–3 gives us the eigenvalues of the final $\mathbf{R}$† matrix (after all the iterations). We note that the fourth eigenvalue is less than one and therefore does not meet one of the criteria for retention. However, it accounts for 9.5% of the variance included in these four factors. It is a borderline case.

Table 7–4 shows the varimax rotated matrix. As would be expected, this is the cleanest matrix we have encountered, in the sense that the entries in each column are either relatively high or relatively low in absolute value.

I interpret the matrix of table 7–4 in the following way (others are free to develop their own interpretations).

Factor 1 distinguishes the "believers" from the "nonbelievers" in social work research. Since negative items are positively loaded on this factor, a low score on this factor indicates a student who tends to believe that social work research should be encouraged and relied upon. Such students do not take research courses just because they are required, and they tend not to find research articles incomprehensible (at least in comparison to other students).

Factor 2 seems to distinguish students who believe that research is valid (low scores) from those who question its validity (high scores). The questioning of validity is in relation to its connection to practice. It should be noted that the analysis forces factor 2 to be uncorrelated with factor 1. It is possible that someone could very much believe in social work research and still question the validity of currently available studies.

Factor 3 appears to distinguish those who believe that researchers are actively engaged in the process of distortion (high scores) from those who are not so cynical. I am unable to make much out of factor 4.

At the bottom of table 7-4 is the *transformation matrix.* The varimax rotated factor matrix is found by post multiplying the principal factor matrix by the transformation matrix. The entries may also be thought of as correlations be-

Table 7-5.   Factor Score Coefficients

FACTOR SCORE COEFFICIENTS

	FACTOR 1	FACTOR 2	FACTOR 3	FACTOR 4
VAR410	0.17006	-0.13112	0.09552	-0.04700
VAR411	0.03560	0.03998	0.00029	-0.00860
VAR412	-0.07549	0.00571	-0.00241	0.04297
VAR413	-0.02332	0.00618	0.00049	-0.01261
VAR414	-0.10191	-0.03226	0.15290	-0.11002
VAR415	0.10732	0.08417	-0.04961	0.19761
VAR416	-0.01805	-0.07999	0.03814	0.31453
VAR417	-0.01031	-0.05433	0.20979	-0.07838
VAR418	-0.07226	0.21880	0.10939	-0.10512
VAR419	-0.03591	-0.07292	0.17054	0.05769
VAR420	-0.00017	0.00004	0.00569	0.13800
VAR421	-0.05488	0.00471	0.01539	0.02429
VAR422	-0.21334	0.13534	-0.05146	0.32670
VAR423	-0.00778	0.04548	0.16254	-0.01473
VAR424	-0.07084	-0.00656	0.09475	0.14734
VAR425	0.08351	-0.02399	0.07818	0.22274
VAR426	-0.01650	0.39378	-0.16342	0.10593
VAR427	-0.02407	-0.04623	0.46014	0.06474
VAR428	-0.09322	0.26018	0.00328	0.04176
VAR429	-0.02075	0.12019	-0.01795	-0.06575
VAR430	0.16304	0.01022	-0.01375	0.08237
VAR431	0.03974	0.02487	0.00915	-0.13266
VAR432	0.00027	0.09326	0.03772	-0.09052
VAR433	0.02505	0.07774	-0.08195	0.01980
VAR434	0.05453	-0.01487	0.06526	0.05373
VAR435	0.26229	-0.00112	-0.07805	0.04496

tween the old and the new factors, where the column headings are the new factors and the row labels are the old factors. This matrix has limited usefulness.

Finally, table 7–5 shows the coefficients to be used to obtain factor scores for the rotated factors. It is the matrix $\mathbf{R}^{-1}\mathbf{A}$. These are the coefficients used to obtain scores for individuals on each of the factors. The coefficients are applied to the standard score values of the variables. For example, to obtain a score for an individual for factor 1, we would multiply the values in the first column of this matrix by that individual's standard scores for the variables and add up these products. Note that although these values are much smaller than those in the rotated factor matrix their relative sizes are similar. This matrix is often not obtained, as it tells us little more than is contained in the factor matrix. If you wish SPSS will print out, punch on cards, or store on disk or tape the factor scores for each individual. These scores may then be input to other analyses such as regression.

8 MULTIVARIATE TESTS OF MEANS

Investigators in the human services almost always have more than one outcome variable. Frequently in such studies the researcher simply performs separate statistical tests on all of the dependent variables. There are, however, serious drawbacks to such a procedure. The first is that the overall probability of Type I error will be larger than the decision level set for each separate test. To put this simply, if we test lots of hypotheses separately at the .05 level, there is a high probability that at least one of them will be rejected "just by chance." Thus, it is desirable that some way be found to test all of the hypotheses simultaneously. We thus come to one of the core motivations for multivariate analysis: the problem of multiple dependent variables. It turns out that the procedure for the multivariate test of means closely parallels that for single variables. So we begin with a review of the test for single variables.

Single-Sample Mean Test

Univariate Test

A univariate, single-sample mean test arises most often when we have matched pairs or when we are using difference scores computed from values of the same

147

variable measured at two points in time. In the case of matched pairs, the data we actually analyze are differences between the dependent variable values for the cases in each pair. This might be written as

$$y_{di} = y_{2i} - y_{1i}$$

where y_{2i} and y_{1i} represent the values for each member of the ith pair. The same expression may be used to represent a difference score for a single individual. That is, y_{2i} and y_{1i} could represent the scores of the ith individual at two points in time. We will drop the first subscript and just represent the dependent variable to be analyzed as y_i, with the understanding that this is usually a difference of raw scores.

In the situation described, the usual hypothesis to be tested is that the mean of these y_i's (or differences) in the population is zero: H_0: $\mu = 0$.

The test of this hypothesis proceeds by finding the mean of the sample y_i's, the estimated standard deviation (s_y, using $n - 1$ in the denominator), and the estimated standard deviation of means (the *standard error* $s_{\bar{y}} = s_y/\sqrt{n}$), and then constructing the t statistic:

$$t = \frac{\bar{y}}{s_{\bar{y}}}$$

This statistic is then referred to a table of the t statistic (with $n - 1$ degrees of freedom, where n is the number of pairs) to determine the probability of obtaining our particular sample $\bar{y}$ under the null hypothesis.

The normal distribution plays a heavy role in the theoretical development of the t test. The test assumes that the distribution of means of samples of this particular size is normal, which would usually be the case only if the population y_i's were normal. However, the central limit theorem assures us that means of large samples from nonnormal populations are asymptotically normal; and, thus, for moderately large samples from nonnormal populations the error in the procedure is modest (the technique is said to be *robust* for the assumption of normality for large samples). How large is large enough depends on how nonnormal the original population is.

Multivariate Test

In the multivariate situation we have a single sample with a series of dependent variable values for each case. The values for a particular case can be arranged in a vector:

$$\mathbf{y}_i{}' = (y_{i1}, y_{i2}, \ldots, y_{ip})$$

where y_{ij} represents the value of the jth variable for the ith case (we have p variables). In our situation, the variables are assumed to be difference scores. We will be interested in the vector of means (the *mean vector*):

$$\bar{y}' = (\bar{y}_1, \bar{y}_2, \ldots, \bar{y}_p)$$

The null hypothesis is that the vector of means for the population is zero:

$$\mu' = (\mu_1, \mu_2, \ldots, \mu_p) = (0, 0, \ldots, 0) = \mathbf{0}'$$

If we imagine taking a large number of samples of the same size from a population in which the null hypothesis is true, the mean vectors for those samples (the vectors of means) will have a *multivariate normal distribution*, if the parent population is multivariate normal. If not, the vector of means will be asymptotically multivariate normal.

It is perhaps easiest to proceed if we deal first with the situation of two dependent variables, y_1 and y_2. Let us assume that the parent population of these values is multivariate (here bivariate) normal. In that case the distribution looks something like a very smooth and perfectly formed hill as in figure 8-1. In this three-dimensional figure, volumes under various segments of this surface represent probabilities. If the y's are in deviation score form, the height of the surface at any point (y_1, y_2) is represented by

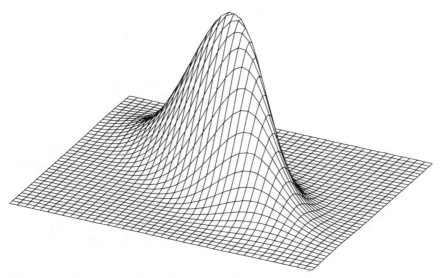

Figure 8-1. Bivariate Normal Distribution.

$$p(y_1,y_2) = \frac{1}{(2\pi)^{p/2}|\Sigma|^{1/2}} \exp \frac{-y'\Sigma^{-1}y}{2}$$

where $\bar{\Sigma}$ is the population covariance matrix of the y's (it has the variances of the y's in the diagonal and covariances of pairs of y's in the off-diagonal cells), p is the number of variables (here 2) and where $\exp(-y'\Sigma^{-1}y/2)$ means e to the power contained in the parentheses. $|\Sigma|^{1/2}$ is the square root of the determinant of the covariance matrix. The quantity $y'\Sigma^{-1}y$ is a quadratic form (and thus reduces to a scalar for given y. It can be shown that this quadratic form $(y\Sigma^{-1}y)$ has a chi-square distribution with p degrees of freedom. That is, if I take a random vector y from a distribution in which the mean of the y vectors is 0 and their variance-covariance matrix is Σ, compute the quantity $y\Sigma^{-1}y$ and look this up in a table of the χ^2 distribution, the resulting figure is the probability of getting that particular y vector or a more extreme one. This fact is important in the theoretical treatment of the problem at hand. This expression holds for any number of dependent variables, not just two. The reader will note some similarities of this expression to the normal probability function for one variable:

$$p(y) = \frac{1}{\sqrt{2\pi}\sigma} \exp\left(\frac{-y^2}{2\sigma^2}\right)$$

The picture we drew of the bivariate normal distribution (figure 8-1) is a picture of a perfectly formed hill. It can be of different shapes, sometimes round, other times elongated and elliptical. Sometimes it will be oriented with its long dimension parallel to one of the y axes, other times not. The shape it takes and its orientation will depend on the variances of the y's and on their covariances (or correlations).

It is hard to look at and even harder to draw such three-dimensional figures. Let's look instead at a contour map. The contour map of our hill will be a lot simpler to draw and interpret than a drawing of a real hill. Figure 8-2 shows a contour drawing in which y_1 and y_2 are assumed to both have means of zero, so the center of the hill is at the origin. In this drawing, as in all contour maps, the ellipses represent lines on the hill that are at the same height all the way around the hill (they are at the same distance from the y_1 and y_2 plane; mathematicians sometimes call such lines *level curves*). These ellipses have a fancy name: *isodensity ellipses*. We will not actually try to determine the height of any particular isodensity ellipse, rather we will be interested in something else. Each ellipse encloses within it a certain amount of the volume of the hill. Since we are treating volumes of our hill as probabilities, the total volume of the hill will be one and the volume within any particular ellipse will be a fraction.

Now the big step: If we were to take a random case from the population, the probability that the values of y_1 and y_2 for that case will lie within a particular ellipse is given by the volume of the hill within that ellipse. Conversely, the

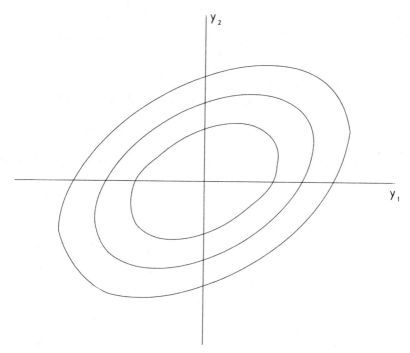

Figure 8-2. Contour Map of Bivariate Normal Distribution.

probability that the case will lie outside the ellipse will be given by the volume outside the ellipse; obviously this is one minus the volume inside.

Of course, we usually will not be interested in the probability of a particular set of values, rather we will focus on means of samples. This suggests that we concern ourselves not with the distribution of cases but with the distribution of means, more precisely with the distribution of mean vectors of samples from populations. In the univariate situation, the distribution of means is taller and narrower than the distribution of values, since the variance of means is the variance of the values divided by the sample size. Similarly, the hill representing the distribution of mean vectors of two variables will be taller and narrower than the distribution of cases. It will have a multivariate normal distribution whose mean vector will be μ and whose variance-covariance matrix will be Σ/n, where n is the sample size. This may be written as $N(\mu, \Sigma/n)$. The mathematical expression for this, in p variables, is:

$$p(\bar{y}_1, \bar{y}_2, \ldots, \bar{y}_p) = (2\pi)^{-p/2} n^{p/2} |\Sigma|^{-1/2} \exp\left[\frac{-n(\bar{y}'\Sigma^{-1}\bar{y})}{2}\right]$$

Now to go back to our original problem in two variables. We are testing the null hypothesis that the mean vector in the population is zero $[\mu' = (\mu_1, \mu_2) = (0,0) = 0]$. In our particular sample we have obtained a mean vector $\bar{y} = (\bar{y}_1, \bar{y}_2)$.

We ask, "What is the probability that we would have gotten this particular sample mean vector, or a more extreme one, if the null hypothesis is true?" To answer that question, we construct the distribution of sample mean vectors under the assumption that the null hypothesis is true (the center of the hill is at the origin where $y_1 = 0$ and $y_2 = 0$). Our particular sample mean vector will fall on a particular isodensity ellipse. The probability outside that ellipse will be the answer to our question.

Obviously we need a numeric example. Suppose that we have done a study in which we have randomly assigned 25 matched pairs to two treatment conditions. We have two outcome measures, and for each of these outcome measures we compute the difference between the values for the two members of each pair. For the ith pair, these difference scores are y_{i1} and y_{i2}. The mean of y_1 is 1.5 and the mean of y_2 is 2. The variance of y_1 is 7.5 and the variance of y_2 is 8. The covariance is 4. (The reader may verify that the correlation between y_1 and y_2 is .52.) The Σ matrix is estimated by the C matrix, which in this case is

$$C = \begin{pmatrix} 7.5 & 4 \\ 4 & 8 \end{pmatrix}$$

The reader will recall that in the univariate case, if the variance is known, the test statistic

$$z = \frac{\bar{y} - \mu_0}{\sigma/\sqrt{n}}$$

is normally distributed. In the likely situation in which σ is not known, the same test statistic (with s estimating σ) has a t distribution. We could write the square of the t statistic like this:

$$t^2 = \frac{(\bar{y} - \mu_0)^2}{s^2/n} = n(\bar{y} - \mu_0)(s^2)^{-1}(\bar{y} - \mu_0)$$

The only reason for wanting to write this in such a strange way is to be able to see the parallels with what follows. If Σ is estimated by C, we have a test statistic Hotelling's T_1^2:

$$T_1^2 = n(\bar{y} - \mu_0)'C^{-1}(\bar{y} - \mu_0)$$

where μ_0 is the vector of hypothesized means. In our case, this vector is 0 so T_1^2 reduces to $T_1^2 = n\mathbf{y}'C^{-1}\mathbf{y}$. The subscript 1 in T_1^2 indicates that this is a one-sample test.

To work through our example we must compute the inverse of $\mathbf{C}$:

$$\mathbf{C}^{-1} = \begin{pmatrix} .1818 & -.0909 \\ -.0909 & .1705 \end{pmatrix}$$

Then,

$$T_1^2 = n\bar{\mathbf{y}}'\mathbf{C}^{-1}\bar{\mathbf{y}} = 25(1.5 \quad 2)\begin{pmatrix} .1818 & -.0909 \\ -.0909 & .1705 \end{pmatrix}\begin{pmatrix} 1.5 \\ 2 \end{pmatrix} = 13.6438$$

It turns out, happily, that T_1^2 is closely related to the F distribution. In fact,

$$\frac{n-p}{(n-1)p} T_1^2 = F(p, n-p)$$

where $F(p, n-p)$ means an F statistic with p degrees of freedom for the numerator and $n-p$ degrees of freedom for the denominator. (The reader should note that in the case of a single variable, $p = 1$, this expression is equal to F with one degree of freedom in the numerator and $n-1$ d.f. in the denominator, which is the square of a univariate t.)

In our example, $F = 6.5377$ with 2 and 23 degrees of freedom, which is significant at the .01 level.

Now to generalize the situation. First, at times the null hypothesis may not be that $\mu' = \mathbf{0}$ but rather that the population mean vector is at some other point μ_0, in which case we could write $H_0: \mu_0'$. The test statistic in this case is

$$T_1^2 = n(\bar{\mathbf{y}} - \mu_0)'\mathbf{C}^{-1}(\bar{\mathbf{y}} - \mu_0)$$

and F is found in the same way as before.

In the case of more than two dependent variables, all of the algebra is the same (we have used $\bar{\mathbf{y}}$ vectors and $\mathbf{C}$ matrices that can be of order greater than 2), only the geometric visualization is more problematic. In fact, we can no longer draw pictures. In more than two dimensions, we would have to talk about such things as isodensity ellipsoids, so we will not pursue that. It is hoped that the reader has a visual picture of the situation in two dependent variables, and is confident that the algebra will provide the right answers for more variables than that.

Two-Sample Mean Test

We begin with a review of the univariate two-sample mean test. The hypothesis usually tested is that the means of y for the two populations from which the samples were drawn are equal:

$$H_0: \mu_1 = \mu_2$$

where the subscripts 1 and 2 represent the two populations. A t statistic is then computed from the sample data:

$$t = (\bar{y}_1 - \bar{y}^2) \bigg/ \sqrt{\frac{s^2}{n_1} + \frac{s^2}{n_2}}$$

where s^2 is a *pooled variance estimate* obtained as follows:

$$s^2 = \frac{\sum_i (y_{i1} - \bar{y}_{.1})^2 + \sum_i (y_{i2} - \bar{y}_{.2})^2}{n_1 + n_2 - 2}$$

In other words, we pool the sums of squares from each sample and divide by the pooled degrees of freedom.

Let's look at the square of the above t:

$$t^2 = \frac{(\bar{y}_1 - \bar{y}_2)^2}{s^2\left(\frac{1}{n_1} + \frac{1}{n_2}\right)} = \left(\frac{n_1 n_2}{n_1 + n_2}\right)(\bar{y}_1 - \bar{y}_2)(s^2)^{-1}(\bar{y}_1 - \bar{y}_2)$$

Again, we have chosen to write this in a strange way to show the analogies with what comes next. We want to develop an analogous T_2^2 statistic for the multivariate situation. We replace the y means in the above expression by vectors of observed means $\bar{\mathbf{y}}_1$ and $\bar{\mathbf{y}}_2$ where $\bar{\mathbf{y}}_1$ denotes the vector of observed means for the first sample and $\bar{\mathbf{y}}_2$ is the same for the second sample. The multivariate generalization of $(s^2)^{-1}$ is a little trickier. It will be the inverse of the pooled within-groups variance-covariance matrix. Analogous with the univariate case, we will determine the sums of squares and cross products (SSCP) matrix within each group separately. Denote these matrices as $\mathbf{S}_1$ and $\mathbf{S}_2$. We then simply add these matrices together, obtaining the pooled within groups sum of squares and cross products matrix, $\mathbf{S}_E$. So $\mathbf{S}_E = \mathbf{S}_1 + \mathbf{S}_2$. The subscript E represents error. This matrix $\mathbf{S}_E$ is of central importance in multivariate analysis and will come up frequently later in this book. The analogy to s^2 is then $\mathbf{S}_E$ divided by its degrees of freedom:

$$[(1/(n_1 + n_2 - 2)] \mathbf{S}_E$$

The analogy to $(s^2)^{-1}$ is

$$[(1/(n_1 + n_2 - 2)(\mathbf{S}_E)]^{-1}$$

which is equal to $(n_1 + n_2 - 2)\mathbf{S}_E^{-1}$.

Finally, the multivariate T^2 is

$$T_2^2 = \frac{n_1 n_2 (n_1 + n_2 - 2)}{n_1 + n_2} (\bar{y}_1 - \bar{y}_2)' S_E^{-1} (\bar{y}_1 - \bar{y}_2)$$

where the subscript 2 on T_2^2 means a test for two samples. It turns out that this T_2^2 is also related to an F in this way:

$$\frac{n_1 + n_2 - p - 1}{(n_1 + n_2 - 2)p} T_2^2 = F(p, n_1 + n_2 - p - 1)$$

Again, in this expression, the reader should see what happens when we have a single dependent variable, that is, when $p = 1$.

Three or More Samples

The case of three or more samples requires a mulivariate analogy to one-way analysis of variance. The reader will recall that in the analysis of variance the between- and within-groups sums of squares are obtained. The within-groups sum of squares is found by computing the sum of squares within each group [for group j this is $\Sigma_i(y_{ij} - \bar{y}_{.j})^2$] and summing over all groups. The between-groups sum of squares is the sum of the squared deviations of group means from the grand mean, each squared deviation multiplied by the number of cases in the group [$\Sigma_j n_j (\bar{x}_{.j} - \bar{x}\cdot\cdot)^2$]. The total sum of squares (found by summing the squared deviation of each observation from the grand mean) is equal to the between sum of squares plus the within sum of squares. An F statistic is constructed as follows:

$$F = \frac{\text{between sum of squares}/(k - 1)}{\text{within sum of squares}/(N - k)}$$

where k is the number of groups and N is the total number of subjects ($N = \Sigma_j n_j$).

We will discuss two approaches to the multivariate analysis of variance resulting in four different statistics for testing the hypothesis. The hypothesis is that the mean vectors for all the populations are equal. We begin with the approach, first suggested by Wilks, called the *likelihood ratio*.

Analysis Based on the Likelihood Ratio

Until this time we have been treating the C matrix (the variance-covariance matrix) as a kind of multivariate analogy to the variance of a single variable. It turns out that the determinant of the C matrix ($|C|$) and of the SSCP matrix

($|S|$) may also be considered as multivariate extensions of the idea of variance. We will not develop the ideas extensively but will simply present the procedure.

In the previous section we defined the matrix S_E, the sum of within-group SSCP matrices. In the case of k groups, we compute SSCP matrices within each group (S_j) and S_E is their sum. So $S_E = S_1 + S_2 + \cdots + S_k$. We relabel the total SSCP matrix (S) computed without reference to group membership as S_T.

The test statistic (Λ) for the null hypothesis that the mean vectors for all groups are the same (H_0: $\mu_1 = \mu_2 = \cdots = \mu_k$) is called *Wilk's lamda* (it is also called the *likelihood ratio criteria*):

$$\Lambda = \frac{|S_E|}{|S_T|}$$

The reader will note that the analogy to the F statistic breaks down in a number of respects. No degrees of freedom appear in the above ratio (S_E and S_T are analogous to sums of squares). We have $|S_T|$ (the determinant of the total SSCP matrix) appearing in the ratio in contrast to the between sum of squares. Finally, lamda decreases as differences among the mean vectors increase (that is, $|S_T|$ becomes larger relative to $|S_E|$) while the F increases in the analogous case.

The lamda statistic is important in much of multivariate work. When the number of groups is equal to one or two, lamda can be shown to be a simple function of T_1^2 or T_2^2. When we have more than two groups, the determination of the probability of an obtained lamda under the null hypothesis is somewhat complicated, due to the complexity of the probability distribution of lamda. Approximate methods of determining this probability are given in appendix E.

Analyses Based on the Matrix $S_H S_E^{-1}$

The second approach depends on a search for that linear combination of dependent variables that maximally discriminates among the groups. A linear combination of the dependent variables may be written as

$$d = a_1 y_1 + a_2 y_2 + \cdots + a_p y_p$$

where p is the number of dependent variables. This may be written in vector terms as

$$d = y'a$$

If I knew the numbers in the vector a I could construct the variable d. I could then do an analysis of variance on d and form an F ratio of the between-groups mean square for d divided by the within-groups mean square. Hence, I operationalize the criteria, "find the vector a such that $y'a$ maximally discriminates among the groups" as "find the vector a that maximizes the F ratio."

In the following, we will need the matrices S_E and S_T. We will also need the between-groups SSCP matrix S_H. The subscript H stands for hypothesis and this SSCP matrix is called the *hypothesis SSCP*. This may be calculated as $S_H = S_T - S_E$. The sum of squares of the linear combination d is equal to $a'S_T a$ (s.s.$_d = (Ya)'(Ya) = a'Y'Ya = a'S_T a$). Similarly, the within-groups sum of squares for d is $a'S_E a$ and the between-groups sum of squares is $a'S_H a$. The degrees of freedom for between groups is $k - 1$ and for within groups is $N - k$. So the F ratio may be written

$$F = \frac{a'S_H a/(k-1)}{a'S_E a/(N-k)} = \frac{a'S_H a(N-k)}{a'S_E a(k-1)}$$

We want to find the a that maximizes this F. Since the factor $(N-k)/(k-1)$ is constant, that is, it stays the same for any choice of values for the vector a, and since it is positive, we can ignore it and simply maximize the ratio:

$$\lambda = \frac{a'S_H a}{a'S_E a}$$

The choice of λ to represent this ratio is not accidental, it turns out that the ratio is an eigenvalue of a matrix we shall shortly encounter.

We want to find the vector a such that λ is maximized. We need to find the partial derivatives of λ with respect to each of the a_i's, set the partial derivatives equal to zero, and solve for the a's. The partial derivatives of λ may be written as follows (see appendix C):

$$\frac{\partial \lambda}{\partial a} = \frac{2(a'S_E a)(S_H a) - 2(a'S_H a)(S_E a)}{(a'S_E a)^2}$$

Setting this equal to zero, multiplying through by the denominator, and dividing by 2 we have

$$(a'S_E a)(S_H a) - (a'S_H a)(S_E a) = 0$$

Dividing through by $a'S_E a$ gives us

$$S_H a - \frac{a'S_H a}{a'S_E a}(S_E a) = 0$$

but

$$\frac{a'S_H a}{a'S_E a} = \lambda$$

so we have

$$S_H a - \lambda S_E a = 0$$

Now multiply through by S_E^{-1} (trusting that S_E has an inverse!):

$$S_H S_E^{-1} a - \lambda S_E S_E^{-1} a = 0$$

(since λ is a scalar, its multiplication is commutative), and finally we have

$$(S_H S_E^{-1} - \lambda I) a = 0$$

This is an eigenvector equation, similar to those we encountered in earlier chapters.

The task is now to find the eigenvectors of the matrix $S_H S_E^{-1}$. The job is a little more complicated than in earlier chapters because unlike those examples, $S_H S_E^{-1}$ is generally not a symmetric matrix. Nonetheless, a number of solutions for the scalar λ and the **a** vector may be found. The maximum number of non-zero λ's will be the rank of $S_H S_E^{-1}$. The **a** associated with the largest λ is the one that will maximize F but it turns out that the other λ's are of interest also. The matrix $S_H S_E^{-1}$ and its eigenvalues are important and will be encountered again in later chapters.

Statistics Based on $S_H S_E^{-1}$. We will discuss three different statistics that have been developed to test the hypothesis of equivalent mean vectors, all depending on the eigenvalues of the matrix $S_H S_E^{-1}$ (the λ's which are the roots of the above equation). The first is called *Roy's largest root criteria.* It focuses on the probability distribution of the largest λ. The probability distribution of the largest root is complicated. It depends on three degrees of freedom. The degrees of freedom are $s = \min(d.f._H, p)$ which means $d.f._H$ or p whichever is smaller; $m = (|d.f._H - p| - 1)/2$; and $n = (d.f._E - p - 1)/2$ where $d.f._H$ and $d.f._E$ are the degrees of freedom for the entries in S_H and S_E respectively. Tables of this distribution may be found in Heck (1960), Pillai (1965, 1967) and Harris (1975). The tables are entered with the value $\theta = \lambda/(1 + \lambda)$ which is the eigenvalue of $S_H(S_H + S_E)^{-1} = S_H S_T^{-1}$. Bock (1975) provides tables in the form of a "generalized F statistic" which is $F_0 = t\lambda_1/r$ where $r = |d.f._H - p| + 1$, $t = d.f._E - p + 1$ and where the degrees of freedom are r, t, and the s defined above.

The second statistic is a generalization of Hotelling's T^2 involving the sum of the eigenvalues:

$$T^2 = \sum_i \lambda_i$$

Since the sum of the eigenvalues is equal to the trace of $S_H S_E^{-1}$, we can also write

$$T^2 = \text{tr}(S_H S_E^{-1})$$

The probability distribution of this statistic, multiplied by $d.f._E$, may be found in Pillai (1960). It has the same degrees of freedom as Roy's largest root statistic.

The final statistic is one proposed by Pillai (Morrison, 1976 p. 223). It is the sum of the values $\lambda_i/(\lambda_i + 1)$:

$$V = \frac{\sum_i \lambda_i}{\lambda_i + 1}$$

which is also the trace of the matrix $S_H(S_H + S_E)^{-1}$.

Approximate probabilities of the obtained statistics may be computed for Hotelling's T and for Pillai's statistic by transforming them into F statistics. For details, see appendix E.

Each of the four statistics are legitimate tests of the hypothesis that the populations mean vectors are equal. All have their advocates (see Harris, 1975). In the case that either the number of variables or the degrees of freedom of S_H is one (this is the quantity $s = \min(d.f._H, p)$) they lead to identical results. Their powers differ depending on the situation (such as the number of variables and groups and the relative sizes of the eigenvalues, see Morrison, 1976 and Harris, 1975).

Step-down Tests

If one is able to reject the null hypothesis of equal population mean vectors it is natural to inquire as to which samples deviate significantly from others and which dependent variables are responsible for the differences. The exploration of differences among groups leads to the multivariate analogy of post-hoc contrasts in univariate analysis of variance (see Harris, 1975, Morrison, 1976). The analysis of which dependent variables are most important could take two tacks: first a linear transformation of the variables into new variables (usually orthogonal) and secondly, the computation of step-down tests. In a step-down test, we begin by ordering the variables, usually from most important to least important or most interesting to least. A univariate F test is performed on the first variable. The first variable is then used as a covariate in a test of the second variable (the second variable is controlled for the first). That is, an analysis of variance is performed on the residuals from a regression of the second variable on the first. The first two variables are then used as covariates for the third and so on. We then go backwards through the resulting list of F's until we reach a significant F. Any variables that were insignificant up to that point may be discarded. All other variables should be thought of as jointly significant.

Assumption of Equal Covariance Matrices

Analogous with the univariate case, the assumption of equal covariance matrices across groups is important to the tests of this chapter. A test for this assumption is given by Bock (1975, p. 413).

Example

We next present a series of computer output illustrating the ideas in this chapter. All of this output was produced using the SPSS Manova program. The example used in previous chapters concerned the effects of a new way of teaching social work research. In this chapter we will be concerned with three outcome variables, knowledge of research, attitudes toward empirically based practice, and plans to do empirically based practice after graduation. We begin with a single sample test of mean vectors. We computed change scores by subtracting the scores at the beginning of the year from scores at the end of the year. These change scores were called XKSCORE, XTOTALAT, and XPLANEBP. The output shown in tables 8-1 and 8-2 was produced by the following commands.

MANOVA   XKSCORE,XTOTALAT,XPLANEBP/
             PRINT=SIGNIFICANCE(STEPDOWN)
             CELLINFO(MEANS)/

Actually, only the first line is absolutely needed.

Table 8-1 shows the means, standard deviations, and 95% confidence intervals for each variable. Note that research knowledge has increased, but the other two variables have decreased. None of the confidence intervals includes 0, so on a univariate basis, all three of the means are significantly different from zero.

Table 8-2 shows the multivariate tests of significance. All show identical results since $s = 1$. Hotelling's T_1^2 is computed as described above. It is highly significant. We can, therefore, conclude that the mean vector is significantly different from zero. The next part of the table shows univariate tests for each of the variables. All are highly significant. Finally, the results of the stepdown tests are shown. Note that change in plans to do EBP is not significant once change in knowledge and attitudes has been controlled. We might conclude from this that changes in plans to do EBP are not significant once changes in the other variables have been taken into account. Hence, we would conclude that there have been significant changes in average knowledge and attitudes, the first positive and the second negative.

In the next analysis, we look at the levels of the three dependent variables at

Table 8-1. Cell Means and Standard Deviations

CELL MEANS AND STANDARD DEVIATIONS

VARIABLE .. XKSCORE   CH SCORE FOR TOTAL KNOWLEDGE SCORE

	MEAN	STD. DEV.	N	95 PERCENT CONF. INTERVAL	
FOR ENTIRE SAMPLE	14.48509	12.91194	123	12.18038	16.78980

VARIABLE .. XTOTALAT   CH SCORE FOR ATITS ABT RES-TOTAL SCORE

	MEAN	STD. DEV.	N	95 PERCENT CONF. INTERVAL	
FOR ENTIRE SAMPLE	-5.09720	9.30117	123	-6.75741	-3.43700

VARIABLE .. XPLANEBP   CH SCORE FOR PLAN TO DO EBP-SUBSCORE

	MEAN	STD. DEV.	N	95 PERCENT CONF. INTERVAL	
FOR ENTIRE SAMPLE	-4.51219	15.97749	123	-7.36409	-1.66030

Table 8-2. Multivariate Tests of Significance

EFFECT .. CONSTANT

MULTIVARIATE TESTS OF SIGNIFICANCE (S = 1, M = 1/2, N = 59)

TEST NAME	VALUE	APPROX. F	HYPOTH. DF	ERROR DF	SIG. OF F
PILLAIS	.61655	64.31556	3.00	120.00	0.0
HOTELLINGS	1.60789	64.31556	3.00	120.00	0.0
WILKS	.38345	64.31556	3.00	120.00	0.0
ROYS	.61655				

UNIVARIATE F-TESTS WITH (1,122) D. F.

VARIABLE	HYPOTH. SS	ERROR SS	HYPOTH. MS	ERROR MS	F	SIG. OF F
XKSCORE	25807.60771	20039.61287	25807.60771	166.71814	154.79784	0.0
XTOTALAT	3195.72272	10554.43666	3195.72272	86.51178	36.93974	.000
XPLANEBP	2504.26705	31144.18323	2504.26705	255.28019	9.80988	.002

EFFECT .. CONSTANT   (CONT.)

ROY-BARGMAN STEPDOWN F - TESTS

VARIABLE	HYPOTH. MS	ERROR MS	STEP-DOWN F	HYPOTH. DF	ERROR DF	SIG. OF F
XKSCORE	25807.60771	166.71814	154.79784	1	122	0.0
XTOTALAT	1540.29888	87.18322	17.66738	1	121	.000
XPLANEBP	80.68947	224.76361	.35900	1	120	.550

time 2 (KSCORE2, TOTALAT2, and PLANEBP2) within each of the seven sections of the research course. These sections were taught by different instructors, each with a somewhat different concept about empirically based practice and with a different approach to research teaching. One of the principal objectives of the evaluation study was to investigate differences in outcome among the sections, a task that was facilitated by the fact that students were randomly assigned to the sections.

This analysis was produced by the following control commands:

MANOVA   KSCORE2, TOTALAT2,PLANEBP2 BY SECTION(1,7)/
          PRINT=SIGNIFICANCE(STEPDOWN,HYPOTH)
          CELLINFO(MEANS)
          ERROR(SSCP)/

Again, only the first line is absolutely necessary. The other lines produce optional output. The command CELLINFO(MEANS) produces the means, standard deviations, and 95% confidence intervals for each of the three outcome variables for each of the seven sections. It is not reproduced here but it is handy to have available. The within-groups (WITHIN CELLS) SSCP matrix (S_E) and the between-groups SSCP (S_H) are shown in table 8-3. Only the lower triangles of the matrices are printed out since they are symmetric.

The top tabulation of table 8-4 shows the four multivariate tests of significance. All are as described above. Wilk's lambda is equal to the ratio of the determinant of S_E to the determinant of $S_T = S_E + S_H$. The other tests are based on the eigenvalues of the matrix $S_H S_E^{-1}$. Hotelling's T^2 is the sum of the eigenvalues of the matrix; Roy's statistic is $\lambda_1/(1 + \lambda_1)$, where λ_1 is the largest

Table 8-3. Within-Groups and Between-Groups SSCP Matrix

WITHIN CELLS SUM-OF-SQUARES AND CROSS-PRODUCTS

	KSCORE2	TOTALAT2	PLANEBP2
KSCORE2	17410.04495		
TOTALAT2	5010.27937	9462.74333	
PLANEBP2	3911.19039	7847.23599	24028.32675

ADJUSTED HYPOTHESIS SUM-OF-SQUARES AND CROSS-PRODUCTS

	KSCORE2	TOTALAT2	PLANEBP2
KSCORE2	1128.75606		
TOTALAT2	611.67892	1014.77833	
PLANEBP2	492.60572	1078.31102	2339.48296

Table 8-4. Tests of Significance

MULTIVARIATE TESTS OF SIGNIFICANCE (S = 3, M = 1, N = 56)

TEST NAME	VALUE	APPROX. F	HYPOTH. DF	ERROR DF	SIG. OF F
PILLAIS	.21180	1.46861	18.00	348.00	.098
HOTELLINGS	.23016	1.44062	18.00	338.00	.110
WILKS	.80196	1.45592	18.00	322.93	.104
ROYS	.10325				

EIGENVALUES AND CANONICAL CORRELATIONS

ROOT NO.	EIGENVALUE	PCT.	CUM. PCT.	CANON. COR.
1	.11513	50.02371	50.02371	.32132
2	.06882	29.90141	79.92512	.25375
3	.04620	20.07488	100.00000	.21015

DIMENSION REDUCTION ANALYSIS

ROOTS	WILKS LAMBDA	F	HYPOTH. DF	ERROR DF	SIG. OF F
1 TO 3	.80196	1.45592	18.00	322.93	.104
2 TO 3	.89429	1.31176	10.00	317.61	.223
3 TO 3	.95584	1.31682	4.00	305.91	.264

UNIVARIATE F-TESTS WITH (6,116) D. F.

VARIABLE	HYPOTH. SS	ERROR SS	HYPOTH. MS	ERROR MS	F	SIG. OF F
KSCORE2	1128.75606	17410.04495	188.12601	150.08659	1.25345	.284
TOTALAT2	1014.77833	9462.74333	169.12972	81.57537	2.07329	.062
PLANEBP2	2339.48296	24028.32675	389.91383	207.14075	1.88236	.090

ROY-BARGMAN STEPDOWN F - TESTS

VARIABLE	HYPOTH. MS	ERROR MS	STEP-DOWN F	HYPOTH. DF	ERROR DF	SIG. OF F
KSCORE2	188.12601	150.08659	1.25345	6	116	.284
TOTALAT2	125.29370	69.74679	1.79641	6	115	.106
PLANEBP2	206.33562	153.65587	1.34284	6	114	.244

eigenvalue; and Pillai's statistic is the sum of $\lambda_i/(1 + \lambda_i)$ for all the eigenvalues λ_i. Approximate F's are given for Pillai's statistic, Hotelling's T^2, and Wilk's lambda. Each gives slightly different probability levels since they have different powers (the order of these probabilities will not necessarily be the same in all situations). It seems reasonable to use the lowest of these for a decision, perhaps after looking up the probability of Roy's statistic in the appropriate table. In this case, we can conclude that the mean vectors of the seven sections are not significantly different from each other since the lowest of these probabilities is about .1.

The next section shows the eigenvalues of the matrix $S_H S_E^{-1}$. This section also provides the canonical correlations that are discussed in a later chapter. Briefly, we imagine six dummy variables representing the seven sections. We imagine constructing linear combinations of the dependent variables and other linear combinations of the dummy variables. Out of all the possible pairs of such linear combinations we select that pair that has the highest correlation with each other. The first canonical correlation is that correlation. We will discuss the other canonical correlations in a later chapter. The canonical correlations and the next table DIMENSION REDUCTION ANALYSIS are of little use in the current situation.

The next table, UNIVARIATE F TESTS, shows univariate analyses of variance for each of the three dependent variables. Note that for none of the dependent variables are there significant differences among the sections at the .05 level although TOTALAT2 comes close ($p = .062$). Note also that this value is lower than the smallest multivariate probability discussed above. However, even if it had been less than .05 it would be improper to conclude that there was a difference between the sections in the absence of a significant multivariate test. This is because of the problem of the increase in Type I error that occurs when we look at more than one dependent variable. Thus, if the multivariate test had proven significant we might use the univariate tests to give us guidance as to which of the independent variables were responsible.

However, if the overall test were significant, it would be better to go on to look at the step-down analysis (the last tabulation in table 8-4). Here, each variable is controlled for the previous variables. Note that the first line is identical to that of the univariate table, since no earlier variables are being controlled. We focus on the last column of this table, starting at the bottom and moving up until we reach a significant value, concluding that all of the variables at and above that point are important to the discrimination among the groups. Unfortunately, here we have no significant values.

9 DISCRIMINANT ANALYSIS

Discriminant analysis is concerned with the situation in which we have two or more groups of subjects and a number of equal-interval variables measured on each of those subjects. We want to develop a linear function of those variables such that the groups are maximally separated on that function. We can think about the equal-interval variables as independent variables and about membership in the groups as a dependent variable. We want that linear combination of the interval variables that best predicts membership in the groups. Put in this way, discriminant analysis is like multiple regression except that the dependent variable is categorical rather than interval (in fact, when we have only two groups, discriminant analysis will yield the same results as a regression, in which we treat group membership as a dichotomous dependent variable). As we shall see, discriminant analysis also has similarities to principal component analysis.

Geometric Representation

Our job is to find the a_j's in the linear combination:

$$d(\mathbf{x}) = \Sigma a_j x_j$$

167

where we have p interval variables, x_j and where $\mathbf{x}$ represents the vector of these variables. The function d is called the discriminant function and the a's are called discriminant coefficients.

We begin with the simplest possible situation—two groups and two variables—and we assume the variables are in deviation score form. We might then diagram the situation as in figure 9-1, where the dots represent members of group A and the x's represent members of group B. The two ○'s represent the centroids of each group. The *centroid* of a group is the point whose coordinates are the means of the variables for that group.

We want a function (called a *discriminant function*):

$$d = a_1 x_1 + a_2 x_2$$

The function d will have a value for each case (depending on the values of x_1 and x_2 for that case) and thus, we can talk about the mean of d for each group. We will designate these means as $\bar{d}_A$ and $\bar{d}_B$. We could choose lots of different values for a_1 and a_2. We want that pair of values that will make $\bar{d}_A$ and $\bar{d}_B$ as far apart as possible relative to the within groups variation in d.

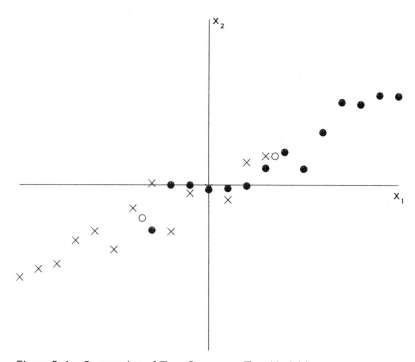

Figure 9-1. Scatterplot of Two Groups on Two Variables.

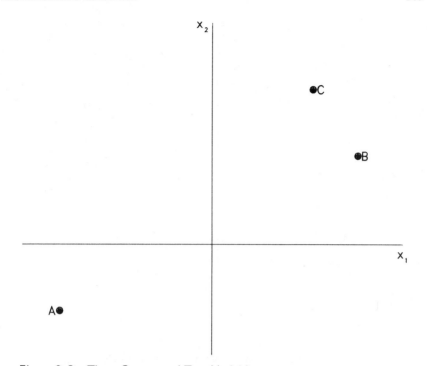

Figure 9-2.   Three Groups and Two Variables.

We know (see chapter 6) that linear combinations can be represented as new coordinate axes in the variable space. So we want to locate a new coordinate axis in this two-dimensional space. In the case of p independent variables and two groups we have a space of p dimensions but otherwise the imagery is the same; that is, we want to locate a coordinate axis for the space such that the averages of the groups for that variable are as far apart as possible relative to the within-groups variation.

In the case of three or more groups, the situation is a little more complicated. If we have two variables and three groups, we can still diagram things in two dimensions. This is illustrated in figure 9-2, where only the centroids of the three groups are shown.

Now suppose that we find a discriminant function that maximally separates these three groups. That discriminant function might be located as in figure 9-3. I have dropped perpendiculars from the centroids of the groups to the axis d. The points $\bar{d}_A$, $\bar{d}_B$, and $\bar{d}_C$ are the means of the groups on the function d.

The reader will notice that the function d does a very good job of separating group A from groups B and C, but not a very good job of separating group B

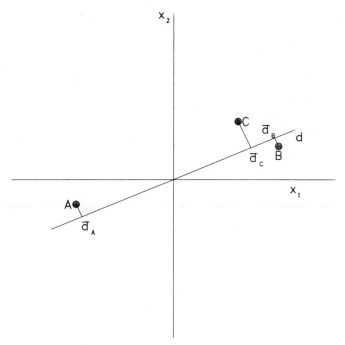

Figure 9-3. Discriminant Function for Three Groups and
Two Variables.

from group C ($\bar{d}_B$ and $\bar{d}_C$ are very close together). But groups B and C are different, their centroids are at two quite separated points. Hence our function d
does not adequately capture the distinctions among the three groups. We solve
this problem by constructing a second axis, representing a second discriminant
function $d_2 = a_{21}x_1 + a_{22}x_2$ as in figure 9-4 (in the process, we rename d as d_1).
In this situation, d_1 separates A from B and C while d_2 separates B from C.

   I located the groups above so as to dramatically make the point that we need
two discriminant functions. Suppose the group centriods were located as in figure 9-5. Here, d does separate the three groups; but, again, it captures only one
of the two dimensions of their differences. A second dimension is still needed as
shown in figure 9-6.

   It is possible, however, that with three groups only one dimension will be
necessary. This will happen if all three groups line up on one discriminant function as in figure 9-7.

   In general, the number of discriminant functions necessary to distinguish the
groups will depend on the number of groups (k) and the number of variables (p).
The maximum number of functions necessary will be the lesser of the number of

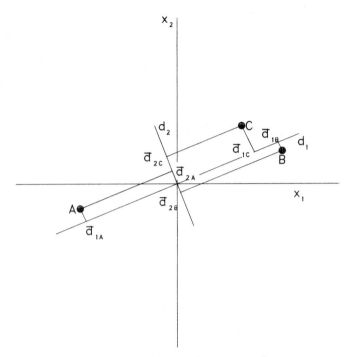

Figure 9-4. Two Discriminant Functions.

variables or the number of groups minus one [this can be written min($p,k-1$)].

As in principal components analysis, it is possible that one or more of the discriminant functions may be insignificant, that is, that they distinguish the groups only slightly. Hence, we will try to find the smallest number of discriminant functions that adequately represents the differences among the groups.

The Algebra of Discriminant Analysis

The algebra of discriminant analysis was introduced in the last chapter. In this chapter the notation is slightly different. In the last chapter group membership was the independent variable and we had a series of interval dependent variables labeled y. Our matrix of the values of those variables was $\mathbf{Y}$. In this chapter group membership is the dependent variable and we have a series of interval independent variables x_j the values of which are in a matrix $\mathbf{X}$.

We want to find the vector $\mathbf{a}$ in the expression

$$d(\mathbf{x}) = \mathbf{Xa}$$

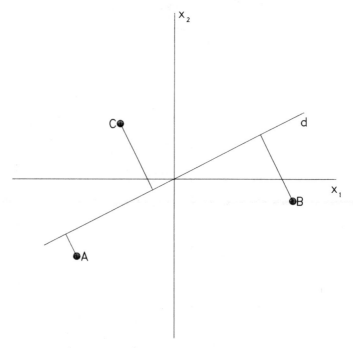

Figure 9-5. One Discriminant Function.

such that an analysis of variance of the variable d produces the largest possible F. As we saw in the last chapter, the solution to this problem is to find the eigenvalues and eigenvectors of the matrix $\mathbf{S}_H \mathbf{S}_E^{-1}$ where $\mathbf{S}_H$ is the SSCP matrix of the x variables for between groups and $\mathbf{S}_E$ is the pooled within groups SSCP matrix of the x's. The largest possible F is provided by the eigenvector associated with the largest eigenvalue. This provides us with the discriminant function that maximally separates the groups. The other discriminant functions are provided by the other eigenvectors. The maximum number of nonzero λ_i's will be $\min(p, k-1)$.

The Discriminant Coefficients

As in principal components analysis, there are a number of ways to scale the vectors of discriminant coefficients. Probably the most useful is to generate *standardized discriminant coefficients,* that is, coefficients computed from independent variables that have been put into standard score form and scaled so

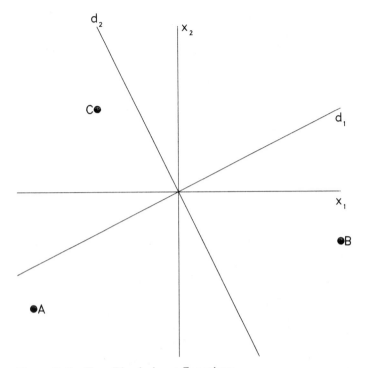

Figure 9-6.   Two Discriminant Functions.

that the individual scores on the discriminant function are also standardized. Most computer programs produce such standardized coefficients. These co-efficients may be interpreted in much the same way as regression coefficients or principal components loadings; that is, they indicate the relative weight of vari-ables in discriminating among the groups along the dimension represented by that discriminate function. When there is more than one discriminant function, it may be desirable to describe the different dimensions represented, in the same way as in principal components analysis. It is possible to rotate discriminant functions to make them more interpretable, but this is usually not done.

Significance Testing

The various discriminant functions account for varying amounts of difference among the groups. These differences are reflected in the values of the eigen-

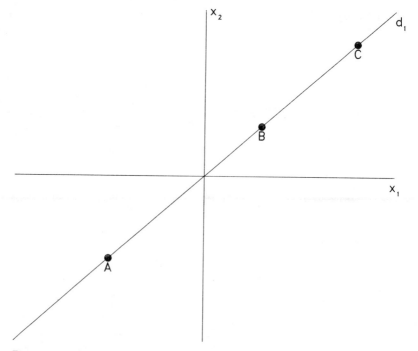

Figure 9-7.   Three Groups Lined Up on One Discriminant Function.

values associated with the functions. Thus, the functions may be ordered in terms of their importance. Tests of significance of the functions proceed through computation of a series of Wilk's lambdas. First, a Wilk's lambda is constructed to determine how much discriminating power there is in the independent variables, that is, to determine whether the group centroids are significantly distinct in the space of independent variables. This Wilk's lambda is $\Lambda = |S_E|/|S_T|$. If this Λ is insignificant, it makes no sense to try to construct any discriminant functions, the variables do not significantly discriminate the groups. If the Λ is significant, the first discriminant function (d_1) is extracted (the one with the largest eigenvalue) and its effects are partialled out of the independent variables. We can then construct the SSCP matrices for the residuals of the independent variables (the residuals after the effects of d_1 are removed). Call these matrices S_{E1} and S_{T1}. A second lambda ($\Lambda_1 = |S_{E1}|/|S_{T1}|$) is now constructed. If this Λ_1 is significant, a second discriminant function may be extracted (there are discriminating elements in the variables beyond those captured by the first discriminant function). If Λ_1 is insignificant, we should stick to one function. The procedure continues until we have an insignificant Λ or until the maximum number of functions is obtained.

It is also possible to test the significance of individual x variables, that is, to test whether they contribute at all to discrimination among the groups, after accounting for all the other variables. Some programs provide stepwise procedures for selecting a subset of variables based on these significance levels.

Classification

One of the objectives of discriminant analysis is to try to classify cases on the basis of their values on the independent variables. That is, we will want to see how good our analysis is at predicting group membership.

When we have only two groups and thus one discriminant function, classification is relatively simple. We find the point along the axis of the discriminant function that best separates the groups, that is, that results in the fewest errors of classification (the fewest numbers of cases falling on the wrong side of the point).

When we move to more than one discriminant function, the situation is a bit more complicated. Here we would need to locate regions of the space of discriminant functions that we could identify with each group and thus we would need to find the boundaries of these regions. A simpler means of classification is through the construction of *classification functions*. Classification functions are another set of linear combinations of the original variables. A classification function is developed for each of the groups. A value is computed for each case on each group's classification function. The case is assigned to that group for which it has the highest value.

Sometimes it is very clear as to which group a case should be assigned, other times the two highest classification function scores for a case may be very close, making us less confident of our classification. Under the assumption of multivariate normality, it is possible to compute, using the classification functions, the probability of membership of each case in each group, thereby enabling us to talk about how much confidence we have in our classification.

Having made our classifications, we will want to check to see how accurate they are. This is usually accomplished by constructing a table like this:

	Actual Group	*Predicted Group*		
		A	B	C
	A			
	B			
	C			

We can then say what proportion of cases were correctly classified by our discriminant analysis (the sum of the diagonal of the above table divided by the total number of cases).

Finally, we may wish to apply our classification functions to cases not included in the original analysis, either as a check on the functions (if we know the correct classification of the new cases) or to predict membership of cases whose classification is unknown. It should be noted that the application of classification functions to a new group of cases invariably results in poorer prediction than for the original cases, since the functions are optimal only for the particular group on which they were generated.

10 OTHER MULTIVARIATE TECHNIQUES

Multivariate Multiple Regression

In chapters 3 and 4 we considered multiple regression, a common technique for exploring the relationship between a number of independent variables and a single dependent variable. In this chapter we consider two procedures to use when we have several dependent variables and several independent variables (all of which are equal interval): multivariate multiple regression and canonical correlation. The latter will be dealt with only briefly.

As indicated in chapter 8, in evaluation work and in other social research we often have more than one outcome measure. It would be possible, in such situations, to compute multiple regression equations for each dependent variable, to find the regression coefficients, and to determine the significance of each equation and the significance of each predictor. The problem with that approach lies in the increase in Type I error rate caused by the large number of statistical tests required. In multivariate multiple regression, that problem is at least partially solved.

The reader will recall the basic model in multiple regression:

$$y = X\beta + \epsilon$$

where y is a vector of the values of y for the n cases, X is the matrix of values for the p independent variables, β is the vector of regression coefficients and ϵ is the vector of residuals or errors. In this chapter, a regression involving a single dependent variable will be referred to as a univariate regression. The basic model for multivariate multiple regression is very similar. Again we assume that we are dealing with variables in deviation score form. Instead of a single dependent variable we have several (say q) so y will be replaced by a matrix of values for the dependent variables, which we will designate Y. Y has q columns, each having the values for one of the dependent variables. The matrix of values of the independent variables X will be the same. We will need a vector of regression coefficients for each dependent variable, so the vector β will be replaced by a matrix of q columns (β, capital beta), each with regression coefficients for one of the dependent variables. Finally, the vector ϵ of residuals must be replaced by a matrix (E, capital epsilon) of q columns, each of which holds the residuals for each case for a particular variable.

The model for multivariate multiple regression is, then,

$$\underset{n\times q}{Y} = \underset{(p\times q)}{\beta} \quad \underset{(p\times q)}{\Gamma} + \underset{n\times q}{E}$$

where n is the number of cases, q is the number of dependent variables, and p is the number of independent variables. This equation summarizes q univariate multiple regression equations, one for each dependent variable.

Our first task is to find estimates for the regression coefficients, that is, for the entries in the matrix B. These estimates are found through a process very similar to that sketched in chapter 3 for the univariate situation. The solution is

$$B = (X'X)^{-1}X'Y$$

which, of course, is identical to the solution in the univariate case except that b is replaced by B and y by Y.

It turns out that the regression coefficients found by the above equation will be exactly the same as if we performed q univariate analyses, one for each dependent variable. What then is the usefulness of multivariate multiple regression, if it gives us the same results as a series of univariate analyses? The answer does not lie in this step (the estimation step) but rather in the next, that of testing significance.

Three kinds of statistical significance questions may be asked. First, is there a relationship between the dependent variables as a whole and the independent variables as a whole? Second, is a particular independent variable or set of independent variables related to the dependent variables, taken as a whole? Third, is the equation for a particular dependent variable significant?

The first step is to determine whether or not there is any relationship between the two sets of variables. If there were no relationship, then all of the entries in B would be zero so the null hypothesis is B = 0. This is similar to the test of the significance of the equation as a whole in univariate regression (there the null hypothesis is $\beta = 0$, or equivalently $R = 0$).

We need concepts analogous to those used in the analysis of variance in univariate regression (see chapter 3). Analogous to the total sum of squares of the dependent variable ($\mathbf{y}'\mathbf{y}$) will be the sum of squares and cross products matrix of the y's which we will designate as $\mathbf{S_T}$ and which is computed as $\mathbf{S_T} = \mathbf{Y}'\mathbf{Y}$. Analogous to the sum of squares for regression ($\mathbf{b}'\mathbf{X}'\mathbf{Xb}$) is the SSCP matrix of the predicted y values, $\mathbf{S_{\hat{T}}}$. Since $\hat{\mathbf{Y}} = \mathbf{XB}$, $\mathbf{S_{\hat{T}}} = \mathbf{B}'\mathbf{X}'\mathbf{XB}$. Finally, analogous to the sum of squares of residuals or errors ($\mathbf{y}'\mathbf{y} - \mathbf{b}'\mathbf{X}'\mathbf{Xb}$) we have the SSCP matrix for the residuals, $\mathbf{S_E} = \mathbf{Y}'\mathbf{Y} - \mathbf{B}'\mathbf{X}'\mathbf{XB}$. This may also be computed from the matrix of residuals $\mathbf{E}$: $\mathbf{S_E} = \mathbf{E}'\mathbf{E} = (\mathbf{Y} - \mathbf{XB})'(\mathbf{Y} - \mathbf{XB})$. The degrees of freedom for the $\mathbf{S_T}$ matrix are $N - 1$, for $\mathbf{S_{\hat{y}}}$, p and for $\mathbf{S_E}$, $N - p - 1$.

The test of the hypothesis that none of the independent variables predict any of the dependent variables ($\mathbf{H_0}$: B = 0) makes use of a Wilk's lambda which is the ratio of the determinant of the residual SSCP matrix divided by the determinant of the total SSCP matrix:

$$\Lambda = \frac{|\mathbf{S_E}|}{|\mathbf{S_T}|}$$

We may understand this ratio by recognizing that if the independent variables do little to help predict the dependent variables, the $\mathbf{E}$ matrix of residuals will be very similar to the original $\mathbf{Y}$ matrix, and therefore the $\mathbf{S_E}$ and $\mathbf{S_T}$ matrices will be similar, as will be their determinants. Therefore, Λ will be close to 1. On the other hand, if the independent variables do predict the dependent variables the absolute values of the cells in the $\mathbf{E}$ matrix will be smaller than those in the $\mathbf{Y}$ matrix and consequently $\mathbf{S_E}$ will have smaller values than $\mathbf{S_T}$. The determinant of $\mathbf{S_E}$ will be smaller than the determinant of $\mathbf{S_T}$ and Λ will be smaller than 1. The other statistics discussed in chapter 8 (Pillai's, Hotelling's, and Roy's) could also be used.

A similar approach may be used to determine the significance of one or more independent variables. This test may be thought of as determining the significance of one or more rows of B. It is based on the assumption that the variables of interest are added after the other variables. We can think of the B matrix as being *partitioned* like this:

$$\frac{\mathbf{B_0}}{\mathbf{B_H}}$$

where $\mathbf{B_H}$ has regression coefficients for the variables being tested. Our hypothesis then is H_0: $B_H = 0$. We will need the SSCP matrix for the residuals from the equation with all the variables included (call this the S_E matrix) and the SSCP matrix from the equation without the variables being tested (call this the S_0 matrix). Then a Wilk's lambda is formed as follows:

$$\Lambda = \frac{|S_E|}{|S_0|}$$

If the new variables add little to the prediction of the y's, the two matrices, and thus their determinants, will be similar and Λ will be close to 1. If the new variables are effective in predicting the y's, over and above the other variables, S_E will have smaller values than S_0, $|S_E|$ will be smaller than $|S_0|$ and Λ will be smaller than 1. The degrees of freedom for S_E are $N - p - r - 1$, where r is the number of new variables being tested while the degrees of freedom for S_0 are $N - p - 1$.

For methods of determining the significance of an obtained Λ see appendix E.

The test of the significance of new variables may be performed on more than one set of independent variables. Such tests, however, are not independent (unless the variables are uncorrelated). If the independent variables can be ordered in some way, the problem can be dealt with by transforming the variables into a new set of uncorrelated variables. This process is called *Gram-Schmidt ortho-normalization* and makes use of what are called *Cholesky factors* (See Finn, 1974 or Bock, 1975). In this procedure, the last set of variables in the ordering is tested first. If it is insignificant, then we may proceed to test the next-to-last set. If the last set is significant then technically we are not allowed to proceed to test earlier sets (their tests would be "confounded" with that of the set already tested). In this way, we may step back through the independent variables until we reach a significant set.

The Dependent Variables

It is also possible to test each dependent variable to see if it is significantly predicted by the independent variables. Such tests may be thought of as tests of the columns of B, that is, the null hypothesis would be that a column of B is zero. Since each column of B contains the regression coefficients for a regression involving one of the dependent variables, it would be possible to simply test the significance of each regression equation (the null hypothesis that $R = 0$ or $\beta = 0$). However, as with the independent variables, the tests of the various dependent variables are not independent, due to associations among them. If the dependent variables can be ordered in some way (over time, or from most important to least important) it is possible to get around this problem through a technique called *step-down analysis*. The analysis again uses Cholesky factors to obtain un-correlated variables. The F ratio for the first equation is determined. Then the first dependent variable is treated as one of the independent variables and the F ratio for the second variable is found. In this way, the effects of the first variable are eliminated from the second, that is, the first variable is controlled. The procedure continues through all of the dependent variables. The F's are then evaluated for significance in a backward fashion, that is, moving backward through them until a significant F is encountered. Technically, at that point one should stop.

Steps in Multivariate Multiple Regression

In practice, multivariate multiple regression should start with an overall test of the relationship between two sets of variables. If that is significant (which it usually will be if we have a relatively large number of variables) then further investigation may proceed. Usually one begins with the independent variables, eliminating those that are insignificant and determining those that are most important in the prediction of the dependent variables as a whole. Then the dependent variables are examined to determine if any are insignificantly related to the independent variables and to see which ones are better predicted than others. After all that, the individual standardized regression coefficients, and their significance levels, may be used to indicate the relative importance of particular independent variables in the prediction of particular dependent variables.

Example

As an example of multivariate multiple regression we will consider a study of parental coping with the death of a child.[1]

The study was concerned in part with how certain coping mechanisms are related to the adaptation of parents following the death of a child. Parents completed questionnaires shortly after the death of a child and again a year later. There were three outcome measures at the second point in time: two measures of depression and a measure of "personal growth." The measures of depression were the Hopkins Symptom Check List (HSCL), a list of psychosocial symptoms (called HSCLDEP2 in the computer program),[2] and a projective sentence completion test coded for negative affect (SCDEP2).[3] The personal growth measure (EVALCH2) was derived from an open ended question about how the respondents had been affected by the experience. Responses were coded as to whether they indicated positive or negative change. The independent variables to be considered here were indications of coping strategies: preoccupation (the continued "presence" of the child for the parent, called **PREOC**); escape (conscious efforts to rid oneself of thoughts of the child or the use of alcohol or drugs, called **AVOID**); religiousness (turning to religion as a source of comfort, called **RE-LIG**); altruism (volunteering to assist other parents, **ALTRU**); replacement with another child (extra attention to surviving children or the birth of another child, **REP**); and replacement with a new role (either changing to a more meaningful job, returning to school or acquiring a new work role, **ROLE**). The analysis shown here concerned the relationship between coping strategies at time 1 with adjustment at time 2. There were three dependent variables and six independent variables (the six coping strategies).

The following tables were produced using the **SPSS MANOVA** program with the following control lines:

```
MANOVA    HSCLDEP2,SCDEP2,EVALCHA2
          WITH AVOID, PREOC,RELIG,ALTRU,REP,ROLE/
          PRINT=SIGNIFICANCE(HYPOTH STEPDOWN) ERROR(SSCP)/
```

The first tabulation in table 10-1, "Adjusted within cells sum-of-squares and cross products," is the SSCP matrix of the residuals, $\mathbf{S_E}$. The "Adjusted hypothesis sum-of-squares and cross products" is the SSCP matrix for the predicted y values $\mathbf{S_T^\wedge}$. Next are the multivariate tests of significance. Notice that all three of the tests result in probabilities less than .01, indicating that as a whole the independent variables are related to the dependent variables; the hypothesis that the matrix of regression coefficients in the population is zero is rejected. In table 10-2 we have the univariate tests of significance, that is, the tests that each of the dependent variables treated separately are related to the independent variables. Next we have step-down tests. Since it was ordered first, the test for **HSCLDEP2** is identical to the univariate test for that variable since none of the other dependent variables are being controlled. The test for **SCDEP2** is performed by treating **HSCLDEP2** and the six coping strategies as independent variables. The test for **EVALCH2** moves both **HSCLDEP2** and **SCDEP2** to the independent side of the equation. The column for **SIG OF F** should be read from the bottom. We move up the column until we reach a significant value. Here we conclude that **EVALCH2** and **SCDEP2** are not significantly predicted by the independent variables after accounting for **HSCLDEP2**. However, we can conclude that **HSCLDEP2** is related significantly to the independent variables. This result is in conformity to the univariate results displayed above.

Finally, in table 10-3 we have the regression equations for each of the dependent variables. The regression coefficients are shown in the column headed **B**, the standardized coefficients are in the **BETA** column. Next are the standard

Table 10-1. Multivariate Multiple Regression

ADJUSTED WITHIN CELLS SUM-OF-SQUARES AND CROSS-PRODUCTS

	HSCLDEP2	SCDEP2	EVALCHA2
HSCLDEP2	56.09736		
SCDEP2	7.06483	4.56720	
EVALCHA2	-54.69087	-8.40782	578.17763

ADJUSTED HYPOTHESIS SUM-OF-SQUARES AND CROSS-PRODUCTS

	HSCLDEP2	SCDEP2	EVALCHA2
HSCLDEP2	11.90030		
SCDEP2	1.47548	.37014	
EVALCHA2	-4.27163	-2.06575	30.36522

MULTIVARIATE TESTS OF SIGNIFICANCE (S = 3, M = 1, N = 64 1/2)

TEST NAME	VALUE	APPROX. F	HYPOTH. DF	ERROR DF	SIG. OF F
PILLAIS	.27673	2.25255	18.00	399.00	.003
HOTELLINGS	.32428	2.33602	18.00	389.00	.002
WILKS	.74153	2.29861	18.00	371.01	.002
ROYS	.18300				

Table 10-2. Univariate and Stepdown Tests

UNIVARIATE F-TESTS WITH (6,133) D. F.

VARIABLE	SQ. MUL. R	MUL. R	ADJ. R-SQ.	HYPOTH MS	ERROR MS	F	SIG. OF F
HSCLDEP2	.17501	.41834	.13779	1.98338	.42178	4.70236	.000
SCDEP2	.07497	.27380	.03324	.06169	.03434	1.79643	.104
EVALCHA2	.04990	.22338	.00704	5.06087	4.34720	1.16417	.329

ROY-BARGMAN STEPDOWN F - TESTS

VARIABLE	HYPOTH. MS	ERROR MS	STEP-DOWN F	HYPOTH. DF	ERROR DF	SIG. OF F
HSCLDEP2	1.98338	.42178	4.70236	6	133	.000
SCDEP2	.03121	.02786	1.12010	6	132	.354
EVALCHA2	5.12495	4.00175	1.28068	6	131	.271

Table 10-3. Regression Equations for Dependent Variables

REGRESSION ANALYSIS FOR WITHIN CELLS ERROR TERM

DEPENDENT VARIABLE ..HSCLDEP2   T2 HSCL DEPRESSION

COVARIATE	B	BETA	STD. ERR.	T-VALUE	SIG. OF T	LOWER .95 CL	UPPER .95 CL
AVOID	.2856714257	.3381943636	.06740	4.23852	.000	.15236	.41898
PREOC	-.0025973509	-.0034434518	.06006	-.04324	.966	-.12140	.11620
RELIG	.0680814049	.1338822521	.04055	1.67877	.096	-.01213	.14830
ALTRU	-.0602959905	-.0426185203	.11319	-.53272	.595	-.28417	.16358
REP	-.2225519418	-.1578175122	.11351	-1.95800	.052	-.44677	.00227
ROLE	-.2666925837	-.1110640448	.19486	-1.36864	.173	-.65212	.11873

DEPENDENT VARIABLE ..SCDEP2   T2 G&G DEPRESSION

COVARIATE	B	BETA	STD. ERR.	T-VALUE	SIG. OF T	LOWER .95 CL	UPPER .95 CL
AVOID	.0480712270	.2111958014	.01923	2.49964	.014	.01003	.08611
PREOC	-.0092664439	-.0455907765	.01714	-.54070	.590	-.04316	.02463
RELIG	.0097578204	.0712111221	.01157	.84326	.401	-.03265	.01313
ALTRU	.0400770169	.1051249567	.03230	1.24094	.217	-.02380	.10396
REP	-.0229251979	-.0604120026	.03239	-.70783	.480	-.08699	.04114
ROLE	-.0533265161	-.0824150009	.05560	-.95911	.339	-.16330	.05665

DEPENDENT VARIABLE ..EVALCHA2

COVARIATE	B	BETA	STD. ERR.	T-VALUE	SIG. OF T	LOWER .95 CL	UPPER .95 CL
AVOID	-.3683966998	-.1457862891	.21638	-1.70256	.091	-.79638	.05959
PREOC	.0129078437	.0057202955	.19282	.06694	.947	-.36849	.39431
RELIG	.2536020203	.1667049888	.13020	1.94785	.054	-.00392	.51112
ALTRU	-.0046353676	-.0010952052	.36337	-.01276	.990	-.72337	.71410
REP	-.2427276536	-.0576142979	.36441	-.66608	.507	-.96352	.47806
ROLE	.0510112104	.0071011643	.62558	.08154	.935	-1.18636	1.28838

errors of the B's, the t statistics for testing the significance of the B's, their significance and the upper and lower 95% confidence limits for the B's. These are all univariate tests. It appears from this table that HSCLDEP2 is related to the avoidance coping strategy and perhaps slightly to the replacement with another child strategy. Since SCDEP2 and EVALCH2 are not significantly predicted by the set of predictors it is risky to attempt to interpret the regression coefficients for those variables. However, it is of interest that avoidance is at least moderately related to these variables as well.

Canonical Correlation

As with multivariate multiple regression, canonical correlation deals with two sets of equal interval variables. However, in canonical correlation no distinctions are made as to independent and dependent variables. The objective is to find linear combinations of the variables within each set such that the two linear combinations have maximum correlation. That is, we find a linear combination of set X (call this combination x) and a linear combination of set Y (call this combination y) such that x and y have the highest possible correlation. We will call these linear combinations *canonical variates.*

As with other techniques in this book (principal components, discriminant analysis), in general more than one pair of canonical variates are required to fully represent the relationships between the two sets of variables. The maximum number of pairs will be equal to the number of variables in the smallest set (if p and q are the number of variables in each set, this can be written as $\min(p,q)$). Again it is possible that the number of significant pairs will be less than $\min(p,q)$. Each pair of canonical variates is orthogonal to previous pairs (e.g., y_2 is orthogonal to both y_1 and x_1 but is correlated with x_2).

Thus, canonical correlation can be thought of as something like performing principal components analysis on two sets of variables, except that the criteria for the pairs of linear combinations is that they have the highest possible correlation while being orthogonal to "earlier" pairs.

Program Output

Computation of canonical correlations proceeds by means of eigenvalue equations. Details will not be given here. The output of computer programs includes the coefficients for the significant pairs of linear combinations, the eigenvalue associated with each pair, the correlation between each pair (called the "canonical correlation"), and Wilk's lambda for each pair (used in significance testing).

It turns out that each eigenvalue is equal to the square of the corresponding canonical correlation. The canonical variate coefficients can be used to interpret or name the variates, just as in principal components and discriminant analysis.

In this author's view, canonical correlation is of limited value in human services research and evaluation. When we have sets of independent and dependent variables we would rarely be satisfied with letting a mathematical procedure determine a linear combination of the dependent variables on purely statistical grounds. For example, if the dependent variables are program outcome measures, it is likely that some will be more important than others for theoretical, practical, or political reasons. The canonical correlation procedure does not pay attention to such reasons. Hence, a procedure like multivariate multiple regression or some a priori weighting would seem to be more appropriate in this situation. However, there may be times when we want some measure of association between two sets of variables that are relatively homogeneous and cannot be ordered theoretically. In this situation, canonical correlation may be appropriate.

Multivariate Analysis of Covariance

Frequently in evaluation work we want to compare two or more groups on some set of variables while controlling for the effects of some other variables. For example, we may want to compare groups of individuals exposed to different treatments on some set of outcome (dependent) variables while controlling for prior levels of those variables and perhaps other variables that might affect the outcome. We call the variables we want to control *covariates* and employ the analysis of covariance to deal with the problem. Since we have several dependent variables, we use a multivariate analysis of covariance. It is a combination of multivariate multiple regression and the multivariate test of means.

In fact, the multivariate analysis of covariance may be thought of as a multivariate test of means with the dependent variables having been adjusted for the control variables. This can be written as

$$H_0: \; \mu_{1\text{ADJ}} = \mu_{2\text{ADJ}} = \cdots = \mu_{k\text{ADJ}}$$

We designate the matrix of dependent variable values $\mathbf{Y}$ and the matrix of covariate values as $\mathbf{X}$. The dependent variable values controlled for the covariates is the matrix of residuals from a regression analysis which is $\mathbf{Y} - \mathbf{BX}$.

The test of the hypothesis requires the construction of a Wilk's lambda involving the ratio of determinants of within and total residual SSCP matrices. We will designate the total residual SSCP matrix as $\mathbf{S}_{Y \cdot X}$. It is found as follows:

$$\mathbf{S}_{Y \cdot X} = (\mathbf{Y} - \mathbf{BX})'(\mathbf{Y} - \mathbf{BX})$$

Similar matrices may be developed within each group, that is, the residual matrix $\mathbf{Y} - \mathbf{BX}$ is partitioned into submatrices corresponding to the groups, and SSCP matrices are constructed from each of these submatrices. These within-groups residual SSCP matrices are then added together to form a pooled within-groups SSCP matrix. Call this matrix $\mathbf{W_{Y \cdot X}}$. Wilk's lambda is then

$$\Lambda = \frac{|\mathbf{W_{Y \cdot X}}|}{|\mathbf{S_{Y \cdot X}}|}$$

If the groups do not differ on the residual variables $\mathbf{S_{Y \cdot X}}$ and $\mathbf{W_{Y \cdot X}}$ will be similar and Wilk's lambda will be close to 1. If the groups differ, $\mathbf{W_{Y \cdot X}}$ will have entries that are smaller than those in $\mathbf{S_{Y \cdot X}}$ (in absolute value), and lambda will be less than one.

For the determination of the significance of Λ see appendix E. The degrees of freedom for $\mathbf{S_{Y \cdot X}}$ are $N - p - 1$ and for $\mathbf{W_{Y \cdot X}}$, $N - p - k - 1$, where k is the number of groups.

The assumptions behind this test include population multivariate normality, equivalence of within groups covariance matrices (in the populations), and parallel group regression hyper-planes. The latter means that the population regressions of the dependent variables and the covariates are the same in all groups, except for the constant (intercept) term. This can be imagined best when we have a single covariate. Then the regression involving that covariate and one of the dependent variables within one of the groups is a line in two-dimensional space. The assumption says that the lines for the various groups are parallel.

The analysis of covariance is a powerful and useful technique. In many circumstances it is, however, tricky to interpret. It is most problematic when we have a nonequivalent group comparison design, as frequently happens when we are unable to randomly assign subjects to treatments. Of course, that is the situation in which we would most like to use the technique, to adjust for the differences in the groups before treatment. In this situation, what are known as *regression effects* can occur, resulting in groups appearing to be similar when they are not and vice versa.

Notes

1. Lynn Videka-Sherman, *Coping with the death of a child: A study over time,* Unpublished Ph. D. Dissertation, The University of Chicago, School of Social Service Administration, December 1981.

2. L.R. Derogatis et al. The Hopkins Symptom Checklist (HSCL): A Self Report Symptom Inventory, *Behavioral Science* 29(1974): 1–15.

3. S.S. Tobin and M.A. Lieberman, *Last Home for the Aged* (San Francisco: Jossey-Bass, 1976).

11 REPEATED MEASURES ANALYSIS

Repeated measures analysis is concerned with a common problem in social science research and evaluation. Often we have a situation in which we have measured the same thing at two or more points in time (called *occasions*), all of the measures having been taken on the same sample. Usually we assume that there are equal time periods between the occasions. For example, in the study of research teaching discussed earlier in this book we measured several outcome variables (knowledge of research, attitudes toward empirically based practice, etc.) at three points in time, the beginning of the school year, the end of the year, and again a year later. In chapter 8 we discussed the simplest kind of repeated measures analysis, one involving only two points in time and we used t tests and multivariate extensions of the t test to test for the differences in the two points in time. Now we will extend the analysis to more points in time.

Repeated measures analysis can also be used in other situations in which several measurements are taken of the same subjects, for example, when we apply two or more treatments to the same subjects (in which case we might systematically vary the order of the treatments for different cases so that the effects of ordering could be detected). One of the problems that must be dealt with in repeated measures analysis is that the observations for a particular case are not independent of each other. That is, a person's score at one point in time bears some relationship to that person's score at another point in time.

189

The simplest repeated measures analysis involves a single group of subjects and a single dependent variable measured at two or more points in time. More complex analyses involve two or more groups and several variables. In our example, students were in seven sections of a research class and were measured on several outcome variables.

Single-Group Designs

We begin with single-group designs involving one variable. In this situation our primary interest is in determining whether there has been a change over time, so our null hypothesis is that the means at the various points in time are not significantly different. We will discuss two approaches to the problem, the *univariate* and *multivariate* approaches.

Univariate Approach

The univariate approach is the simplest but it is limited to special circumstances, which will be discussed later. The data for such an analysis may be thought of as being laid out in an array like the following:

| | Occasions | | |
Case	Time 1	Time 2	Time 3
1			
2			
.			
.			
.			
N			

Suppose that we have observed each of N cases on p occasions (here $p = 3$). We have pN observations (the table has pN cells). The univariate approach utilizes a two-way analysis of variance with occasions as one factor and cases forming the other factor. That is, the factor "occasions" has p categories while the factor "cases" has N categories. The design is called a *mixed model* analysis of variance. This means that one of the factors (occasions) has fixed categories or levels (we determine when the measurements are to be taken) while the other factor (subjects) is sampled. That is, we do not determine which subjects to take before hand but rather use some kind of sampling procedure to select them. Other subjects might have been selected. There is only one observation per cell (we have a two-way analysis of variance *without replication*). Hence, there is no within-cells variation so a within-cells sum of squares cannot be computed.

For our example, using research knowledge as the dependent variable, the analysis of variance table for 105 cases looks like this:

	Sum of Squares	d.f.	Mean Squares	F
Subjects	36,477.91	104	350.75	
Occasions	14,033.73	2	7016.87	100.26
Subjects by Occasions (Interaction)	14,558.87	208	69.99	
Total	65,070.50	314		

We have a total of 315 observations, so the total degrees of freedom are 314. There are three occasions so the degrees of freedom for occasions is 2 (p - 1). There are 105 subjects so the degrees of freedom for subjects is 104 (N - 1). The degrees of freedom for interaction is the product of the degrees of freedom for occasions and subjects. Mean squares are computed as usual by dividing the sums of squares by their degrees of freedom.

In two-way analysis of variance with replication (two or more cases per cell) we use the within-cells mean square (the error mean square) to test for the main effects. That is, the mean squares for rows and columns are divided by the within-cells mean square to form an F statistic. In this case we have no within-cells mean square so we use the interaction mean square instead. The F for occasions is shown in the table (it is 7016.87/69.99). It has 2 and 208 d.f. and is highly significant, indicating that there are differences in mean knowledge at the three points in time. We would say that there is a significant "occasions effect." We could also test for a "subjects effect" by dividing the mean squares for subjects by the interaction mean squares; but we usually assume that there are differences among subjects, so we are not concerned with proving that.

If we have established that there are differences among occasions, we will be interested in characterizing those differences. One approach would be to look at differences between successive occasions, that is, to examine the difference in means between time 2 and time 1 and between time 3 and time 2. Although that approach can be used, a technical problem arises because statistical tests of such successive differences are not independent, the significance or nonsignificance of one difference has an impact on the significance or nonsignificance of another.

The way out of this problem is to examine orthogonal contrasts of the means for occasions. A *contrast* of the means is a linear combination of the means:

$$a_1\mu_1 + a_2\mu_2 + a_3\mu_3$$

where the μ's represent means of the three occasions and the a's are coefficients we choose. The a's must add to zero (so one or more must be negative while others are positive). The a's are chosen in such a way that they give us contrasts or comparisons among the means that are interesting. For example, the contrast

$$1\mu_1 - .5\mu_2 - .5\mu_3$$

gives us the difference between the mean of time 1 and the average of the means of time 2 and 3. We use this contrast to test the null hypothesis that the mean of time 1 is equal to the average of the means of time 2 and time 3:

$$H_0: \quad 1\mu_1 - .5\mu_2 - .5\mu_3 = 0$$

We can test more than one contrast in a given analysis; but to stay on the up and up with statistical theory, the contrasts must be independent or orthogonal. Two contrasts are *orthogonal* if the sum of the cross products of the corresponding coefficients is equal to zero. To put this in vector terms, we can think of the coefficients of two contrasts as forming two vectors, say a and b. The two contrasts are orthogonal if the vector product $a'b$ is equal to zero. For example, the two contrasts:

$$1\mu_1 - .5\mu_2 - .5\mu_3$$
$$0\mu_1 + 1\mu_2 - 1\mu_3$$

are orthogonal since $(1)(0) + (-.5)(1) + (-.5)(-1) = 0$. There is a limit to how many orthogonal contrasts we can test at one time. That is, it is impossible to write more than $p - 1$ (where p is the number of occasions) contrasts, each of which is orthogonal to all the others. Each of the contrasts has one degree of freedom associated with it and these degrees of freedom cannot add to more than the degrees of freedom for occasions. Finally, contrasts are usually normalized, that is, the sums of squares of their coefficients are made to be equal to one. (This can be accomplished by dividing each coefficient by the square root of the sum of the squared coefficients in the contrast.) The normalized versions of the above contrasts are

$$.816\mu_1 - .408\mu_2 - .408\mu_3 \quad \text{and} \quad 0\mu_1 + .707\mu_2 - .707\mu_3$$

One particular set of contrasts frequently used in repeated measures analysis is called *polynomial contrasts*. We can plot the means of the occasions. Figure 11–1 shows two of the possible ways a plot of three occasions might look. With three occasions, the plot will either be a straight line (or almost a straight line) or it will have one bend. Of course, a straight line could be horizontal or slant down and a curved line could bend in the other direction. With four occasions, we could have two bends as in figure 11–2.

The tendency of the line to slope up or down is called the *linear component*

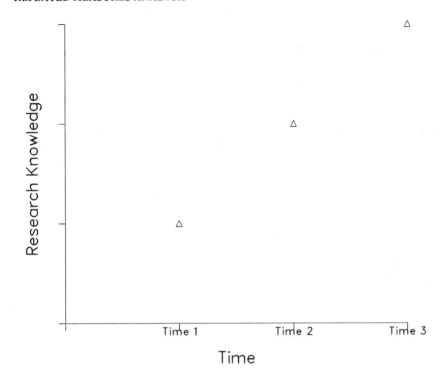

Figure 11-1a.   Linear Plot of Occasions.

of the occasions effect. The presence of a single bend in the plot is called a *quadratic component,* while a tendency to have three bends is called a *cubic effect.* Higher order effects are possible with more points in time. Statisticians call all of this a "single degree of freedom polynomial decomposition of the occasions effect."

In computer programs the analysis of orthogonal contrasts is accomplished by computing linear transformations of the values of the dependent variable. This may be thought of as the matrix product $Y^* = YA$, where Y^* is the matrix of transformed values, Y is the matrix of original values, and A is a matrix with the coefficients of the linear transformations. For example, with three occasions, the matrix A for orthogonal polynomials would be

$$
\begin{matrix}
.57735 & .57735 & .57735 \\
.70711 & 0 & -.70711 \\
-.40825 & .81650 & -.40825
\end{matrix}
$$

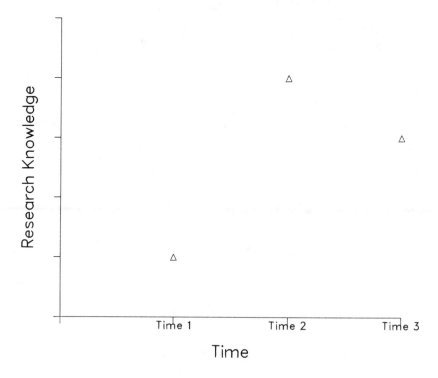

Figure 11-1b.   Curved Plot of Occasions.

The vector of means of the y variables will be transformed in the same way. In our example, the means for the three points in time are 53.97, 68.06, and 68.19, so the transformed means are

$$(53.97 \quad 68.06 \quad 68.19) \begin{pmatrix} .57735 & .57735 & .57735 \\ .70711 & 0 & -.70711 \\ -.40825 & .81650 & -.40825 \end{pmatrix} = (109.82 \quad -10.05 \quad 5.7)$$

The values 109.82, -10.05, and 5.7 are the means of the new transformed variables.

The first row of the **A** matrix (the values .57735) is not a contrast, although it is orthogonal to the other rows. It forms a new variable which is a kind of average of the values at the three points in time. If we used 1/3 as this value, we would have the average (adding up one third of each observation for a case is the same thing as adding up all the observations and then dividing by three). However, we want these coefficients to be normalized (the sum of their squares should add to one), so we divide each 1/3 by the square root of $3(1/3)^2$. That

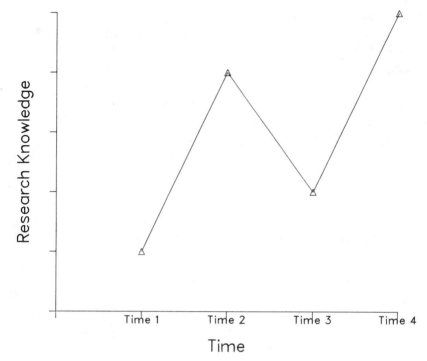

Figure 11-2. Plot of Four Occasions.

gives us .57735. In general, the values of this row will be $\sqrt{1/p}$ and the mean of this transformed variable will be $\sqrt{p}$ times the mean of the occasions.

This first transformed variable, called the *constant* or *overall* effect, is usually not of much interest when we have only one group of cases, as in the present example. It can be used to test the hypothesis that the mean of the three occasions is zero; usually, however, we are confident that it is not zero and do not bother with that test. The overall effect is of more importance when we get to the analysis of more than one group.

The second row of the **A** matrix has coefficients for a contrast of the first and third occasions. It is used to test the linear component. The third row is a contrast of the second occasion with the mean of the first and third. It is used to test the quadratic component.

The full analysis of variance table for our data, with the occasions variation divided up into linear and quadratic components is shown below.

	Sum of Squares	d.f.	Mean Squares	F
Subjects	36,477.90	104	360.75	

Occasions	14,033.73	2		
(Linear)	(10,619.27)	(1)	(10,619.27)	(112.69)
(Quadratic)	(3,414.46)	(1)	(3,414.46)	(74.62)
Subjects by occasions	14,558.87	208		
(Linear)	(9,800.19)	(104)	(94.23)	
(Quadratic)	(4,758.69)	(104)	(45.76)	
Total	65,070.50	314		

Note that both the occasions and the subjects by occasions sums of squares are partitioned. The linear and quadratic effects are tested by dividing the mean squares for linear occasions and the mean squares for quadratic occasions by the mean squares for linear and quadratic subjects by occasions respectively.[1]

These tests are essentially t tests of the hypothesis that the mean of each transformed variable is zero ($t = (\bar{x} - 0)/s_{\bar{x}}$). In this example, both the linear and quadratic components are significant.

Interpretation of these results is helped by a plot of the means over time (the means of the original variables), as shown in figure 11-3. The upward (linear) trend is obvious in the picture and statistically significant. The time 3 mean is virtually the same as the time 2 mean, so we have a bend in the curve; and that quadratic bend is also significant. Obviously, as a whole the students did not increase their knowledge of research in the year after the research course (the second year of the graduate program).

Assumptions of This Approach. The univariate approach presented here assumes that the covariance matrix of the error components of the transformed variables is diagonal. In the case of a single group, this means that there should be no correlations among the transformed variables in the population. (An even more restrictive assumption is that the variances of the transformed contrasts, linear, quadratic, etc., are equal. This assumption leads to a more powerful test of the hypothesis than that given above. For details, see Bock, 1975, pp. 459–460). Of course, in a sample there may be some correlation due to sampling variation even if there is none in the population. For a test of this assumption see Bock p. 462.

Multivariate Approach

The assumption required for the univariate approach is often not met in real data; that is, there are often correlations among the transformed variables. The multivariate approach provides a means of exploring the trends over time without making the assumption. In the multivariate approach, orthogonal transformations of the original variables continue to be needed; and we will pursue the

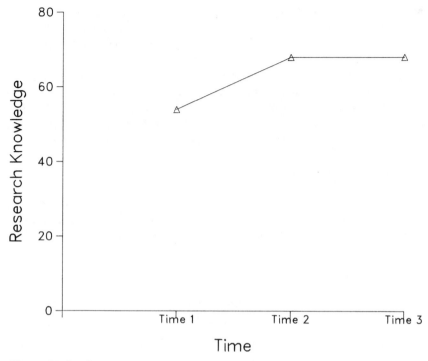

Figure 11-3. Plot of Means over Time.

discussion in the context of orthogonal polynomials, although other orthogonal contrasts could be used.

In order to pursue the multivariate approach, we need to introduce a broadened view of the idea of sum of squares. Throughout this book we have talked about the sum of squares of a variable as the sum of the squared deviations of the values around the mean, that is, $\Sigma(x_i - \bar{x})^2$. We could also talk about the sum of squares of the original values, that is, simply Σx_i^2. The sum of squared deviations can be written as $\Sigma x_i^2 - n\bar{x}^2$. The first of these two terms is the sum of squares of the original values. The second is called the sum of squares "due to the mean" or "due to the constant" (it is the mean squared and summed over all cases). The sum of squares of the original values is equal to the sum of squares for deviations plus the sum of squares for the constant. We can symbolize this as: $s.s._O = s.s._D + s.s._C$ where C stands for constant. The degrees of freedom for the constant sum of squares is one, the one degree of freedom that is lost in the degrees of freedom for the sum of squares for deviations (the degrees of freedom for deviations sum of squares is $n - 1$). Mean squares can be computed by dividing these sums of squares by their degrees of freedom and the hypothesis that the mean of the variable is equal to zero can be tested by the F ratio of the mean square for the constant (which is equal to the sum of squares, since we are dividing by one) divided by the mean square for deviations.

We can think about sums of squares and cross products matrices in a similar way. If X_O is a matrix of the original scores for several variables and X_D is the matrix of deviation scores (called just X until now) then $S_O = X_O'X_O$ is the SSCP matrix of original scores and $S_D = X_D'X_D$ is the SSCP matrix of deviation scores (called S until now). The SSCP matrix for the constant term is the difference between these: $S_C = S_O - S_D$.

In repeated measures analysis we transform our original scores matrix of repeated measures, Y_O by an orthogonal transformation matrix A (that is, we perform the multiplication $Y_O A$). The total, deviation, and constant SSCP matrices for the transformed scores will be $A'S_O A$, $A'S_D A$ and $A'S_C A$. (Proof for total: SSCP of transformed y's $= (Y_O A)'Y_O A = A'Y_O'Y_O A = A'S_O A$.)

For the example used above the SSCP matrices of the polynomial transformations are:

		Overall	Linear	Quadratic
S_O	Overall	1302934.85		
	Linear		20419.45	
	Quadratic		-9001.85	8173.15
	(d.f. = N)			
S_D	Overall	36477.90		
	Linear		9800.19	
	Quadratic		-2980.30	4758.69
	(d.f. = $N - 1$)			
S_C	Overall	1266456.95		
	Linear		10619.27	
	Quadratic		-6021.55	3414.46
	(d.f. = 1)			

The matrices are symmetric, so only the bottom halves are shown. In addition, the last two entries in the overall column are not of much use and are not printed out by the computer, so they are not shown.

To test the hypothesis that there is a difference among the means of the three occasions we pay attention to the submatrices without the row and column for overall. We can test this hypothesis by forming the Wilk's lambda:

$$\Lambda = \frac{|S_D^*|}{|S_C^* + S_D^*|} = \frac{37753808.38}{85857817.87} = .43972$$

where the asterisks indicate the submatrices. This Wilk's lambda is significant, indicating that there is a difference among the occasions. Alternatively, other tests discussed in chapter 8 (Pillai's, Hotelling's, and Roy's tests) may be performed. These tests require the S_H and S_E matrices. In this context, the S_H is the submatrix for the constant (S_C) and S_E is the submatrix of deviation scores (S_D). The test that more than a linear component is present would be conducted by eliminating both the overall and linear columns from the above matrices and proceeding as above. In this case we are left with single numbers rather than matrices so the test could be performed as an ordinary t or F test. Similarly, if we have enough repetitions of the measurement, we could test to see if any higher order components are needed.

N-Sample Case

We turn now to the situation in which we have two or more groups of subjects each measured at several points in time. In our example, the students were divided into seven sections. We have two main parts to the design. First, all subjects are measured at three points in time, this is called the *within-subjects design*. Second, subjects are divided into seven groups. This is called the *between-subjects design*. As in the single-group case, orthogonal transformations of the occasions values are needed; and we will continue to use orthogonal polynomials for these transformations, although others could be used. The univariate analysis of the *n* sample case may be thought of as a process of transforming the values, then performing a one-way analysis of variance across groups for each of the transformed variables (the linear, quadratic, cubic, etc. variables). We will not pursue the univariate approach further, but rather will turn immediately to the multivariate approach.

In the *n*-sample case, we can plot the means of each group in time. Figure 11-4 shows such a plot for the seven sections.

In the analysis of repeated measures for several groups we might be interested in one or more of the following questions:

1. Are there differences over time in the whole group?

This is the same question we were asking above in the single-group case. However, the test of the null hypothesis may be more sensitive because we will remove the differences among groups from the error term.

2. Are there differences among groups in their average levels across all occasions?
3. Are the curves for the groups all shaped about the same way (i.e., are they parallel) or is there an interaction between occasions and groups?

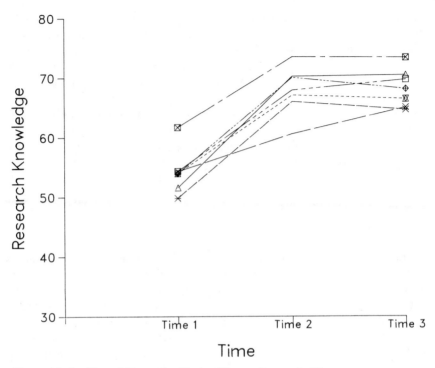

Figure 11-4. Plot of Means for Each of Seven Groups in Time.

This last question is the same as asking whether all the groups change by the same amount. For example, if the sections had different impacts on students' learning of research we would expect that the change from time 1 to time 2 would differ for different sections and thus the slope of the lines from time 1 to time 2 would be different.

The multivariate analysis requires that three SSCP matrices be computed on the transformed variables. That is, the total SSCP S_O is partitioned into three matrices: S_C (the same SSCP for constant as before); an SSCP for between groups, S_B; and an SSCP for within groups, S_W (our previous $S_D = S_B + S_W$). The degrees of freedom for the terms in S_B and S_W are $k - 1$ (where k is the number of groups) and $N - k$ respectively. In our example, the S_B and S_W matrices for the transformed variables are

		Overall	Linear	Quadratic
	Overall	2507.11		
S_B	Linear		321.73	

		Quadratic		-263.04	457.68
		Overall	33970.80		
S_W		Linear		9478.45	
		Quadratic		-2717.27	4301.01

The degrees of freedom are 6 and 98 respectively. The various hypotheses are tested through Wilk's lambdas involving submatrices of these matrices. The hypothesis that the sections do not differ in their averages over time is tested by focusing on the overall variable (an average of the three points in time). An F ratio of the mean square for between groups to the mean square for within groups is formed:

$$F = \frac{2507.106/6}{33907.80/98} = 1.205$$

This F is insignificant, so we cannot conclude that there is a difference among groups in their overall averages.

The hypothesis that there are differences over time is tested by the Wilk's lambda of the submatrices involving the linear and quadratic variables:

$$\Lambda = \frac{|S_W|}{|S_C + S_W|} = \frac{\begin{vmatrix} 9478.45 & -2717.27 \\ -2717.27 & 4301.01 \end{vmatrix}}{\begin{vmatrix} 20097.72 & -8738.82 \\ -8738.82 & 7715.47 \end{vmatrix}} = .4242$$

This Wilk's lambda is significant (as before), so we conclude that there is an occasions effect. Again, the other test statistics (Pillai's, Roy's, and Hotelling's) could be used.

The hypothesis that there is no interaction between section and occasion is tested with the following Wilk's lambda:

$$\Lambda = \frac{|S_W|}{|S_B + S_W|} = \frac{\begin{vmatrix} 9478.45 & -2717.27 \\ -2717.27 & 4301.01 \end{vmatrix}}{\begin{vmatrix} 9800.18 & -2980.31 \\ -2980.31 & 4758.69 \end{vmatrix}} = .8842$$

This Λ is not significant. Thus, in this data there is no reason to conclude that the shapes of the curves for the various sections are different.

If a significant interaction between sections and occasions were found it would not make sense (and it would be improper statistically) to attempt to interpret differences among the sections in their means across occasions (differences among the sections on the transformed overall variable). Instead, we should describe how the curves for the various groups differ.

Computer Output

We turn now to a presentation of computer output of an analysis of repeated measures in the study we have been discussing. The analysis to be presented is slightly more complex than that we have been discussing. It involves the simultaneous analysis of two dependent variables, research knowledge and attitudes toward empirically based practice, each measured at the three points in time. Such an analysis is called *doubly multivariate*. As we shall see, the additional complications are minor.

The output in tables 11-1 to 11-3 was produced by the MANOVA program in the SPSS system with the following control lines:

```
MANOVA    KSCORE,KSCORE2,KSCORE 3,
          TOTALATT,TOTALAT2,TOTALAT3
          BY SECTION(1,7)/
          WSFACTOR=OCCASION(3)/
          WSDESIGN=OCCASION/
          ANALYSIS(REPEATED)/
          RENAME=KOVERALL,KLIN,KQUAD,
          AOVERALL,ALIN,AQUAD/
          PRINT SIGNIF(BRIEF)/
          PRINT ERROR(COR)/
          DESIGN=SECTION/
```

The first two lines list the dependent variables, making sure that the three knowledge scores are listed together and in order, then the three attitude scores. BY SECTION means that we want an analysis of variance by the variable section. WSFACTOR=OCCASION(3) indicates that we have an analysis in which there is a within-subjects design. The within-subjects factor is to be called "occasion" and has three categories, for the three points in time. The 3 in parentheses also indicates that the dependent variables listed on the first line are to be taken in groups of three (that is KSCORE, KSCORE2, and KSCORE3 are to be taken as a single within-subjects repeated measure and similarly for the attitude scores). WSDESIGN=OCCASION calls for a transformation of the data. In the case of two or three occasions, SPSS performs orthogonal polynomial transformations.[2]

The command ANALYSIS(REPEATED) invokes a repeated measures analysis. The RENAME command gives names to the new transformed variables. If the RENAME command is not used, the transformed variables are given the same names as the old variables, which is very confusing.

PRINT SIGNIF(BRIEF) asks for abbreviated output, which is usually sufficient for repeated measures analysis. It does not, however, produce output necessary for a complete univariate analysis and so may be omitted to obtain more complete output. It is also possible to obtain the various SSCP matrices involved through the command PRINT ERROR(SSCP) SIGNIF(HYPOTH) (that is how I produced the matrices that appear earlier in this chapter). The command PRINT ERROR(COR) produces a test of the assumptions underlying the univariate approach.

The program first prints out the transformation matrix in transposed form (table 11-1). Note that the matrix is composed of two submatrices. The upper left 3X3 submatrix transforms the knowledge scores while the lower right transforms the attitude scores.

Next, the program prints out the tests of significance for the between-groups part of the design. It utilizes the transformed overall variables (KOVERALL, AOVERALL). The first line, labeled CONSTANT provides a test of the hypothesis that the means of the variables for the entire group are zero (that the mean vector for KOVERALL and AOVERALL is zero). This line is usually of little interest. The second line tests the hypothesis that the sections differ in their mean vectors for KOVERALL and AOVERALL. Note that the multivariate F used to test the significance of Wilk's lambda is barely significant ($p = .048$). This differs from the insignificant results obtained when only knowledge scores were being examined. The inclusion of attitudes leads to the conclusion of significant differences among sections. The last two columns of this table present the AVERAGED F and its significance. These figures refer to the results that would be obtained if the most restrictive assumptions about the data hold, that is, if the covariance matrix of the error terms is diagonal and all entries in the diagonal are the same. In that case, these columns provide an adequate test of the hypothesis.[3]

Note that the result for the averaged F is different from the multivariate analysis in that this procedure produces an insignificant effect for section.

The program next presents the estimates for the transformed overall variables (table 11-2). These estimates are shown in the column labeled COEFF. In line 1 the value of 109.88 is the mean of the means of the sections for the variable KOVERALL (when the sections do not have the same numbers of cases this will not be equal to the grand mean of all cases). In the lines labeled 2 through 7 are the differences between the means of sections one to six and the mean of the means. This is the *effect* of being in a particular section. The effect of being in section seven is minus the sum of the effects of the other sections. The other columns provide univariate t-tests of the hypothesis that a particular effect is equal to zero. Note that for KOVERALL, section six (parameter 7) is the only section to have a significant effect (although we do not know about section seven) and that effect is positive (+10.47). For AOVERALL, sections one and three (parameters 2 and 4) have significant effects in opposite directions.

Table 11-1. Orthonormalized Transformation Matrix

ORTHONORMALIZED TRANSFORMATION MATRIX (TRANSPOSED)

	1	2	3	4	5	6
1	.57735	.70711	-.40825	0.0	0.0	0.0
2	.57735	0.0	.81650	0.0	0.0	0.0
3	.57735	-.70711	-.40825	0.0	0.0	0.0
4	0.0	0.0	0.0	.57735	.70711	-.40825
5	0.0	0.0	0.0	.57735	0.0	.81650
6	0.0	0.0	0.0	.57735	-.70711	-.40825

TESTS OF SIGNIFICANCE FOR WITHIN CELLS USING SEQUENTIAL SUMS OF SQUARES

SOURCE OF VARIATION	WILKS LAMBDA	APPROX MULT F	SIG. OF F	AVERAGED F	SIG. OF F
CONSTANT	.00364	13265.73310	0.0	6596.71525	0.0
SECTION	.80860	1.81181	.048	1.39369	.171

Table 11-2. Estimates for Transformed Overall Variables

ESTIMATES FOR KOVERALL

CONSTANT

PARAMETER	COEFF.	STD. ERR.	T-VALUE	SIG. OF T	LOWER .95 CL	UPPER .95 CL
1	109.8816712657	1.83851	59.76678	0.0	106.23321	113.53013

SECTION

PARAMETER	COEFF.	STD. ERR.	T-VALUE	SIG. OF T	LOWER .95 CL	UPPER .95 CL
2	-6.0388238081	4.90036	-1.23232	.221	-15.76342	3.68577
3	-5.7322252786	4.23614	-1.35317	.179	-14.13870	2.67425
4	1.0778192785	4.34225	.24822	.804	-7.53924	9.69488
5	-1.6655175244	4.73564	-.35170	.726	-11.06325	7.73221
6	10.4736384944	4.73564	2.21166	.029	1.07591	19.87137
7	.9054149230	4.45946	.20303	.840	-7.94425	9.75508

ESTIMATES FOR AOVERALL

CONSTANT

PARAMETER	COEFF.	STD. ERR.	T-VALUE	SIG. OF T	LOWER .95 CL	UPPER .95 CL
1	115.6338147535	.76030	152.09063	0.0	114.12503	117.14260

SECTION

PARAMETER	COEFF.	STD. ERR.	T-VALUE	SIG. OF T	LOWER .95 CL	UPPER .95 CL
2	-5.2093979928	2.02649	-2.57065	.012	-9.23090	-1.18789
3	1.1320937914	1.75181	.64624	.520	-2.34432	4.60850
4	4.6669324251	1.79569	2.59896	.011	1.10344	8.23043
5	.6645035491	1.95837	.33931	.735	-3.22183	4.55083
6	-.8709161916	1.95837	-.44471	.658	-4.75725	3.01542
7	-2.5405535878	1.84416	-1.37762	.171	-6.20024	1.11913

Table 11-3. Tests of Within-Subjects Part of Design

WITHIN CELLS CORRELATIONS WITH STD. DEVS. ON DIAGONAL

	KLIN	KQUAD	ALIN	AQUAD
KLIN	9.83458			
KQUAD	-.42558	6.62479		
ALIN	-.15845	.05401	10.46165	
AQUAD	-.17298	.06116	.51325	7.91753

DETERMINANT = .58099
BARTLETT TEST OF SPHERICITY = 52.04035 WITH 6 D. F.
SIGNIFICANCE = .000

F(MAX) CRITERION = 2.49377 WITH (4,98) D. F.

TESTS OF SIGNIFICANCE FOR WITHIN CELLS USING SEQUENTIAL SUMS OF SQUARES

SOURCE OF VARIATION	WILKS LAMBDA	APPROX MULT F	SIG. OF F	AVERAGED F	SIG. OF F
OCCASION	.29614	56.44873	0.0	63.32050	0.0
SECTION AND OCCASION	.73431	1.28281	.172	1.33990	.133

UNIVARIATE F-TESTS WITH (6.98) D. F.

VARIABLE	HYPOTH. SS	ERROR SS	HYPOTH. MS	ERROR MS	F	SIG. OF F
KLIN	321.73169	9478.45451	53.62195	96.71892	.55441	.765
KQUAD	457.67706	4301.00993	76.27951	43.88786	1.73806	.120
ALIN	599.66274	10725.72678	99.94379	109.44619	.91318	.489
AQUAD	1135.17279	6143.34789	189.19546	62.68722	3.01809	.009

The remainder of the output provides tests of the within-subjects part of the design and therefore concerns the analysis of the linear and quadratic transformed variables. At the top of table 11-3 is the within-cells correlation matrix. The interesting thing here is the numbers under the matrix. The BARTLETT TEST OF SPHERICITY tests the assumption that the population error covariance matrix is diagonal (this is equivalent to the test that the error correlation matrix is an identity matrix). The results shown here indicate that the hypothesis that the error covariance matrix is diagonal cannot be accepted since $p < .001$, so that assumption may not be made with our data. If that assumption had been supported, we would go on to test the assumption that the variances of the transformed variables are all equal. That assumption is tested by the F MAX CRITERION. If both of these assumptions held up, we could use the AVERAGED F statistic. If only the first holds up, we could use the univariate F statistics.[4]

The next part of table 11-3 indicates that the occasions effect is highly significant (as was the case when we examined knowledge alone), while there is no significant interaction between sections and occasions. Hence, sections do not differ in the way they change over time on either knowledge or attitudes. The last part of table 11-3 shows a univariate analysis of the interaction. This table cannot be produced in a run requesting SIGNIF(BRIEF), but was produced in another run in which the full output was requested. These results are presented only for illustration, since the assumptions that require their use have not been upheld.

Finally, the program produces estimates for the linear and quadratic transformed variables. These tables are similar to those shown above for the overall variables and so are not reproduced here.

Other designs are possible both for within subjects and between subjects. That is, for between subjects it would be possible to superimpose a two-way analysis of variance on a repeated measures design. In addition, it would be possible to expose each subject to two or more treatments, taking several measurements for each treatment, thereby having a more complicated within-subjects design. Finally, it is possible to also combine repeated measures analysis with the analysis of covariance, that is, to introduce covariates as control variables for the dependent repeated measures.

Notes

1. For each variable, linear and quadratic, the sum of squares for the constant, $(\Sigma x_i)^2/N$, is the occasions sum of squares, while the sum of squares for deviations is the subjects by occasions sum of squares $\Sigma x_i^2 - (\Sigma x_i)^2/N$.)

2. For four or more occasions, the transformations invoked by WSDESIGN are not orthogonal polynomials. It is possible to obtain orthogonal polynomial transformations by

using the TRANSFORM command and then leaving out the next card. The output produced by such a procedure is somewhat more difficult to interpret than that presented here but it will be correct.

3. The averaged F is equal to

$$[\text{tr}(S_B^*)/(\text{d.f. for } S_B)]/[\text{tr}(S_W^*)/(\text{d.f. for } S_W)]$$

where S_B^* and S_W^* are the SSCP submatrices concerned only with KOVERALL and AOVERALL.

4. The F max statistic tests for the equivalence of two or more variances. It is the ratio of the largest estimated variance to the smallest. The degrees of freedom for the statistic are the number of variances and the degrees of freedom for the S_W matrix. Critical values for the F max statistic are given in Winer, 1971.

APPENDIXES

A THE GREEK ALPHABET

A	α	Alpha
B	β	Beta
Γ	γ	Gamma
Δ	δ	Delta
E	ϵ	Epsilon
Z	ζ	Zeta
H	η	Eta
Θ	θ	Theta
I	ι	Iota
K	κ	Kappa
Λ	λ	Lambda
M	μ	Mu
N	ν	Nu
Ξ	ξ	Xi
O	o	Omicron
Π	π	Pi
P	ρ	Rho
Σ	σ	Sigma
T	τ	Tau
Υ	υ	Upsilon
Φ	ϕ	Phi
X	χ	Chi
Ψ	ψ	Psi
Ω	ω	Omega
	∂	Delta (old)

B RANDOM VARIABLES, EXPECTED VALUES, AND VARIANCE

Random Variables

The idea of a random variable is basic to probability theory and the mathematical development of statistics. A nontechnical definition of a random variable is that it is a variable whose values have certain probabilities.

Random variables can be derived, that is, formed from combinations of other random variables. Thus, the mean of a random sample is a random variable; each possible value it might take has a certain probability. Technically, the values of random variables do not have to be numbers, but I will assume here that they are. Random variables can be either *continuous* or *discrete*. By a discrete random variable I mean one that takes only certain values like zero or one to stand for male or female, or a count of the number of objects that fall into a certain category. Discrete random variables have only a finite number of possible values between any two specified values. A continuous random variable is one that can have any possible numerical value within a certain range. The technical definition of continuousness is that for any two values of the variable, no matter how close, it is possible to find a value between those two values which the variable could take. There are no gaps in a continuous variable, and thus there are an infinite number of possible values. An example of a continuous random variable

213

might be age. In this book we usually assume that our random variables are at least theoretically continuous although the way we measure them might be somewhat inexact and yield only certain values. For example, although we can think of age as continuous, the clock we use to measure time might only measure down to a tenth of a second.

Expected Values

The idea of expected values is an extension and an abstraction of the idea of a mean. It is an idea that is applied to random variables and their probability distributions. For discrete random variables it is defined as

$$E(x) = \sum_i x_i p(x_i)$$

Where the summation is over all possible values of the random variable x, and $p(x)$ is the probability function of x. This expression means that we multiply each possible value of x times the probability of that value and add up all those products. For example, suppose we are tossing a coin and assign the value 0 to heads and 1 to tails. The probability of each of these values is assumed to be $1/2$. The expected value of the variable is $(0)(1/2) + (1)(1/2) = 1/2$. The expected value may be thought of as the average value over an infinite number of trials or cases. (Although the random variable can take only a finite number of values, we can think of an infinite number of cases or, in this case, flips of the coin.) To see the relationship of expected value to the mean, imagine that we plan to flip the coin 100 times. We expect that about half of the time it will be heads, the other half tails. Therefore, the value of our variable will be 1 about 50 times and 0 the other 50. The formula for the mean is

$$\bar{x} = \frac{\sum_i x_i}{n}$$

If we get 50 tails Σx_i will be 50. $N = 100$, so $\bar{x}$ will be .5. Although $\bar{x}$ will not usually be exactly .5 for any finite number of flips, the larger the number of flips the closer $\bar{x}$ will be to .5 ($\bar{x}$ is said to *converge* on .5).

The expected value of a continuous distribution is somewhat more complicated to define, in fact it requires the idea from calculus of an integral. For readers who are familiar with integrals the definition is

$$E(x) = \int xp(x)\,dx$$

where the limits of integration are minus infinity to plus infinity. This can be thought of as a way of writing the sum of an infinite number of things, in this case the sum of the product of the infinite number of possible x's times their $p(x)$'s.

The idea of the mean of a population is sometimes defined in terms of an expectation:

$$\mu = E(x)$$

And it can be shown that

$$E(\bar{x}) = \mu$$

Which means that the expected value of the mean of a sample from a population is the mean of the population. Roughly speaking, if we were to take an infinite number of samples from the population and compute the mean of each, the mean of those means would be the population mean μ.

There is an algebra of expectations that enables us to manipulate them. There are a couple of rules (these can be proven mathematically, the reader should be able to verify them intuitively). The first rule is

$$E(cx) = cE(x)$$

That is, the expectation of a constant times a random variable is equal to the constant times the expectation of the random variable.

The second rule is

$$E(x + y) = E(x) + E(y)$$

if x and y are independent. That is, the expectation of the sum of two independent random variables is the sum of their expectations. Both of these formulas can be proven by making use of the properties of summations, i.e., $\Sigma cxp(x) = c\Sigma xp(x)$ and $\Sigma(x + y) = \Sigma x + \Sigma y$.

Variance

The idea of variance can be defined in expectation terms. Recall the formula

$$\sigma_x^2 = \frac{\Sigma(x - \bar{x})^2}{n}$$

for computing variance in a sample.

We will define the variance as

$$V(x) = E[x - E(x)]^2$$

that is, the expectation of the square of the difference between a value and its expectation. An equivalent definition is: $V(x) = E(x^2) - [E(x)]^2$. Since expectations are like means, the variance defined this way is like the average of the squares of the differences between values and their mean, so it conforms to the formula for σ^2 above. The mathematical advantage to this definition is that it applies to an infinite number of cases or trials, while it is hard to think of a summation of such an infinite number of trials.

There is also an algebra of variance. In particular, $V(cx) = c^2 V(x)$, $V(x + y) = V(x) + V(y)$, and $V(x - y) = V(x) + V(y)$, if x and y are independent.

It can be shown (by probability theory) that the expected value of

$$\sigma^2 = \frac{\Sigma(x_i - \bar{x})^2}{n}$$

where this is computed from sample data, is not the population variance. Symbolically,

$$E\left(\frac{\Sigma(x_i - \bar{x})^2}{n}\right) \neq V(x)$$

The formula $\Sigma(x - \bar{x})^2/n$ is thus said to be a *biased* estimator of $V(x)$ in the population. However, $n - 1$ in the denominator fixes things up. That is,

$$E\left(\frac{\Sigma(x_i - \bar{x})^2}{n - 1}\right) = V(x)$$

where $V(x)$ is the population variance.

Covariance

The covariance of two variables is a measure of how much they vary together. For a population, covariance is defined as

$$\text{cov}(x, y) = E[(x - E(x))(y - E(y))] = E(xy) - E(x)E(y)$$

In a sample the covariance is found by

$$\text{cov}(x, y) = \frac{\Sigma(x - \bar{x})(y - \bar{y})}{n}$$

and the unbiased estimator of the population covariance is

$$\frac{\Sigma(x - \bar{x})(y - \bar{y})}{n - 1}$$

The covariance takes the value of zero when there is no relationship between the variables, it is positive if the variables are positively related and negative if they are negatively related. The covariance is often used in statistics, but it is hard to interpret standing by itself, because its size is affected by the variances of the variables. We need a concept that better reflects the relationship, that gives us an index of relationship between variables that is not dependent on their variances. We thus define the correlation coefficient for populations:

$$\rho = \frac{\text{cov}(x, y)}{\sqrt{V(x)V(y)}}$$

that is, the covariance of the variables divided by the square roots of the variances of the variables (the standard deviations).

For samples, the correlation coefficient r is defined as

$$r = \frac{[\Sigma(x_i - \bar{x})(y_i - \bar{y})]/(n - 1)}{\sqrt{\Sigma(x_i - x)^2/(n - 1)}\sqrt{\Sigma(y_i - y)^2/(n - 1)}}$$

which reduces to

$$r = \frac{\Sigma(x_i - \bar{x})(y_i - \bar{y})}{\sqrt{\Sigma(x_i - x)^2 \Sigma(y_i - y)^2}}$$

Some Proofs of Commonly Used Variance and Expectation Formulas

1. Show that $E(\bar{x}) = E(x)$:

$$E(\bar{x}) = E(\Sigma x/n) = (1/n)E(\Sigma x)$$
$$= (1/n)[E(x_1) + E(x_2) + \cdots + E(x_n)]$$

but $E(x_1) = E(x_2) = \cdots = E(x_n)$, so we have

$$E(\bar{x}) = (n/n)E(x) = E(x)$$

2. Show that $V(cx) = c^2 V(x)$:

$$V(cx) = E[cx - E(cx)]^2 = E[cx - cE(x)]^2$$
$$= E[c(x - E(x))]^2 = c^2 E[x - E(x)]^2 = c^2 V(x)$$

3. Show that $V(x + y) = V(x) + V(y)$ if x and y are independent:

$$V(x + y) = E[(x + y)^2] - [E(x + y)]^2$$
$$= E(x^2 + 2xy + y^2) - [E(x) + E(y)]^2$$
$$= E(x^2) + 2E(xy) + E(y^2) - [E(x)]^2 - 2E(x)E(y) - [E(y)]^2$$

Consider the term $E(xy)$. This is equal to

$$\sum_i \sum_j x_i y_j p(x_i, y_j)$$

If x_i and y_j are independent, the multiplication rule holds and we have

$$p(x_i, y_j) = p(x_i) p(y_j)$$

therefore

$$E(xy) = \sum_i \sum_j x_i y_j p(x_i) p(y_j) = \sum_i x_i p(x_i) \sum_j y_j p(y_j) = E(x)E(y)$$

so the $2E(xy)$ and $-2E(x)E(y)$ terms drop out and we have

$$E(x^2) - [E(x)]^2 + E(y^2) - [E(y)]^2 = V(x) + V(y)$$

4. It is left to the reader to prove that $V(x - y)$ is also equal to $V(x) + V(y)$.
5. Show that $V(\bar{x}) = V(x)/n$:

$$V(\bar{x}) = V(\Sigma x/n) = (1/n^2) V(\Sigma x)$$

Above we found that $V(x + y) = V(x) + V(y)$. Extending this to a sum of n x_i's we have

$$V(\bar{x}) = (1/n^2)[V(x_1) + V(x_2) + \cdots + V(x_n)]$$

All of the $V(x_i)$ are the same, so we have

$$V(\bar{x}) = (n/n^2) V(x) = V(x)/n$$

6. Now we will show that $[\Sigma(x_i - \bar{x})^2]/[n - 1]$ is an unbiased estimator of $V(x)$. To simplify the algebra, we assume first of all that $\mu = 0$ (i.e., $E(x) = 0$). We can do this without affecting our argument because changing the mean of a distribution does not change its variance. We want to find

$$E\left(\frac{\Sigma(x_i - \bar{x})^2}{n - 1}\right) = [1/(n - 1)] [E(\Sigma x^2) - 2E(\bar{x}\Sigma x) + E(n\bar{x}^2)]$$

But $\Sigma x = n\bar{x}$, so we have

$$[1/(n - 1)] [E(\Sigma x^2) - nE(\bar{x}^2)]$$

$$= [1/(n - 1)] [E(x_1^2 + x_2^2 + \cdots + x_n^2) - nE(\bar{x}^2)]$$

$$= [1/(n - 1)] [E(x_1^2) + E(x_2^2) + \cdots + E(x_n^2) - nE(\bar{x}^2)]$$

The $E(x^2)$ are all the same, so we have

$$[1/(n-1)] [nE(x^2) - nE(\bar{x}^2)] = [n/(n-1)] [E(x^2) - E(\bar{x}^2)]$$

Since $E(x) = 0$, $E(x^2) = V(x)$ and $E(\bar{x}^2) = V(\bar{x}) = V(x)/n$, so we have

$$[n/(n-1)] [V(x) - V(x)/n] = V(x)[n/(n-1)] [1 - 1/n] = V(x)$$

7. Show that $V(b) = (X'X)^{-1}\sigma^2$:

$$b = (X'X)^{-1}X'y$$

so

$$V(b) = V[(X'X)^{-1}X'y]$$

But $(X'X)^{-1}X'$ is a matrix of constants, so

$$V[(X'X)^{-1}X'y] = (X'X)^{-1}X'[V(y)]X(X'X)^{-1}$$

If the y_i's are independent, then $V(y) = \sigma^2 I$ where σ^2 is the variance of the y's at each combination of x values. Therefore,

$$V(b) = (X'X)^{-1}X'\sigma^2 IX(X'X)^{-1}$$
$$= \sigma^2(X'X)^{-1}(X'X)(X'X)^{-1}$$
$$= \sigma^2(X'X)^{-1}$$

C A LITTLE CALCULUS

In the development of statistical theory it is sometimes necessary to maximize or minimize a function of some variable or variables. That is, it is necessary to find the value or values of the variable or variables that maximize or minimize the function. We call on the differential calculus to find the values that do this.

To get to the point that we can easily find the values that maximize or minimize a function requires the development of a number of ideas.

Slopes of Functions

The differential calculus is concerned with slopes of functions. Consider the simple linear function $f(x) = 2 + .5x$ shown in figure C-1.

The y intercept (the value of $f(x)$ at $x = 0$) of this function is 2 and the slope is .5. By the slope we mean the amount of change in $f(x)$ for an increase of one unit in x. Therefore the slope of a function is also called its rate of change.

Slopes of linear functions (functions represented by straight lines) are easy, they are the same all along the line, and if that were the only kind of function that existed we would not need the differential calculus. But some functions are

221

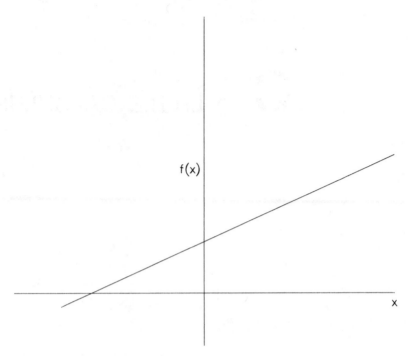

Figure C-1. Simple Linear Function.

not linear, they are represented by curved lines. For example, we might have an $f(x)$ represented as in figure C-2. Here the slope of the curve is different at different points or at different values of x. In fact, we even need a definition of what the slope is. We will say that the slope of a function at x_0 is the slope of the tangent to the curve at x_0. The tangent of the above curve at x_0 has been drawn in.

Given a function of x (that is, given the rule that gives us a value of $f(x)$ for values of x), we need a way to determine the slope at various values of x. Since the slope takes different values at different values of x, we can think of that as another function of x, which we will designate $f'(x)$ (the *derivative* of $f(x)$).

We get at the determination of derivatives through the concept of limits.

Limits

The limit of the function $f(x)$ as x approaches some number x_0 is the number that $f(x)$ gets closer and closer to as x gets closer and closer to x_0. The function

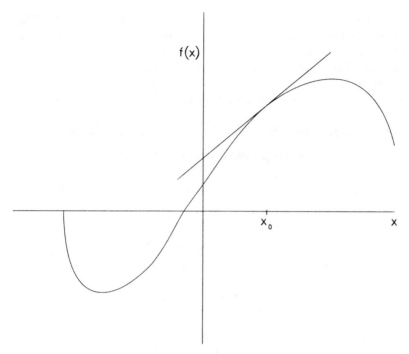

Figure C-2. Curved Function.

$f(x)$ may or may not actually touch its limit. For example, if $f(x) = 2x$, as x
approaches 0, $f(x)$ also approaches 0, so we say that the limit of $f(x)$ as x approaches 0 is 0. We, however, never let x actually get to x_0. We write limits
like this,

$$\lim_{x \to x_0} f(x) = L$$

which is read, "The limit of $f(x)$ as x approaches x_0 is L." A limit is formally
defined as follows:

$\lim_{x \to a} f(x) = L$ means that for any ϵ, no matter how small, there is a δ, such that
if $0 < |x - a| < \delta$ then $|f(x) - L| < \epsilon$.

Basically, this means that we can get $f(x)$ as close to L as we want by choosing
x properly. This definition does not provide us a way of determining what the
limit is in a particular situation. However, if we have an idea about what the
limit is, we can determine whether that idea is right by applying the definition.

Sometimes a function has a different limit at a particular point, depending on the direction from which we approach the point. An example is shown in figure C-3. As x approaches 0 from the positive side, the function has a limit of +1, if from the negative side the limit is –1. Luckily, we will not deal further with such functions here.

There is an algebra of limits. In particular:

- The limit of the sum of two functions is equal to the sum of the limits:

$$\lim_{x \to c} [f(x) + g(x)] = \lim_{x \to c} f(x) + \lim_{x \to c} g(x)$$

- The limit of the product of two functions is equal to the product of their limits:

$$\lim_{x \to c} [f(x)g(x)] = \lim_{x \to c} f(x) \lim_{x \to c} g(x)$$

- The limit of the reciprocal of a function is equal to the reciprocal of its limit:

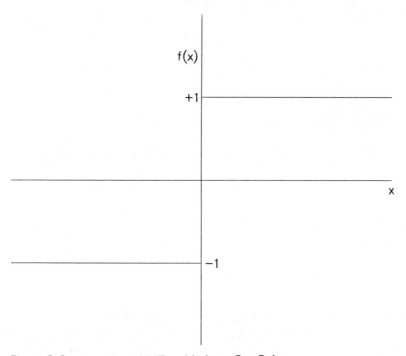

Figure C-3.   Function with Two Limits at One Point.

$$\lim_{x \to c} \frac{1}{f(x)} = \frac{1}{\lim_{x \to c} f(x)}$$

if $\lim_{x \to c} f(x) \neq 0$.

It should be obvious that $\lim_{x \to 0} x$ and $\lim_{x \to 0} x^n$ (for n equal to any positive number) are both zero.

In what follows, we must deal with situations in which we have to find the limit of something divided by x, as x goes to zero. That is:

$$\lim_{x \to 0} \frac{something}{x}$$

This may look like a big problem since we can never divide by zero. The above does not require us to divide by zero, however; rather we are supposed to figure out what happens when x gets closer and closer to zero. Sometimes the problem is solved when the something is equal to zero already; in that case, the limit is also zero. Other times, x will divide evenly into the something so nothing is left in the denominator. (We can perform this division because we never let x actually become zero.)

Derivatives

Imagine a function $f(x)$ such as that shown in figure C-4 whose slope at $x = x_0$ we wish to determine. At x_0 the function has the value $f(x_0)$. Imagine also the value of x at $x_0 + b$. The function at that value has the value $f(x_0 + b)$. In the above diagram, I have drawn in the straight line connecting the points $[x_0, f(x_0)]$ and $[x_0 + b, f(x_0 + b)]$. Consider the slope of this line. It is the average rate of change in $f(x)$ from x_0 to $x_0 + b$. The slope of that line may be written as

$$\frac{f(x_0 + b) - f(x_0)}{b}$$

That is, how much $f(x)$ changes from x_0 to $x_0 + b$ divided by the change in x, which is b.

Now imagine that we let the point $x_0 + b$ get closer and closer to x_0, that is, let b get smaller and smaller. As that happens, $f(x_0 + b)$ gets closer and closer to $f(x_0)$, but more importantly to us, the line connecting the two points gets closer

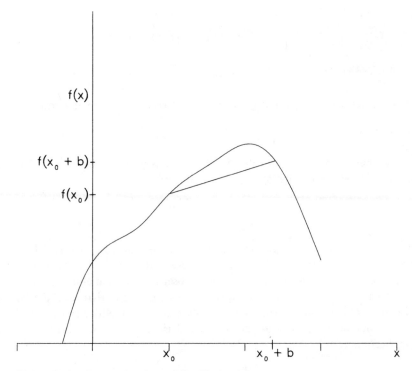

Figure C–4.   Determination of the Derivative.

and closer to the tangent line at x_0. Therefore, the slope gets closer and closer to the slope of the tangent. Thus, as b approaches 0 the limit of the slope of the line is the slope of the tangent. We therefore define the derivative of $f(x)$ at x_0 [represented by $f'(x_0)$] as

$$f'(x_0) = \lim_{b \to 0} \frac{f(x_0 + b) - f(x_0)}{b}$$

As mentioned above, this can be thought of as a new function of x. That is, we can often easily find a rule that will give us the slope for any value of x we plug into the rule, so we will drop the subscript from x_0 and just talk about $f'(x)$ as the derivative of $f(x)$. The process of finding derivatives is often called *differentiation*.

We will need a number of derivatives in statistical work, so let's see if we can apply the above definition to some functions of x. Begin with the simplest:

$f(x) = c$ ($f(x)$ is a constant, no matter what x is.

                      The graph is a horizontal line.)

Plugging this into the definition, we get

$$f'(x) = \lim_{b \to 0} \frac{f(x+b) - f(x)}{b} = \lim_{b \to 0} \frac{c - c}{b} = 0$$

The numerator is 0 no matter how close the denominator is to 0, and b is never allowed to become 0, so the limit of the ratio is 0. Of course, this conforms to what we know, that the slope of a horizontal line is 0.

Let's try $f(x) = cx$:

$$f'(x) = \lim_{b \to 0} \frac{[c(x+b) - cx]}{b} = \lim_{b \to 0} \frac{cx + cb - cx}{b} = \lim_{b \to 0} c = c$$

In the final step, b has dropped out and only c remains. Now let $f(x) = x^2$. We have

$$f'(x) = \lim_{b \to 0} \frac{(x+b)^2 - x^2}{b} = \lim_{b \to 0} \frac{x^2 + 2bx + b^2 - x^2}{b}$$

$$= \lim_{b \to 0} (2x + b) = 2x$$

This is our first function with a derivative that differs for different x.

Now let $f(x) = x^n$. We have

$$f'(x) = \lim_{b \to 0} \frac{(x+b)^n - x^n}{b}$$

There is a bit of a problem here. The expansion of $(x+b)^n$ is tedious. It turns out, however, that we only have to worry about a few terms. This is the expansion of a binomial. The reader may remember that it looks like this: $x^n + nx^{n-1}b +$ terms involving a number times x to a power less than $n - 1$ times b to a power greater than 1, ending in the term b^n, so the limit looks like this:

$$\lim_{b \to 0} \frac{(x^n + nx^{n-1}b + cx^{n-2}b^2 + dx^{n-3}b^3 + \cdots + b^n) - x^n}{b}$$

For our purposes, it does not matter what c, d, etc., are (they are binomial coefficients). The x^n's cancel each other out. So we have

$$\lim_{b \to 0} \left(\frac{nx^{n-1}b}{b} + \frac{cx^{n-2}b^2}{b} + \frac{dx^{n-3}b^3}{b} + \cdots + \frac{b^n}{b} \right) = \lim_{b \to 0} (nx^{n-1} + cx^{n-2}b$$

$$+ dx^{n-3}b^2 + \cdots + b^{n-1})$$

In this expression, since b is going to 0, all the terms except the first (which doesn't contain b) go to 0 so we are left with $f'(x) = nx^{n-1}$.

Putting this rule together with an earlier one, we have for the derivative of $f(x) = cx^n$,

$$f'(x) = ncx^{n-1}$$

Rather conveniently, the derivative of a sum of two functions is equal to the sum of the separate derivatives. This may be shown as follows: If $F(x) = f(x) + g(x)$,

$$F'(x) = \lim_{b \to 0} \frac{F(x+b) - F(x)}{b}$$

$$= \lim_{b \to 0} \frac{[f(x+b) + g(x+b)] - [f(x) + g(x)]}{b}$$

$$= \lim_{b \to 0} \frac{f(x+b) - f(x)}{b} + \lim_{b \to 0} \frac{g(x+b) - g(x)}{b}$$

$$= f'(x) + g'(x)$$

The derivatives of products and ratios of functions are more complicated. We will not try to prove them. For products, if $F(x) = f(x)g(x)$ then $F'(x) = g(x)f'(x) + f(x)g'(x)$. For ratios, if $F(x) = f(x)/g(x)$ then $F'(x) = [g(x)f'(x) - f(x)g'(x)]/[g(x)]^2$.

There are a number of other notations in use for derivatives. One common one that we will use is

$$\frac{df(x)}{dx}$$

This is not to be interpreted as a fraction. (It is not $df(x)$ divided by dx.) Sometimes we abbreviate this notation as df/dx.

Second Derivatives. Sometimes we will want to find the derivative of a derivative. This is called a second derivative and is symbolized $f''(x)$ or $d^2f(x)/dx^2$. For example, if $f(x) = x^2$, $f'(x) = 2x$ and $f''(x) = 2$.

Functions of Functions. At times we will deal with functions of functions. That is, we may have f as some function of y [that is, $f(y)$], and y as some function of x [that is, $y(x)$]. For example, if $f(y) = y^2$ and $y(x) = 2x$, then $f[y(x)] = (2x)^2 = 4x^2$. The derivative of a function of a function is $df/dx = (df/dy)(dy/dx)$, where df/dy means the derivative of f with respect to y and dy/dx means the derivative of y with respect to x. For our example,

$$\frac{d(y^2)}{dy} = 2y \quad \text{and} \quad \frac{d(2x)}{dx} = 2$$

so

$$\frac{df(y)}{dx} = (2y)(2) = 4y$$

But $y = 2x$, so we can plug that in and get

$$\frac{df(y)}{dx} = 8x$$

Of course, we could have gotten this another way by taking the derivative directly:

$$\frac{d(4x^2)}{dx} = 8x$$

The procedure for finding the derivative of a function of a function is called the *chain rule*.

Other Derivatives. A few other derivatives that are useful are:

$$d(\ln x)/dx = 1/x$$

that is, the derivative of the natural log of x is $1/x$ and

$$d(e^x)/dx = e^x$$

that is, the derivative of e^x is itself.

Minima and Maxima

One of the most important uses of derivatives is to find maxima and minima of functions. The reason we can do that is that when a function is a maximum or minimum, the slope of the tangent line is zero so the derivative is zero. Hence, if we can find the derivative of a function, set it equal to zero, and solve for x, we have the value of x at which the original function is either a maximum or minimum. Let's take an example:

Suppose $f(x) = (x - 1)^2 + 3$. This function looks like figure C-5. We want to find the point at which $f(x)$ is a minimum.

We can use the chain rule by letting $x - 1$ equal a function (say $g(x)$). Then

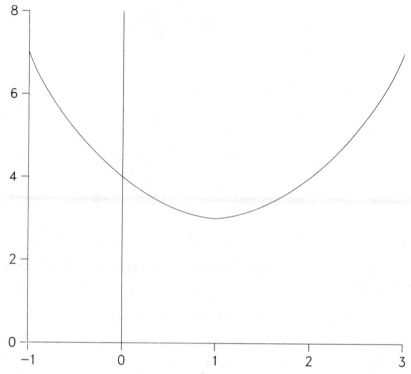

Figure C-5.   Graph of $f(x) = (x - 1)^2 + 3$.

$f[g(x)] = [g(x)]^2 + 3$. Then $df/dx = (df/dg)(dg/dx) = [2g(x) + 0] 1 = 2(x - 1) =$ $2x - 2$. Set this equal to 0 and solve for x:

$$2x - 2 = 0 \quad \text{and} \quad x = 1.$$

Usually this is as much as we want, but we could also find the value of $f(x)$ at the minimum by substituting this value of x into our original function. When we do that here we find $f(1) = 3$.

When we find the value of x that makes the derivative zero, we do not know on the face of it whether the function is a maximum or minimum at that point. To find out, we could plug in some values of x on either side of our value to see if the function is higher or lower at these points. However, there is a better way. That is to look at the value of the second derivative at that point. If the second derivative is positive the point will be a minimum. For example, in the above function on the left side of the curve, the slope is negative. It gets less negative as we move to the right until at $x = 1$ the slope is zero. Then the slope gets more and more positive. Therefore, the slope is increasing (i.e., the rate of change of the slope is positive), so the derivative of the slope is positive, so the second derivative of $f(x)$ is positive.

On the other hand, if the second derivative is negative where the first derivative is zero the point will be a maximum. The algebra of this, for our example, is

$$\frac{d^2f}{dx^2} = \frac{d(2x-2)}{dx} = 2 \qquad \text{(which is positive for all } x)$$

However, this is not quite the whole story, because there is one other situation in which the slope (and derivative) can be zero, yet the function is neither a maximum nor a minimum. This is when the function has a *point of inflection*. That situation looks like figure C-6. When that happens, the second derivative at that point is also equal to 0. It should be noted that this process finds "local" maxima and minima, that is, points at which the curve reaches its highest or lowest level in a neighborhood. These points are not necessarily the highest or lowest points for the whole curve.

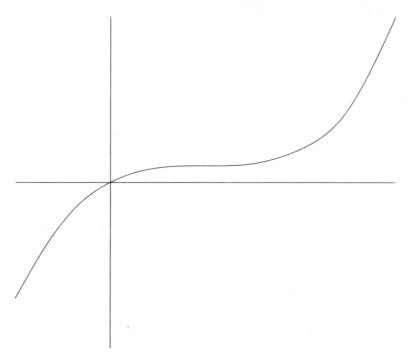

Figure C-6. Point of Inflection.

Problems

1. Find the derivatives of the following functions (find df/dx).
   a. $f(x) = 2x^3 + 3x^2 - 5x + 4$
   b. $f(x) = 3x^{-2}$
   c. $f(x) = \sqrt{x}$
   d. $f(x) = 1/\sqrt{x}$
   e. $f(x) = e^{2x}$
   f. $f(x) = \ln x^r$

(Use a rule regarding logarithms before trying to take derivatives.)

   g. $f(x) = (x^2 + 3x + 2)^3$ (Use the chain rule.)

2. Determine the maximum, minimum, or points of inflection of 1a. Functions 1b through 1f do not have maximum or minimum. How can you tell that from the derivative? (Facile students may be able to find the maximum and minimum of g.)

3. If $df/dx = 2x$, what is $f(x)$? (This is called finding *antiderivatives* and is essentially the process of *integration* in the integral calculus. It turns out that there is no one answer to this question. See if you can express in some way the infinite number of possible answers.)

Partial Derivatives

The functions we have talked about up to now have been functions of only one variable, x. In statistics we deal with functions of more than one variable so we need to know how to take their derivatives. Let's take as an example the function $f(x_1,x_2) = x_1^2 + x_2^2$. This function looks like figure C-7. Now we can take the derivative of $f(x_1,x_2)$ "with respect to" either x_1 or x_2. When we take the derivative with respect to x_1, x_2 will be treated as a constant and vice versa. We call such derivatives *partial derivatives* and symbolize them like this:

$$\frac{\partial(fx_1,x_2)}{\partial x_1} \quad \text{or} \quad \frac{\partial(fx_1,x_2)}{\partial x_2}$$

Another notation for partial derivatives is $f_1(x_1,x_2)$ or $f_2(x_1,x_2)$. So, for the above function, we have two possible partial derivatives:

$$f_1(x_1,x_2) = \partial f/\partial x_1 = 2x_1 \quad \text{and} \quad f_2(x_1,x_2) = \partial f/\partial x_2 = 2x_2$$

To find the point at which $f(x_1,x_2)$ is a minimum (or maximum) we set both partial derivatives equal to zero and solve the set of equations for x_1 and x_2. For our example, this is easy:

$$\frac{\partial f}{\partial x_1} = 2x_1 = 0$$

$$\frac{\partial f}{\partial x_2} = 2x_2 = 0$$

so

$$x_1 = 0 \quad \text{and} \quad x_2 = 0$$

Finding the Regression Coefficients

Now let's apply these ideas to finding the b's in a regression equation with one independent variable. The desired equation is:

$$\hat{y}_i = b_0 + b_1 x_i$$

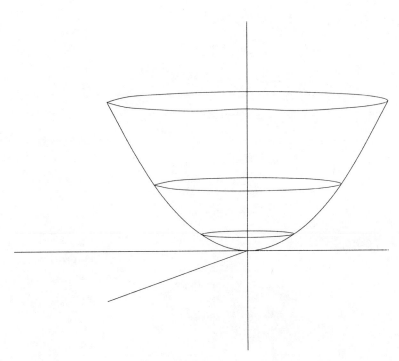

Figure C-7. Function of Two Variables.

We want to find the b's such that

$$L = \sum_i (y_i - \hat{y}_i)^2 \quad \text{is minimized}$$

Substitute $b_0 + b_1 x_i$ for $\hat{y}_i$:

$$L = \sum_i [y_i - (b_0 + b_1 x_i)]^2$$

In this expression the y_i's and x_i's are assumed to be given (that is our data), b_0 and b_1 are unknown. So L is a function of b_0 and b_1 and we want to know what values of b_0 and b_1 will minimize it. L looks like figure C–8. Unfortunately we have to go through some algebra before we can take derivatives. First, expand the square:

$$L = \sum_i (y_i - b_0 - b_1 x_i)^2$$

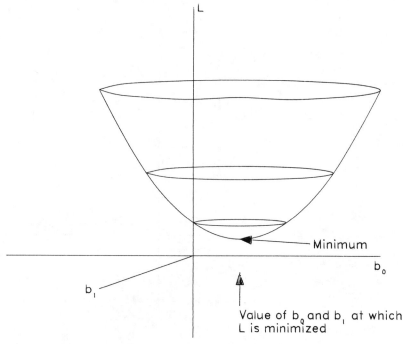

Function C-8.   The Least Squares Solution for Regression Coefficients.

$$= \sum_i (y_i^2 + b_0^2 + b_1^2 x_i^2 - 2b_0 y_i - 2b_1 x_i y_i + 2b_0 b_1 x_i)$$

Then distribute the summation to get

$$L = \Sigma y_i^2 + \Sigma b_0^2 + \Sigma b_1^2 x_i^2 - \Sigma 2b_0 y_i - \Sigma 2b_1 x_i y_i + \Sigma 2b_0 b_1 x_i$$

The summations are over the y_i's and x_i's so the 2's, b_0's and b_1's can be brought in front of the summation signs. We have then

$$L = \Sigma y^2 + nb_0^2 + b_1^2 \Sigma x_i^2 - 2b_0 \Sigma y_i - 2b_1 \Sigma x_i y_i + 2b_0 b_1 \Sigma x_i$$

Now take the partial derivatives of this with respect to b_0 and b_1:

$$\frac{\partial L}{\partial b_0} = 2nb_0 - 2\Sigma y_i + 2b_1 \Sigma x_i$$

$$\frac{\partial L}{\partial b_1} = 2b_1 \Sigma x_i^2 - 2\Sigma x_i y_i + 2b_0 \Sigma x_i$$

Setting each of these equations equal to zero, dividing through by two, and rearranging terms we have

$$\Sigma y_i = nb_0 + b_1 \Sigma x_i$$
$$\Sigma x_i y_i = b_i \Sigma x_i^2 + b_0 \Sigma x_i$$

These equations are sometimes called the *normal* equations. We have two simultaneous equations which if solved will produce the familiar expressions for b_0 and b_1.

Problems

1. Find $\partial f/\partial x_1$ and $\partial f/\partial x_2$:
$$f(x_1, x_2) = 3x_1^3 + 2x_1^2 x_2 + 5x_1 x_2^2 + 4x_2^3 + 6$$

2. Find $\partial f/\partial x_1$ and $\partial f/\partial x_2$ and find the minimum or maximum:
$$f(x_1, x_2) = 6x_1^2 + 4x_1 x_2 + 3x_2^2 + 3x_1$$

3. Find all partial first derivatives:
$$f(x_1, x_2, x_3) = 4x_1^2 + 8x_2^2 + 6x_3^2 + 2x_1 x_2 + 4x_1 x_3 + 4x_2 x_3$$

(This is called a quadratic form and can be written as $x'Ax$ where $x' = (x_1, x_2, x_3)$ and A is a symmetric matrix of coefficients. See if you can figure out what A is.)

4. Write the normal equations as an equation involving vectors and matrices where: $\mathbf{b}' = (b_0, b_1)$, $\mathbf{y}$ is a vector of the observations on the dependent variable, and $\mathbf{X}$ is an $n \times 2$ matrix with 1's in the first column and the x observations in the second column.

Vector Derivation

When we get to multiple regression with very many independent variables, we will have long expressions for L with lots of squared terms and cross-product terms. In that circumstance we will want to simplify matters by using matrix and vector algebra. We will have a function L of lots of b's. We will differentiate the function with respect to each of the b's in turn. If we stack all of the b's into a column vector $\mathbf{b}$, we will symbolize all of this partial differentiation in one symbol:

$$\frac{\partial L}{\partial \mathbf{b}}$$

which means we differentiate L with respect to each of the b_i's in $\mathbf{b}$. We will also stack all of the resulting partial derivatives up in a vector. Hence, we are starting with an expression that is not a vector, differentiating with respect to a vector, and we wind up with a vector. Not only that, but we will represent L in the first place as a matrix and vector product.

Suppose we have the function:

$$f(\mathbf{b}) = \underset{1 \times p}{\mathbf{b}'} \underset{p \times 1}{\mathbf{c}}$$

where $\mathbf{b}$ is a vector of variables and $\mathbf{c}$ is a vector of constants. Written out this is

$$f(\mathbf{b}) = (b_1 \quad b_2 \quad \cdots \quad b_p) \begin{pmatrix} c_1 \\ c_2 \\ \cdot \\ \cdot \\ \cdot \\ c_p \end{pmatrix} = b_1 c_1 + b_2 c_2 + \cdots + b_p c_p$$

Now take the partial derivatives with respect to each b_k. The partial derivatives will be constants, c_k, that is $\partial f / \partial b_k = c_k$. We can stack these in a vector, which will be the vector $\mathbf{c}$. So $\partial f / \partial \mathbf{b} = \mathbf{c}$.

Quadratic Forms

Now suppose we have the function $g(\mathbf{b}) = \mathbf{b}'\mathbf{A}\mathbf{b}$, where $\mathbf{A}$ is a $p \times p$ symmetric matrix the entries of which we know. The expression $\mathbf{b}'\mathbf{A}\mathbf{b}$ is called a quadratic form (multiplied out it is a scalar). We want the partial derivatives with respect to each of the b_k's.

Let us write out $\mathbf{b}'\mathbf{Ab}$. We can do this in two steps:

$$\mathbf{b}'\mathbf{Ab} = \mathbf{b}'(\mathbf{Ab})$$

$$= (b_1 \quad b_2 \quad \cdots \quad b_p) \begin{pmatrix} a_{11}b_1 + a_{12}b_2 + \cdots + a_{1p}b_p \\ a_{21}b_1 + a_{22}b_2 + \cdots + a_{2p}b_p \\ \vdots \\ a_{p1}b_1 + a_{p2}b_2 + \cdots + a_{pp}b_p \end{pmatrix}$$

$$= b_1 a_{11} b_1 + b_1 a_{12} b_2 + \cdots + b_1 a_{1p} b_p$$
$$+ b_2 a_{21} b_1 + b_2 a_{22} b_2 + \cdots + b_2 a_{2p} b_p$$
$$+ \quad \cdots \quad + \quad \cdots \quad + \cdots + \quad \cdots$$
$$+ b_p a_{p1} b_1 + b_p a_{p2} b_2 + \cdots + b_p a_{pp} b_p$$

Note that I have arranged this summation so that terms with b_1 are in the first row and first column. Similarly, terms with b_k will be in the kth row and kth column. The derivative of this with respect to b_k ($\partial g / \partial b_k$) will come from those terms that have b_k in them. They can be visualized as follows:

$$+ b_1 a_{1k} b_k +$$
$$+ b_2 a_{2k} b_k +$$
$$\vdots$$
$$b_k a_{k1} b_1 + b_k a_{k2} b_2 + \cdots + b_k a_{kk} b_k + \cdots + b_k a_{kp} b_p$$
$$\vdots$$
$$+ b_p a_{pk} b_k +$$

The sum of the derivatives (with respect to b_k) of the terms in the column will be:

$$a_{1k}b_1 + a_{2k}b_2 + \cdots + 2a_{kk}b_k + \cdots + a_{pk}b_p$$

The sum of the derivatives of the terms in the row will be (leaving out the derivative of $b_k a_{kk} b_k$ which has already been included above):

$$a_{k1}b_1 + a_{k2}b_2 + \cdots + a_{kp}b_p$$

To get the whole partial derivative ($\partial g / \partial b_k$), we add these two lines together. But $\mathbf{A}$ is symmetric, ($a_{kj} = a_{jk}$), so we have pairs of identical terms in the above lines, except for the term $2a_{kk}b_k$. Hence, on adding the two lines, we have

$$2a_{1k}b_1 + 2a_{2k}b_k + \cdots + 2a_{kk}b_k + \cdots + 2a_{kp}b_p$$

This can be written as a vector product. That is,

$$\partial g/\partial b_k = 2a_k' b$$

Where a_k' is the kth row of the A matrix.

We can stack all of the p such partial derivatives up in a vector:

$$2a_1' b$$
$$2a_2' b$$
$$.$$
$$.$$
$$.$$
$$2a_k' b$$
$$.$$
$$.$$
$$.$$
$$2a_p' b$$

Each entry in this vector is two times a row of the A matrix times the vector b. We can represent that by the matrix-vector product $2Ab$. Thus we can summarize the whole thing like this:

$$\partial g/\partial b = 2Ab$$

Now applying this to the regression situation, we want to minimize

$$L = y'y - y'Xb - b'Xy + (XB)'Xb$$

Multiplied out, each of these terms is a scalar. The middle terms are the same. This may be seen by noting that $y'Xb$ is the transpose of $b'X'y$. But since they are both really scalars they must be the same. So we have

$$L = y'y - 2b'X'y + b'X'Xb$$

We take the partial derivatives of this with respect to each of the b_k's. In each of these partial derivatives the term $y'y$ will drop out since it is a constant. The derivatives of the second term $(-2b'X'y)$ may be found by application of the first rule above substituting $-2X'y$ for the vector c. Hence,

$$\frac{\partial(-2b'X'y)}{\partial b} = -2X'y$$

The derivative of the second term $(b'X'Xb)$ may be found from the second rule where we substitute $X'X$ for A (which is legitimate since $X'X$ is a square $p \times p$ symmetric matrix). So we have

$$\frac{\partial (b'X'Xb)}{\partial b} = 2X'Xb$$

Putting these two together, we have

$$\frac{\partial L}{\partial b} = -2X'y + 2X'Xb$$

Setting this equal to zero we have

$$-2X'y + 2X'Xb = 0$$

Dividing through by two and rearranging terms we have

$$X'Xb = X'y$$

This equation involving matrices and vectors is really, once multiplied out, an equation with vectors on both sides. It is the normal equations in matrix form. It represents p equations in p unknown b's (where p is number of independent variables or b's), each equation being a line of the respective vectors. We must solve this system of simultaneous equations for the b's. In other words, we find the b vector.

If $X'X$ is nonsingular, we can multiply both sides of the equation by $(X'X)^{-1}$ to get

$$b = (X'X)^{-1}X'y$$

Hence, finding the b's is reduced to matrix manipulations. We find the SSCP matrix $(X'X)$, take its inverse, and multiply by $X'y$ (which is a column vector). The result is a column vector of b's.

Derivatives of Ratios of Quadratic Forms. The derivative of the ratio of two quadratic forms, $b'Ab/b'Cb$ is similar to that of scalar ratios:

$$[2b'CbAb - 2b'AbCb]/[b'Cb]^2$$

Maximizing a Function Subject to a Constraint

At several points in this book we have the problem of having to maximize a function $F(x_1, x_2, \ldots, x_j)$ subject to some other constraint on the x's which constraint can be written as $g(x_1, x_2, \ldots, x_j) = 0$.

For example, we sometimes want to find the x's that maximize the quadratic form $x'Ax$ subject to $x'x = 1$. The latter condition can be written $g(x_1, x_2, \ldots, x_j) = x'x - 1 = 0$. The problem is sometimes called that of maximizing a function subject to a side condition.

Let's take a two-dimensional example. The quadratic form is

$$F(x_1,x_2) = (x_1,x_2)\begin{pmatrix} a_{11} & a_{12} \\ a_{21} & a_{22} \end{pmatrix}\begin{pmatrix} x_1 \\ x_2 \end{pmatrix} = a_{11}x_1^2 + 2a_{12}x_1x_2 + a_{22}x_2^2$$

assuming that the matrix is symmetric (i.e., $a_{12} = a_{21}$).

The side condition is $g(x_1,x_2) = x_1^2 + x_2^2 - 1 = 0$. This condition may be represented in the two-dimensional x_1,x_2 plane as a circle with the center at 0 and a radius equal to 1.

The function $F(x_1,x_2)$ is either an ellipse, a hyperbola, or a straight line. If the matrix **A** is a SSCP, **C** or **R** matrix computed from real data (and has not been fooled with like the reduced correlation matrices of factor analysis), the figure will not be a hyperbola. (The quadratic form will be *positive definite* or *positive semidefinite*.) If the matrix is also nonsingular, the figure will not be a straight line. Therefore, we will assume that it is an ellipse.

The function $F(x_1,x_2) = a_{11}x_1^2 + 2a_{12}x_1x_2 + a_{22}x_2^2$ then describes an ellipse, or rather it describes a set of ellipses of varying sizes. In order to get it to describe a particular ellipse of a particular size, we have to set it equal to a particular number, say c. So we have $F(x_1,x_2) = c = a_{11}x_1^2 + 2a_{12}x_1x_2 + a_{22}x_2^2$. Choosing different numbers for c will give us different size ellipses; but for given a_{11}, a_{12}, and a_{22}, these different ellipses will all be oriented the same way (they will all be tilted the same direction) and they will all have their centers at the origin.

So we might visualize matters as in figure C-9, where we have drawn the circle representing $g(x_1,x_2) = x_1^2 + x_2^2 - 1 = 0$ and a series of ellipses $F(x_1,x_2) = c$ with different c's.

Our task is to find values of x_1,x_2 such that they fit $g(x_1,x_2) = 0$ and $F(x_1,x_2) = c$ for some c. That means first that our points must lie on the unit circle and that they must also lie on one of the ellipses. They must also allow for c to be as large as possible. The required ellipse is the one that just touches the circle (is tangential to it) as shown in figure C-10. There are two points that fit our requirements.

In the unconstrained maximization problem we would simply find the partial derivatives, set them equal to zero, and solve this set of equations. We would have the same number of equations as unknowns and, as long as the equations were independent, we would have no problems. Now we introduce a constraint in the form of another equation so we have more equations than we have unknowns. The solution would seem to be "overdetermined."

Since we have more equations than we have unknowns, the way out of this problem is to introduce another unknown. This apparent sleight of hand is quite justifiable mathematically. I will attempt to give only an intuitive explanation of the procedure.

Begin with the constraint. In the above example the constraint is $\mathbf{x}'\mathbf{x} - 1 = 0$.

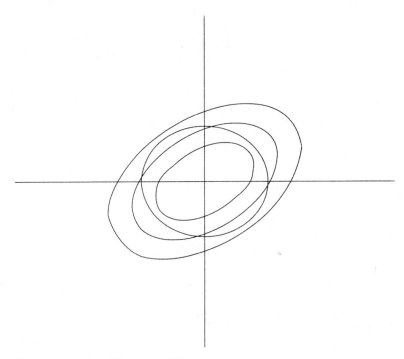

Figure C-9. Unit Circle with Ellipses.

We can multiply both sides of this equation by something and the equation will be the same. Let's multiply it by λ:

$$\lambda(x'x - 1) = 0$$

(My choice of multipliers is not random; mathematicians almost always use λ in this situation; it is called a *Lagrange multiplier.*)

The original function we wanted to maximize was $F(x) = x'Ax$. Since $(x'x - 1)$ is equal to 0, we can add it to $F(x)$ without changing anything. However, although we are adding 0, we still call the sum by a new name, $G(x)$:

$$G(x) = x'Ax + \lambda(x'x - 1)$$

We now find the partial derivatives of G with respect to the j x's and the λ. Setting these expressions equal to zero gives us $j + 1$ equations in $j + 1$ unknowns.

The justification for this procedure is that if the constraint is satisfied (i.e., if $x'x - 1 = 0$), $G(x)$ will act like $F(x)$. That is, for those points for which the constraint is true, $F(x)$ is equal to $G(x)$. The values of x that maximize G will maximize F within the set of points that satisfy the constraint.

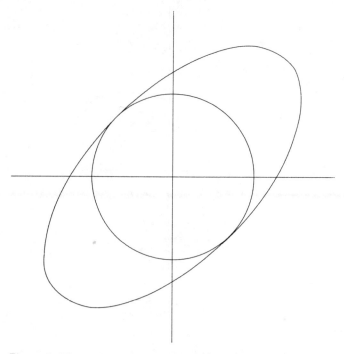

Figure C-10.   Unit Circle with Tangential Ellipse.

Finding the partial derivatives of G with respect to the j x's is the same as differentiating with respect to the **x** vector:

$$\frac{\partial G}{\partial \mathbf{x}} = 2\mathbf{Ax} - 2\lambda\mathbf{x}$$

And the derivative with respect to λ is

$$\frac{\partial G}{\partial \lambda} = -(\mathbf{x}'\mathbf{x} - 1)$$

Setting the last expression equal to 0 and multiplying through by -1 gives us

$$\mathbf{x}'\mathbf{x} - 1 = 0$$

So one of our equations is the same as our constraint.

The text provides an example of solving these equations.

D A LITTLE TRIGONOMETRY

Suppose we have a *unit circle,* that is, a circle whose radius is one as in figure D-1, and suppose we construct an angle θ from the center of the circle as in figure D-2. The angle θ is formed by two radii from the center of the circle, each radius of length 1. We can drop a perpendicular from the intersection of one radius with the circle (I) to the other radius. The cosine of the angle θ is defined as the distance between the center and a. It is written $\cos \theta$. Notice that if the angle is made to be zero degrees, the cosine is 1 ($\cos 0° = 1$); and if the angle is a right angle, the cosine is 0 ($\cos 90° = 0$). Given a situation like Figure D-3, to find the cosine we extend one of the radii as in figure D-4, find the distance between 0 and a on the extended line, and then attach a negative sign to this amount. The cosine is then $-a$. Notice that if the angle is $\theta = 180°$ as in figure D-5, the cosine is -1.

For vectors anywhere in a space of any dimension the scalar product

$$v_1' v_2 = \rho_1 \rho_2 \cos \theta$$

where θ is the angle between them and ρ_1 and ρ_2 are the lengths of the vectors, that is, the distance of the vector to the origin. If the two vectors are of length 1, then the scalar product is equal to the cosine.

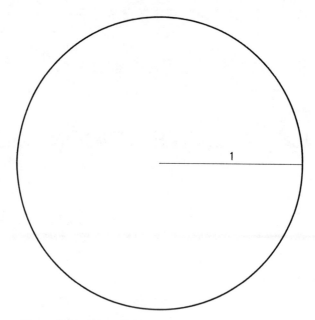

Figure D-1. Unit Circle.

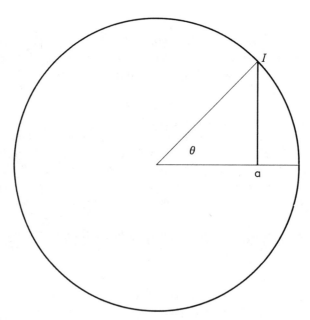

Figure D-2. Unit Circle with Constructed Angle.

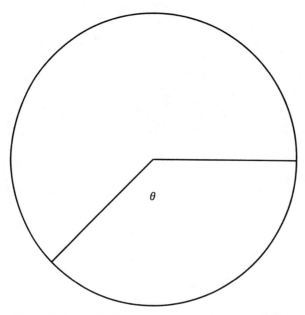

Figure D-3. Unit Circle with Angle of More than 90°.

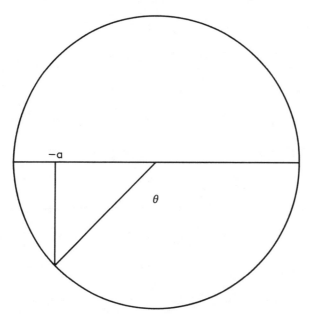

Figure D-4. Finding the Cosine of an Angle of More than 90°.

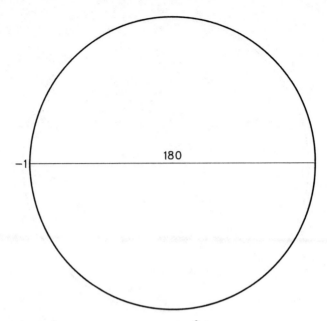

Figure D-5. Unit Circle with $180°$ Angle.

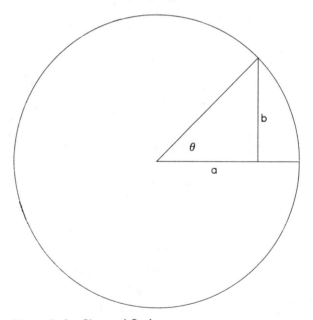

Figure D-6. Sine and Cosine.

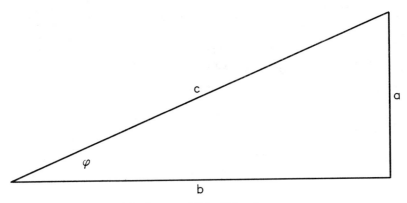

Figure D-7. Sine and Cosine in a Right Triangle.

Sine. Let us go back to our unit circle, but pay attention to the length of another line, the line b in figure D-6. The length b is defined as the sine of θ, written sin θ. The sine of $0°$ is 0 and sin $90° = 1$.

Tangent. Another trigonometric function is the tangent. It is equal to a/b or sin $\theta/\cos \theta$. Still other trigonometric functions have been defined, but they have less use.

Another Way of Looking at Sines and Cosines. In any right triangle (see figure D-7), cos $\phi = b/c$ and sin $\phi = a/c$. This is sometimes put into words like this: For either of the two angles in a right triangle that is not the right angle, the cosine of the angle is the side adjacent to the angle divided by the hypotenuse, and the sine of the angle is the side opposite divided by the hypotenuse.

Relationship Between the Sine and Cosine. The Pythagorean theorem can be used to prove that $\sin^2 \theta + \cos^2 \theta = 1$.

Inverse Trigonometric Functions. Inverse trigonometric functions are just the inverse of trigonometric functions. They are written as

$$\cos^{-1} p \quad \text{or} \quad \arccos p$$
$$\sin^{-1} q \quad \text{or} \quad \arcsin q$$

which mean, respectively, the angle whose cosine is p and the angle whose sine is q.

Tables of Trigonometric Functions.   There are available tables of trigonometric functions that give the values of the functions for given angles and the angles whose trigonometric functions are certain values. Some hand-held calculators are able to compute trigonometric functions and their inverses.

E STILL MORE ON MATRICES

Quadratic Forms

Frequently, in statistical work we encounter a matrix product called a *quadratic form*. It is the product of a row vector times a square matrix times a column vector. Usually the row vector is the transpose of the column vector and the matrix is symmetric:

$$\underset{1 \times p}{\mathbf{a}'} \quad \underset{p \times p}{\mathbf{C}} \quad \underset{p \times 1}{\mathbf{a}}$$

The result will always be a scalar. However, sometimes the vector will consist of a set of unknowns that we want to solve for. Let's take a simple example:

$$\begin{aligned}
\mathbf{x}'\mathbf{C}\mathbf{x} &= (x_1 \quad x_2) \begin{pmatrix} 3 & 1 \\ 1 & 2 \end{pmatrix} \begin{pmatrix} x_1 \\ x_2 \end{pmatrix} \\
&= 3x_1^2 + x_1 x_2 + x_2 x_1 + 2x_2^2 \\
&= 3x_1^2 + 2x_1 x_2 + 2x_2^2
\end{aligned}$$

The reason this is called a quadratic form is that squares of the x_i's and products of one x_i with another appear in the expansion.

249

The expansion of quadratic forms can be written as follows: If x is a column vector of p unknowns, (x_i) and $\mathbf{C}$ is a square matrix of numbers (c_{ij}), then:

$$\mathbf{x}'\mathbf{C}\mathbf{x} = \sum_i \sum_j c_{ij} x_i x_j$$

If the matrix $\mathbf{C}$ is symmetric, then $c_{ij} = c_{ji}$; thus $c_{ij}x_ix_j = c_{ji}x_jx_i$ so we have pairs of identical terms in the above expression. We can collect these terms and write:

$$\mathbf{x}'\mathbf{C}\mathbf{x} = \sum_i c_{ii} x_i^2 + 2 \sum_{\substack{i,j \\ j>i}} c_{ij} x_i x_j$$

where the second summation (multiplied by 2) means we sum over all pairs of i and j where j is greater than i.

Minors and Cofactors

If we have a square matrix $\mathbf{A}$, the minor of any element a_{ij} is a determinant that is found by striking out the ith row and the jth column. We denote this minor as M_{ij}.

The cofactor of a_{ij} is

$$A_{ij} = (-1)^{i+j} M_{ij}$$

which is a fancy way of writing the idea that the cofactor equals the minor if the sum of the number of the row plus the number of the column is even; and the cofactor is the minor with a minus sign if that sum is odd.

Inverse Matrices

If a matrix $\mathbf{A}$ is nonsingular, then there exists another matrix denoted $\mathbf{A}^{-1}$ such that $\mathbf{A}\mathbf{A}^{-1} = \mathbf{A}^{-1}\mathbf{A} = \mathbf{I}$.

$$\mathbf{A}^{-1} = \frac{1}{\det \mathbf{A}} \begin{pmatrix} A_{11} & A_{21} & \cdots & A_{n1} \\ A_{12} & A_{22} & \cdots & A_{n2} \\ \cdots & \cdots & \cdots & \cdots \\ A_{1n} & A_{2n} & \cdots & A_{nn} \end{pmatrix}$$

where the entries in the matrix on the right (A_{ij}) are cofactors of $\mathbf{A}$ and $\det \mathbf{A}$ is the determinant of $\mathbf{A}$. Note that the rows and columns of cofactors in the inverse are interchanged from the original matrix. That is, the element in the ith row and the jth column of $\mathbf{A}^{-1}$ is the cofactor of the element in the jth row and ith column of the original matrix $\mathbf{A}$. This matrix is sometimes called the adjoint of $\mathbf{A}$, written adj($\mathbf{A}$).

Eigenvalues and Eigenvectors

The eigenvalues (also called *characteristic roots*) of the square matrix $\mathbf{A}$ are the λ's which satisfy the equation:

$$|\mathbf{A} - \lambda\mathbf{I}| = 0$$

(the left side of this equation is the determinant of the matrix $\mathbf{A} - \lambda\mathbf{I}$). In the applications in this book, the λ's will be positive real numbers or zero. The number of nonzero eigenvalues is equal to the rank of the matrix.

In this book we deal with eigenvalues of the following three types of matrices:

1. *In principal components analysis* — covariance matrices $\mathbf{C}$: Here the rank of the matrix is equal to the order of the matrix (the number of variables in the analysis) unless one or more of the variables is a linear combination of the others. The matrix $\mathbf{C}$ is always symmetric.

2. *In factor analysis* — correlation matrices or *reduced* correlation matrices: Reduced correlation matrices are correlation matrices with the ones in the diagonal replaced by estimated communalities. If the communalities are estimated correctly the rank of the reduced correlation matrix will be the dimensionality of the common factor space. Correlation matrices and reduced correlation matrices are always symmetric.

3. *In tests of multivariate hypotheses* — the matrix $\mathbf{S}_H\mathbf{S}_E^{-1}$: $\mathbf{S}_H$ and $\mathbf{S}_E$ are square, p by p, SSCP matrices where p is a number of variables, hence the matrix $\mathbf{S}_H\mathbf{S}_E^{-1}$ is square p by p. It is usually not symmetric. The number of nonzero eigenvalues will not exceed p. The rank of $\mathbf{S}_H$ is sometimes less than p, in which case the rank of $\mathbf{S}_H\mathbf{S}_E^{-1}$ is less than p and we have fewer than p nonzero eigenvalues. For example, when the design involves comparisons of mean vectors among groups, $\mathbf{S}_H$ will be the SSCP matrix for between groups. If the number of groups is less than p, the rank of $\mathbf{S}_H$ will be less than p.

Eigenvectors

The eigenvectors of the matrix $\mathbf{A}$ are the vectors $\mathbf{m}_i$, which satisfy the equation

$$\mathbf{A}\mathbf{m}_i = \lambda_i\mathbf{m}_i$$

for each nonzero λ_i. That is, for each nonzero eigenvalue, we find the vector **m** that satisfies the above equation. Actually, for each λ, there are an infinite number of vectors that satisfy this equation, but they are all proportional to each other. That is, if **m** satisfies the equation, then c**m** will also satisfy the equation if c is not equal to zero (prove this by plugging c**m** into the equation in place of **m**). Two particular versions of eigenvectors are used in multivariate analysis: the vector whose sum of squares equals the eigenvalue and the vector whose sum of squared values equals one (called the *normalized* eigenvector).

In tests of multivariate hypotheses, it is usually not necessary to compute the eigenvectors, only the eigenvalues are needed. In principal components analysis and factor analysis eigenvectors are needed.

Some Facts About Eigenvalues and Eigenvectors

Define **D** as the diagonal matrix composed of the eigenvalues of **A**, and define **Z** as a matrix whose columns are the normalized eigenvectors (eigenvectors of length one) in the same order as their corresponding values in **D**. Then the following are true if **A** is symmetric:

1. $$\mathbf{Z'Z = I}$$

that is, the matrix of normalized eigenvectors is an orthogonal matrix.

2. $$|\mathbf{Z}| = |\mathbf{Z'}| = 1$$

This fact holds for all orthonormal matrices.

3. $$\mathbf{A = ZDZ'}$$

A may be factored into a product of matrices involving the eigenvalues and the eigenvectors.

4. $$|\mathbf{A}| = |\mathbf{D}|$$

The product of the eigenvalues is equal to the determinant of **A**, or $|\mathbf{A}| = \Pi\lambda_i$.

5. $$\mathbf{Z'AZ = D}$$

A is transformed into a diagonal matrix by pre- and postmultiplication by **Z**.

6. $$\mathbf{A^{-1} = ZD^{-1}Z'}$$

The inverse of **A** may also be factored into a product of matrices involving the eigenvalues and eigenvectors. This fact can be used to find the inverse of **A**.

7. $$\Sigma\lambda_i = \text{tr}(\mathbf{A})$$

that is, the sum of the eigenvalues is equal to the trace of $\mathbf{A}$.

8. $|\mathbf{A}| = |\mathbf{Z}|\ |\mathbf{D}|\ |\mathbf{Z}'|$

As an exercise, these facts may be verified using

$$\mathbf{A} = \begin{pmatrix} 2 & 1 \\ 1 & 4 \end{pmatrix}$$

In which case

$$\mathbf{D} = \begin{pmatrix} 4.414 & 0 \\ 0 & 1.586 \end{pmatrix} \quad \text{and} \quad \mathbf{Z} = \begin{pmatrix} .3825 & -.9239 \\ .9239 & .3825 \end{pmatrix}$$

Partitioning of Matrices

Sometimes it is useful to think of matrices as being made up of or partitioned into submatrices, so we write things like

$$\mathbf{A} = \begin{pmatrix} \mathbf{A}_1 \\ \hline \mathbf{A}_2 \end{pmatrix} \quad \text{or} \quad \mathbf{A} = \begin{pmatrix} \mathbf{A}_{11} & | & \mathbf{A}_{12} \\ \hline \mathbf{A}_{21} & | & \mathbf{A}_{22} \end{pmatrix}$$

where the $\mathbf{A}$'s with subscripts are matrices. For example, if we have a set of independent and dependent variables, $\mathbf{A}$ might be the covariance matrix of all the variables, $\mathbf{A}_{11}$ the covariance matrix of the dependent variables, $\mathbf{A}_{22}$ the covariance matrix of the independent variables, and $\mathbf{A}_{12} = \mathbf{A}_{21}'$ the matrix of covariances of independent with dependent variables.

It is possible to think of matrix algebra in terms of partitioned matrices. For example, the product of two partitioned matrices works the same way as regular matrix multiplication:

$$\mathbf{AB} = \begin{pmatrix} \mathbf{A}_{11} & | & \mathbf{A}_{12} \\ \hline \mathbf{A}_{21} & | & \mathbf{A}_{22} \end{pmatrix} \begin{pmatrix} \mathbf{B}_{11} & | & \mathbf{B}_{12} \\ \hline \mathbf{B}_{21} & | & \mathbf{B}_{22} \end{pmatrix}$$

$$= \begin{pmatrix} \mathbf{A}_{11}\mathbf{B}_{11} + \mathbf{A}_{12}\mathbf{B}_{21} & | & \mathbf{A}_{11}\mathbf{B}_{12} + \mathbf{A}_{12}\mathbf{B}_{22} \\ \hline \mathbf{A}_{21}\mathbf{B}_{11} + \mathbf{A}_{22}\mathbf{B}_{21} & | & \mathbf{A}_{21}\mathbf{B}_{12} + \mathbf{A}_{22}\mathbf{B}_{22} \end{pmatrix}$$

Tests of Multivariate Hypotheses

Tests of multivariate hypotheses in chapters eight to eleven involve the comparison of two SSCP matrices, $\mathbf{S}_H$, the "hypothesis" SSCP and $\mathbf{S}_E$, the "error" SSCP. The analysis also involves the sum of these matrices, $\mathbf{S}_H + \mathbf{S}_E$. These matrices are all square symmetric p by p matrices where p is a number of varibles. Each of these matrices has associated with it a degrees of freedom, $d.f._H$, $d.f._E$, and $d.f._H + d.f._E$, where the degrees of freedom are the same as the univariate degrees of freedom for any element in the matrix. In the various applications discussed in this book, the matrices have the meanings summarized in table E-1, where k is the number of groups and p is the number of variables. Many other hypotheses can be constructed in more complex designs resulting in other S_E and S_H matrices.

Two approaches have been developed for testing these hypotheses leading to four different statistics. The first approach is Wilk's maximum likelihood method and depends on the calculation of Wilk's lambda:

$$\Lambda = \frac{|S_E|}{|S_E + S_H|}$$

that is, the ratio of the determinant of the error SSCP to the determinant of the sum of the error and hypothesis SSCP matrices. Wilk's lambda is also the product of the reciprocals of one plus the eigenvalues of the matrix $S_H S_E^{-1}$:

$$\Lambda = \prod_i (1/(1 + \lambda_i))$$

It is difficult to determine the exact probability of an obtained Λ under the null hypothesis. However, there are two ways to approximate the probability (Bock, 1975, pp. 152–153). The first involves transforming Λ into an approximate χ^2:

$$\chi^2 = -m(\ln \Lambda)$$

where $\ln \Lambda$ means the natural logarithm of Λ and

$$m = [d.f._H + d.f._E - (p + d.f._H + 1)/2]$$

this χ^2 has degrees of freedom of $p(d.f._H)$.

The second approximation is obtained by transforming Λ into an approximate F statistic:

$$F = \frac{1 - \Lambda^{1/t} mt - 2k}{\Lambda^{1/t} p(d.f._H)}$$

where

$$t = \left(\frac{p^2 (d.f._H)^2 - 4}{p^2 + (d.f._H)^2 - 5} \right)^{1/2}$$

Table E-1. Matrices Used in Multivariate Tests of Significance

Test and Hypothesis	S_H	d.f.	S_E	d.f.	$S_E + S_H$	d.f.
Multivariate tests of means. (Chap. 8)	Between groups SSCP	$k-1$	Pooled within groups SSCP	$N-k$	S_T, the total SSCP SSCP $Y'Y$	$N-1$
Discriminant analysis (Chap. 9)	Between groups SSCP	$k-1$	Pooled within groups SSCP	$N-k$	$X'X$	$N-1$
Multivariate multiple regression (Chap. 10)	SSCP of predicted values $B'X'XB$	p	SSCP of residuals $Y'Y - B'X'XB$	$N-p-1$	S_T, the total SSCP	$N-1$
increments added by new variables	SSCP of increments of variance	s	SSCP of residuals with all variables in	$N-p-s-1$	SSCP of residuals without additional variables	$N-p-1$
Covariance test of hypothesis that means adjusted for covariates are equal (Chap. 10)	Between groups residual from regression	$k-1$	Pooled within in groups residual from regression	$N-k-r$	Total SSCP residual from regression $(Y - BX)'(Y - BX)$	$N-r-1$
Repeated Measures (Chap. 11)						
differences among groups	S_B for overall	$k-1$	S_W for overall	$N-k$	$S_B + S_W$	$N-1$
occasions	S_C (SSCP for occasions without overall entries)	$k-1$	S_W for occasions	$N-k$	$S_C + S_W$	$N-1$
occasions by groups	S_B for occasions	$k-1$	S_W for occasions	$N-k$	$S_B + S_W$	$N-1$

Note: In this table k = number of groups, p = number of independent variables, q = number of dependent variables, r = number of covariates, s = number of added variables (in regression), N = sample size.

(if the denominator is zero, $t = 1$), and

$$k = [p(d.f._H) - 2]/4$$

The F statistic has $p(d.f._H)$ and $mt - 2k$ degrees of freedom.

The second approach uses the matrix $\mathbf{S_H S_E^{-1}}$. Three statistics are based on the eigenvalues of this matrix (the λ's).

Roy's largest root statistic uses the largest of these eigenvalues (λ_1). The distribution of sample values of λ_1 if the null hypothesis is true is complicated but has been tabulated by Heck (1960), Pillai (1965, 1967), and Harris (1975). These tables are entered with the value $\theta_1 = \lambda_1/(1 + \lambda_1)$ which is the eigenvalue of $\mathbf{S_H(S_H + S_E)^{-1}}$. This statistic has three degrees of freedom, $s = \min(p, d.f._H)$ (which means s equals p or $d.f._H$, whichever is smaller), $m = (|d.f._H - p| - 1)/2$, and $n = (d.f._E - p - 1)/2$.

Bock provides tables for a "generalized F" statistic, which is $F_0 = t\lambda_1/r$, where $t = d.f._E - p + 1$ and $r = |d.f._H - p| + 1$; and the F_0 is tabulated in terms of the degrees of freedom t, r, and s, where s is defined as above.

Hotelling's trace criteria is defined as

$$T^2 = \sum_i \lambda_i$$

Since the sum of the eigenvalues is equal to the trace of the matrix, we could also write

$$T^2 = \text{tr}(\mathbf{S_H S_E^{-1}})$$

This statistic is sometimes defined as $T_0^2 = d.f._E [\text{tr}(\mathbf{S_H S_E^{-1}})]$. The probability distribution of this statistic (with the multiplier $d.f._E$) may be found in Pillai (1960). It has the same degrees of freedom as Roy's largest root criteria, that is, s, m, and n.

T^2 can be converted into an approximate F (Hughes and Saw, 1972):

$$F = T^2 \frac{p(d.f._E - p - 1) + 2}{p^2(d.f._H)}$$

where the F has degrees of freedom of $p(d.f._H)$ and $p(d.f._E - p - 1) + 2$.

Finally, we have Pillai's V^S statistic which is equal to the sum of the values $\lambda_i/(\lambda_i + 1)$:

$$V = \frac{\sum\limits_i \lambda_i}{\lambda_i + 1}$$

(Pillai, 1955). This is also the sum of the values θ_i defined above. Probabilities of this statistic under the null hypothesis are approximated by an F:

$$F = \frac{(2n + s + 1)\, V}{(2m + s + 1)\,(s - V)}$$

where s, n, and m are defined as above. This F has degrees of freedom of $s(2m + s + 1)$ and $s(2n + s + 1)$.

These four tests vary in their powers depending on the number of groups, the number of variables, and the relative sizes of the various eigenvalues (see Morrison, 1976, and Harris, 1975).

F LOGARITHMS

Logarithms are simply exponents. The logarithm of a number x is that exponent which, when applied to a number (called the base), produces x. To say it another way, the logarithm of x to the base k satisfies the equation

$$k^{\log x} = x$$

The logarithm here is sometimes written $\log_k x$.

The base cannot be 0 or 1, since, when we raise these numbers to powers, nothing happens. Negative numbers are also never used as bases since we want to be able to use fractional exponents, and strange things happen when we take negative numbers to fractional exponents. Finally, we will define logarithms of only positive numbers, i.e., for $x > 0$.

The logarithm of 1 is 0 no matter what base is used.

There are two bases for logarithms in general use: 10 and e. e is a special number, which, to be circular about matters, is the base of the natural logarithm system. The base 10 is handy since when we take logarithms to the base 10 the digits part of the result is the number of digits in x to the left of the decimal point minus one. In particular:

$$\log_{10} 10 = 1$$

259

$$\log_{10} 100 = 2$$

$$\log_{10} 1000 = 3$$

and so on. Logarithms of decimals are also handy in base 10:

$$\log_{10} 0.1 = -1 \quad (10^{-1} = 0.1)$$

$$\log_{10} 0.01 = -2 \quad (10^{-2} = 0.01)$$

$$\log_{10} 0.001 = -3 \quad (10^{-3} = 0.001) \quad \text{etc.}$$

There is an algebra of logarithms. In particular:

$$\log xy = \log x + \log y$$

$$\log x/y = \log x - \log y$$

$$\log x^y = y \log x$$

The reader may easily prove these rules using the following facts about exponents:

$$a^x a^y = a^{x+y}$$

$$1/a^x = a^{-x}$$

$$(a^x)^y = a^{xy}$$

Logarithms appear occasionally in statistical theory, for example, in maximum likelihood estimation. One of their greatest uses, however, is in transformations of data. If we have original data with a distribution that we do not like, we sometimes apply a nonlinear transformation such as the logarithmic to the data to try to improve the distribution.

G MATRIX ROUTINES IN SAS

The *Statistical Analysis System*[1] (SAS) is a computer software system for data analysis. It has some capabilities that SPSS does not have and vice versa. Perhaps most important for our purposes, it has a set of matrix routines that will allow you to program your own analyses. Thus, although SAS already has built into it programs for regression, multivariate analysis of variance, etc., one can develop programs for those routines from scratch, using the matrix routines. (Of course, it is not really from scratch; the matrix routines of SAS have in them a lot of programming that is already done for you. That programming translates your matrix commands into scalar arithmetic that the computer can handle.)

Besides these notes you will need the *SAS Introductory Guide* and the matrix section of the *SAS User's Guide: Basics* and the MATRIX procedure in the *SAS User's Guide: Statistics,* 1982 edition (p. 271).

The SAS *Statistics,* 1982 edition, has two main steps: the DATA step and the procedure (abbreviated PROC) step. In the DATA step, a set of data is created and/or modified. In the PROC step, various statistical operations may be performed on the data created in a DATA step. An SAS program may include any combination of DATA and steps. As we will see below, the MATRIX subroutine of SAS allows one to input matrices directly, without going through a DATA step.

261

The MATRIX procedure of SAS is called with a line that reads:

PROC MATRIX;

After the word MATRIX, and before the semicolon, you can put various options. The most useful is PRINT, which gives you the results of each statement that follows:

PROC MATRIX PRINT;

Now we are ready to do some matrix arithmetic. The problem is we need some matrices. There are two ways to create matrices. The first and simplest is to give the machine a matrix:

X = 1 2 3 /
    4 5 6;

or

X = 1 2 3 / 4 5 6;

In the above, slashes (/) mean the end of a row, the semicolon means the end of the matrix, and spaces are used between values. You can define one or many matrices at the beginning or at any point along the way. The X above can be any alphabetic character or characters. (In this appendix matrices are not represented by bold-faced letters. They have names, which are all capital letters. The names may be only one letter like X above).

The second way to define matrices for MATRIX is to call them in from a stored data set. This is done with a FETCH command.

FETCH JOHN DATA = CMAT;

In the above, a matrix named JOHN is being created from a data set named CMAT. In the above line, you will put whatever name you have chosen for your matrix in place of JOHN, and whatever the data set name is in place of CMAT. If you have created a new data set in a DATA step just previous to your procedure line, you can leave out the DATA = part and the program will use that data set.

Let's suppose that you have now defined some matrices, and are ready for some matrix arithmetic. It is really very simple: In everything that follows, *letters on the left side of the equals sign are names for new matrices or scalars. Matrices on the right side of the equals sign are assumed to have been previously defined.*

1. To get the matrix C that is the sum of A and B: C = A + B;
   (Always put semicolons at the ends of lines.)
2. Subtraction: C = A - B;
3. Multiplication: C = A * B;
4. Transpose: C = A';
5. Inverse: C = INV(A); or A**(-1);
6. To power a matrix (multiply a square matrix A times itself K times):
   C = A**K;
   (K must be integral and greater than or equal to -1.)
7. To multiply by a scalar: C = A#K;
   (Where K is a scalar.)
8. To divide by a scalar: C = A#/K;
   (Where K is a scalar.)
9. To raise each element of the matrix to a power: C = A##K
   (Where K is a scalar.)

These operations can be run together; for example, I could write:

$$D = (A-B)*C';$$

There are rules of precedence for arithmetic operations. For example, if I write:

$$D = A - B*C;$$

the multiplication will be performed first. I recommend the liberal use of parentheses to make sure the machine does things in the right order.

Besides arithmetic operations, there are many other manipulations available:

1. To create a submatrix from a matrix. The following will create a new matrix S using the entries in rows 1 and 4 and columns 2 and 5:

   $$S = X(1\ 4,2\ 5);$$

   this matrix will have only four cells $(x_{12}, x_{15}, x_{42}, x_{45})$. We can also write S = X(1:7, 2:5); which would create the matrix S out of rows 1 to 7 and columns 2 to 5 of X.
2. To get the determinant: D = DET(A);
3. To create a diagonal matrix from the diagonal elements of a matrix A:
   D = DIAG(A);
   To create a diagonal matrix from a vector V: D = DIAG(V);

4. To create a vector of eigenvalues and a matrix of eigenvectors:

$$\text{EIGEN e a M;}$$

(Where M is the name of the matrix, e is your name for the vector of eigen-values, and a is your name for the matrix of eigenvectors).

5. To create an identity matrix: X = I(d);
    (Where d is the order (dimension) of the identity matrix.)

6. Trace: T = TRACE(X);

7. To find the number of rows: N = NROW(A);
    and columns: C = NCOL(A);

8. To get a row vector of the sums of columns: S = X(+,);

9. To create a matrix of identical values: X = J(R,C,V);
    (Where R is the number of rows, C the number of columns, and V the value. If the value is omitted, 1 is used. J is a function that creates the matrix of identical values).

10. Concatenation: To create a matrix C that is composed of the matrices A and B horizontally joined: C = A||B
    (On some computer terminals the vertical bar is represented by a broken bar.)
    For vertical joining: C = A//B
    (Of course, the matrices must have the right number of rows or columns to be joined.)

Let's use the above in an example. Suppose we have previously defined a data set named MULRAN of 10 columns in which the first column is a case number. We want to generate the deviation score matrix. The program would look like this:

```
PROC MATRIX;
     FETCH RAN DATA = MULRAN;
     MUL = RAN(,2:10);
```

(Omitting the rows, that is, just putting in a comma, means we want all rows; 2:10 means we want to take all columns between 2 and 10.)

```
     N = NROW(MUL);
     MEAN = MUL(+,)#/N;
```

(First get the sums of all columns, then divide by N)

```
     X = MUL-J(N,1)*MEAN;
     PRINT N MEAN X;
```

The last instruction prints the number of rows, the vector of means and the deviation score matrix. We could then get the sum of squares and cross products by:

$S=X'*X;$

Note

1. SAS is the registered trademark of SAS Institute Inc., Cary, N.C.

BIBLIOGRAPHY

Anderberry, M.R. 1973. *Cluster Analysis for Applications*. New York: Academic Press.

Anderson, T.W. 1958. *An Introduction to Multivariate Statistical Analysis*. New York: Wiley.

Barnett, V., and T. Lewis. 1978. *Outliers in Statistical Work*. New York: Wiley.

Bock, R.D. 1975. *Multivariate Statistical Methods in Behavioral Research*. New York: McGraw-Hill.

Cohen, J., and P. Cohen. 1975. *Applied Multiple Regression/Correlation Analysis for the Behavioral Sciences*. Hillsdale, N.J.: Lawrence Erlbaum Associates.

Cooley, W.W., and P.R. Lohnes. 1962. *Multivariate Procedures for the Behavioral Sciences*. New York: Wiley.

Cooley, W.W., and P.R. Lohnes. 1977. *Multivariate Data Analysis*. New York: Wiley.

Darlington, R.B. 1968. Multiple regression in psychological research and practice. *Psychological Bulletin* 69:161–182.

Draper, N.R., and H. Smith. 1981. *Applied Regression Analysis*. 2nd ed. New York: Wiley.

DuBois, P.H. 1957. *Multivariate Correlational Analysis*. New York: Harper.

Dunn, O.J., and V.A. Clark. 1974. *Applied Statistics, Analysis of Variance and Regression*. New York: Wiley.

Finn, J.D. 1974. *A General Model for Multivariate Analysis*. New York: Holt.

267

Fruchter, B. 1954. *Introduction to Factor Analysis.* New York: Van Nostrand.

Gorsuch, R.L. 1974. *Factor Analysis.* Philadelphia: Saunders.

Graybill, F.A. 1976. *Theory and Application of the Linear Model.* North Scituate, Mass.: Duxbury Press.

Harmen, H.H. 1967. *Modern Factor Analysis.* 2nd ed. Chicago: University of Chicago Press.

Harris, R.J. 1975. *A Primer of Multivariate Statistics.* New York: Academic Press.

Heck, D.L. 1960. Charts of some upper percentage points of the distribution of the largest characteristic root. *Annals of Mathematical Statistics* 31:625–642.

Heise, D.R. 1975. *Causal Analysis.* New York: Wiley.

Helwig, Jane T. 1978. *SAS Introductory Guide.* Cary, N.C.: SAS Institute.

Horst, P. 1963. *Matrix Algebra for Social Sciences.* New York: Holt.

Horst, P. 1965. *Factor Analysis of Data Matrices.* New York: Holt.

Hughes, D.T. and J.G. 1972. Saw approximating the percentage points of Hotelling's generalized T_0 statistic. *Biometrika* 59:224–226.

Hull, C.H. and N.H. Nie, 1981. *SPSS Update 7–9.* New York: McGraw-Hill.

Kendall, M.G. 1957. *A Course in Multivariate Analysis.* New York: Hafner.

Kenny, D.A. 1979. *Correlation and Causality.* New York: Wiley.

Kerlinger, F.N., and E.J. Pedhazer. 1973. *Multiple Regression in Behavioral Research.* New York: Holt.

Kim, J., and C.W. Mueller. 1978. *Factor Analysis.* Beverly Hills: Sage.

Kleinbaum, D.G., and L.L. Kupper. 1978. *Applied Regression Analysis.* North Scituate, Mass.: Duxbury.

Lawley, D.N., and A.E. Maxwell. 1971. *Factor Analysis as a Statistical Method.* New York: American Elsevier.

McNeil, K., et al. 1975. *Testing Research Hypotheses Using Multiple Linear Regression.* Carbondale, Ill.: Southern Illinois University Press.

Mardian, K.V., J.T. Kent, and J.M. Bibby. 1979. *Multivariate Analysis.* New York: Academic Press.

Maxwell, A.E. 1977. *Multivariate Analysis in Behavioral Research.* London: Chapman and Hall.

Morrison, D.F. 1976. *Multivariate Statistical Methods.* 2nd ed. New York: McGraw-Hill.

Mosteller, F. and J.W. Tukey. 1977. *Data Analysis and Regression.* Reading, Mass.: Addison Wesley.

Muliak, S.A. 1972. *Foundations of Factor Analysis.* New York: McGraw Hill.

Neter, J. and W. Wasserman. 1974. *Applied Linear Statistical Models.* Homewood, Ill.: Irwin.

Nie, N.H. *et al.,* 1975. *Statistical Package for the Social Sciences.* 2nd ed, New York: McGraw-Hill.

Overall, J.E., and C. Klett. 1973. *Applied Multivariate Analysis.* New York: McGraw-Hill.

Pillai, K.C.S. 1955. Some new test criteria in multivariate analysis. *Annals of Mathematical Statistics* 26:117–121.

Pillai, K.C.S. 1960. Statistical tables for tests of multivariate hypotheses. University of the Philippines Statistical Center.

Pillai, K.C.S. 1965. On the distribution of the largest characteristic root of a matrix in multivariate analysis. *Biometrika* 52:405–414.

Pillai, K.C.S. 1967. Upper percentage points of the largest root of a matrix in multivariate analysis. *Biometrika* 54:189–194.

Press, S.J. 1972. *Applied Multivariate Analysis.* New York: Holt.

Rao, C.R. 1965. *Linear Statistical Inference.* New York: Wiley.

Roberts, H.V., and R.F. Ling. 1982. *Conversational Statistics with IDA.* New York: McGraw-Hill.

Roy, S.N. 1957. *Some Aspects of Multivariate Analysis.* New York: Wiley.

Rulon, P.G., et al. 1967. *Multivariate Statistics for Personnel Classification.* New York: Wiley.

SAS Institute. 1982. *SAS User's Guide: Basics.* Cary, N.C.: SAS Institute.

SAS Institute. 1982. *SAS User's Guide: Statistics.* Cary, N.C.: SAS Institute.

Searle, S.R. 1971. *Linear Models.* New York: Wiley.

Snedecor, G.W., and W.G. Cochran. 1967. *Statistical Methods,* 6th ed. Ames, Iowa: Iowa State University Press.

Tatsuoka, M.M. 1970. *Discriminant Analysis.* Champaign, Ill.: Institute for Personality and Ability Testing.

Winer, B.J. 1971. *Statistical Principles in Experimental Design,* 2nd ed. New York: McGraw-Hill.

Index